THE
21ST-CENTURY
NOVEL

Edinburgh University Press Ltd
The Tun, Holyrood Road, 12(2f) Jackson's Entry, Edinburgh EH8 8PJ

www.euppublishing.com

Typeset in Minion and Chaparral
by Elizabeth McLean
printed and bound in Great Britain by
CPI Group (UK) Ltd, Croydon CR0 4YY

A CIP record for this book is available from the British Library

ISBN 978 0 7486 9834 9 (paperback)
ISBN 978 0 7486 9835 6 (epub)

Editor's note: Except where otherwise stated, the curated discussions have been edited from
the discussions which took place at the Edinburgh World Writers' Conference events by
Jonathan Bastable.

The Edinburgh World Writers' Conference 2012-2013 was a major programming partnership
between the Edinburgh International Book Festival and the British Council and was supported by
The Scottish Government's Edinburgh Festivals Expo Fund, Creative Scotland, Event Scotland and
the City of Edinburgh Council.

PRESENTED BY:

2012-2013 **EDINBURGH WORLD
WRITERS' CONFERENCE**

SUPPORTED BY:

THE 21ST-CENTURY NOVEL

Notes from
THE EDINBURGH WORLD WRITERS' CONFERENCE

Jonathan Bastable and Hannah McGill

CONTENTS

FOREWORD

When the first Edinburgh Writers' Conference was staged in 1962, its organisers couldn't possibly have imagined its far-reaching consequences. Half a century ago, authors who had rarely been seen in public were able to talk about ideas that felt radical and even dangerous against a backdrop of Presbyterian moral rectitude. Hugh MacDiarmid pronounced that he was a communist and a nationalist; Alexander Trocchi, having fled from the US after injecting heroin in front of US television cameras, accused MacDiarmid of being an old fossil. MacDiarmid responded with the accusation that Trocchi was 'cosmopolitan scum'. So toothsome were the exchanges that news articles by bright-eyed arts reporter Magnus Magnusson found their way onto The Scotsman's front page, and large crowds of people gathered to witness the action on the days that followed.

Yet these headline-grabbing exchanges were the froth on a series of conversations between writers who in fact hoped to answer some profound questions. What role did fiction (and the novel in particular) play in a world still coming to terms with the two bloodiest wars in world history? Could the novel, an eighteenth-century invention, still play a meaningful role in a twentieth century characterised by global power struggles and utopian ideologies? And against a backdrop of bans for books by the likes of William Burroughs, DH Lawrence and Henry Miller, should society be allowed to prevent authors from publishing books about subjects that were illegal or taboo at the time, such as drug-taking, sex, or homosexuality?

The 1962 Writers' Conference discussions were part of a broader liberalisation of values, and they helped underline Edinburgh's status as a festival city surfing a wave of social change. Moreover, the Conference made it perfectly clear that people were ready to flock to hear authors talking about ideas. Not only did the events of 1962 provide a snapshot of the state of the novel at the time, but they also helped catapult Edinburgh to attention as an exciting festival city, and paved the way for the tsunami of literary festivals that would follow over the next half-century.

Fifty years on, we wanted to pay homage to the events of 1962; to pay our respects to the courage and swagger of John Calder and his co-organisers Jim Haynes and Sonia Brownell who staged their event despite opposition from forces of conservatism such as the Moral Re-Armament group. Yet we were also struck by how much society – and the context in which authors work – has changed in the intervening years. The Soviet Union broke up twenty years ago and the ideological oppositions of the Cold War have been trumped by global capitalism. The ascendence of the globalised market has been turbocharged by the arrival of a digital age in which communication – and trade – can zip across the world at the touch of a button. Back in 1962 the organisers did their best to be international, but writers from behind the Iron Curtain struggled to secure a visa, and with the best will in the world the majority of the speakers hailed from Britain or America. Today, it is difficult for authors NOT to have international influences and networks.

We decided it was time to organise another Writers' Conference – and this time one that should genuinely reach out to include authors working all over the world. To make this possible, we needed to bring together two organisations with vast experience, both of literary communities and of international collaboration more generally. The British Council and the Edinburgh International Book Festival set up a major partnership and the Edinburgh World Writers' Conference 2012-2013 was born. Fifty writers from across the world were invited to participate in a five-day conference in Edinburgh in August 2012, and then a further fifteen festivals around the world signed up to present conferences of their own, culminating in a final event at the Melbourne Writers' Festival in August 2013.

Organising these events was a monumental task involving hundreds of people. It is not easy securing permission for a public discussion in Beijing, yet five authors from China and Britain all managed to have their say – in Mandarin and in English – at least until the hosts became too nervous about the political nature of the discussion and summarily closed the event down. It is not straightforward to hold public debates in Brazzaville, the capital of the Republic of the Congo, but almost fifty authors managed to take part (and to welcome the President Denis Sassou-Nguesso when he decided to pay a visit). On those humid days in sub-Saharan Africa, there were authors who had travelled from South

Africa, Nigeria, Chad, Mali, Zanzibar, Senegal, Egypt, Sierra Leone, Tunisia, Algeria, Morocco and the Democratic Republic of the Congo, not to mention France and Belgium. It proved unexpectedly challenging to organise a conference in Krasnoyarsk, Siberia – but thanks to the British Council team, writers from Russia and Britain discussed the future of the novel in a city better known for being a gateway to the gulags. Other cities proved less tricky: we were welcomed with open arms by the International Festival of Authors in Toronto; the Bocas Literary Festival in Trinidad & Tobago; the Berlin Literaturfestival and Étonnants Voyageurs in St Malo. We proudly took our place at the Jaipur Literature Festival, the Lisbon Book Fair, the Open Book festival in Cape Town and the Cooler Lumpur Festival in Malaysia. In Belgium we collaborated with the Passaporta festival to stage a special event in Brussels, while Yaşar University in İzmir, Turkey welcomed us for a special conference. Only Egypt eluded us: despite our best efforts, the political unrest there made it impossible for the planned Writers' Conference to go ahead at the University of Cairo. Nevertheless, this book includes some of the keynote speeches that were intended to be delivered there.

The five topics discussed back in 1962 were very much of their time, but if we were to test the health of the novel half a century later, we realised that we should ask the same questions again – albeit couching them in language more appropriate to a twenty-first- century writing community. At times this felt problematic: talking about censorship did not come easily to writers in the UK or Canada, countries that already claim to embrace freedom of speech, and many suggested the idea of 'self-censorship' was something altogether different. Others found the contrast between Style and Content to be tiresome or even redundant. Yet despite the international differences, these were questions that turned out to be remarkably resilient, and the different relevance depending on where they were asked threw up the possibility that globalisation may not be as homogenising a force as some fear. In China the question of censorship was regarded as so sensitive that the authorities in Beijing wouldn't allow it to be discussed at all. In Scotland the relationship between writing and national identity was of great relevance – just as it was in Brazzaville where writers are wrestling with a post-colonial context. By contrast in South Africa 'a national literature' was regarded by many as a deeply unattractive idea.

Just like in 1962, the Writers' Conference generated huge amounts of media coverage – this time also fuelled by social media discussion. But when the BBC News at Ten reported on the Edinburgh discussions, reporter Will Gompertz jokingly complained that there had been no fist-fights; that authors had been much less pugilistic than their predecessors. Perhaps that's a reflection of the fact that authors are much more aware of their public image than they were in Sixties – much more used to appearing on public platforms and discussing their ideas. Nevertheless, the authors were not scared to put forward their profoundly-held and powerfully-argued views.

The resulting book reflects the organisation of the conference sessions: each one kicked off with a keynote speech commissioned by the festival organisers. It was billed as a 'polemic' and in many cases that's exactly what the authors delivered. That speech was followed by discussion among the authors present in the room, and then opened out to members of the audience for their contributions. To reflect this diversity of views, Edinburgh-based writer Hannah McGill was commissioned to write an introductory essay to each chapter of the book. These pieces navigate a sure-footed and entertaining path through the cacophony of opinions. Alongside these, Jonathan Bastable undertook the heroic task of selecting and editing the keynote speeches, and weaving contributions from all sixteen conferences into coherent, curated discussions. We are infinitely grateful to both of them for their excellent work

We would also like to pay tribute to all the people who organised the conferences across the world. Central to everything were Susie Nicklin and Tanya Andrews at the British Council. Equally important were Lisa Craig, Andrew Coulton, Roland Gulliver, Janet Smyth and Julie Weston at the Book Festival in Edinburgh. Without them, the project would never have seen the light of day. We are also grateful to Dr Eleanor Bell and Dr Angela Bartie at the University of Strathclyde, Glasgow, who originally suggested the project to us and whose expert research into the Writers' Conference of 1962 proved vital to our ability to deliver it. Alongside them and the countless other organisers, we would like to pay tribute to the authors who took part in this grand international experiment.

This book distils thousands of hours of discussion, held across the world and over a time period of twelve months, into a document that reflects authors' attitudes to their work at the beginning of the twenty-first century.

Needless to say, novels were not the only topic of the discussions: the conversation ranged in interesting but connected ways beyond the novel to include short-story writing, poetry and other forms of literature. However the fifth and final topic – The Future of the Novel – seemed to indicate that the novel remains central. Clearly, writers working today find it as hard to earn a living wage as they did in 1962, and finding a readership remains a struggle. Yet again and again, across the world, most writers affirmed that the novel itself feels vital to what they do. Even in a digital age when interactivity and the moving image are ubiquitous, writers want to express themselves through a mode of writing developed more than two centuries ago. Will they feel the same in 2062, if a Writers' Conference is organised then? We hope someone will take up the challenge and find out.

Nick Barley
Director, Edinburgh International Book Festival

Cortina Butler
Director Literature, British Council

EDINBURGH WORLD WRITERS' CONFERENCE 2012-2013

Keynote speakers are in highlighted in bold. Page references indicate the inclusion of the full keynote text.

SCOTLAND
EDINBURGH INTERNATIONAL BOOK FESTIVAL
17–21 AUGUST 2012

SHOULD LITERATURE BE POLITICAL?
STYLE VERSUS CONTENT
A NATIONAL LITERATURE
CENSORSHIP TODAY
THE FUTURE OF THE NOVEL

PARTICIPATING WRITERS

ANDREY ASTVATSATUROV	JACKIE KAY	IAN RANKIN
BERNADO ATXAGA	HARI KUNZRU	JAMES ROBERTSON
ALAN BISSETT	NICK LAIRD	JOSÉ RODRIGUES DOS SANTOS
THERESA BRESLIN	MARGO LANAGAN	ELIF SHAFAK
MELVIN BURGESS	MICHEL LE BRIS	PREETA SAMARASAN
JOHN BURNSIDE	YIYUN LI	KAMILA SHAMSIE
XI CHUAN	AONGHAS MACNEACAIL	OWEN SHEERS
SOPHIE COOKE	**CHINA MIÉVILLE** (p.40)	KYUNG-SOOK SHIN
JUNOT DÍAZ	DENISE MINA	**ALI SMITH** (p.290)
NATHAN ENGLANDER	NICOLA MORGAN	DAG SOLSTAD
CARLOS GAMERRO	EWAN MORRISON	**AHDAF SOUEIF** (p.104)
ALAN GIBBONS	**PATRICK NESS** (p.178)	JANNE TELLER
KEITH GRAY	GARTH NIX	KIM THÚY
KIRSTY GUNN	JOYCE CAROL OATES	CHIKA UNIGWE
XIAOLU GUO	BEN OKRI	**IRVINE WELSH** (p.222)
MANU JOSEPH	ELLIOT PERLMAN	SAMAR YAZBEK
KAPKA KASSABOVA	MATTHIAS POLITYCKI	

GERMANY
INTERNATIONALES LITERATURFESTIVAL BERLIN
4–16 SEPTEMBER 2012

THE FUTURE OF THE NOVEL

PARTICIPATING WRITERS

GREG BAXTER	HALLGRÍMUR HELGASON	STEINUNN SIGUROARDOTTIR
SOPHIE COOKE	MARTIN JANKOWSKI	JANNE TELLER
JULIAN GOUGH	**GEORG KLEIN** (p.60)	BARBARA WAHLSTER
XIAOLU GUO	TIM PARKS	CLARE WIGFALL

SOUTH AFRICA
OPEN BOOK, CAPE TOWN
20–24 SEPTEMBER 2012

SHOULD LITERATURE BE POLITICAL?
A NATIONAL LITERATURE
CENSORSHIP TODAY

PARTICIPATING WRITERS

DIANE AWERBUCK	LIESL JOBSON	DON PINNOCK
BULELWA BASSE	**ANJALI JOSEPH** (p.252)	AZILA REISENBERGER
ANDRE BRINK	RUSTUM KOZAIN	PATRICIA SCHONSTEIN
KARINA BRINK	**ANTJIE KROG**	MARTINIQUE SITWELL
IMRAAN COOVADIA	HAIDEE KRUGER	DEON SIMPHIWE SKADE
KEITH CORNELIUS-BRITZ	SIPHIWO MAHALA	FIONA SNYCKERS
CAROL-ANN DAVIDS	RENEILWE MALATJI	KELWYN SOLE
INGRID DE KOK	BRENT MEERSMAN	SAMKELA STAMPER
DOROTHY DYER	ZAHEDA MOHAMED	TONI STUART
JUSTIN FOX	NATALIA MOLEBATSI	RAENETTE TALJAARD
DAMON GALGUT	**NJABULO NDEBELE** (p.112)	MEG VAN DER MERWE
KEITH GRAY (p.187)	FUTHI NTSHINGILA	RACHEL ZADOK
COLLEEN HIGGS	BARBARA NUSSBAUM	
KAREN JENNINGS	MARGIE ORFORD	

CANADA
INTERNATIONAL FESTIVAL OF AUTHORS, TORONTO
18–28 OCTOBER 2012

STYLE VERSUS CONTENT
A NATIONAL LITERATURE
CENSORSHIP TODAY
THE FUTURE OF THE NOVEL

PARTICIPATING WRITERS

BERT ARCHER	JOSHUA KNELMAN	KATRINA ONSTAD
STEVEN BEATTIE	CHAN KOONCHUNG	ANDREW PYPER
HEATHER BIRRELL	KATHRYN KUITENBROUWER	COREY REDEKOP
SHAUGHNESSY BISHOP-STALL	MICHELE LANDSBERG	ANAKANA SCHOFIELD
ANDREW BOROWSKI	REBECCA LEE	LEANNE SHAPTON
LIAM CARD	BEATRICE MACNEIL	ANIA SZADO
MAJORIE CELONA	ALEN MATTICH	KRISTEL THORNELL
FARZANA DOCTOR	KEN MCGOOGAN	**MIRIAM TOEWS** (p.242)
BRIAN FRANCIS	**CHINA MIÉVILLE**	BECKY TOYNE
JAMES GRAINGER	JAY MILLAR	VIKKI VAN SICKLE
DEBORAH HARKNESS	EVAN MUNDAY	IRVINE WELSH
A.L. KENNEDY	JO NESBØ	ZOE WHITTALL
LAUREN KIRSHNER	HAL NIEDZVIECKI	BRIAN WRIGHT-MCLEOD

RUSSIA
KRASNOYARSK BOOK CULTURE FAIR
31 OCTOBER–3 NOVEMBER 2012

SHOULD LITERATURE BE POLITICAL?
A NATIONAL LITERATURE
THE FUTURE OF THE NOVEL

PARTICIPATING WRITERS

ANDREY ASTVATSATUROV	**MELVIN BURGESS** (p.120)	**KIRILL KOBRIN**
THERESA BRESLIN	**TIBOR FISCHER**	**KONSTANTIN MILCHIN**

EGYPT
UNIVERSITY OF CAIRO, DIWAN BOOKSTORE
AND GENERAL EGYPTIAN BOOK ORGANISATION
8–9 DECEMBER 2012

This event was unavoidably cancelled due to the political situation in the region but keynotes on the following topics were published and brought vital voices to the debate:

SHOULD LITERATURE BE POLITICAL?
THE FUTURE OF THE NOVEL

PARTICIPATING WRITERS
TAMIM AL-BARGHOUTI (p.155)
SAHAR EL MOUGY (p.93)

INDIA
JAIPUR LITERATURE FESTIVAL
24–28 JANUARY 2013

A NATIONAL LITERATURE
CENSORSHIP TODAY

PARTICIPATING WRITERS

REZA ASLAN

TAHAR BEN JELLOUN

JOHN BURNSIDE

SHOMA CHAUDHURY

SELMA DABBAGH

JOHN KAMPFNER

BASHARAT PEER

JONATHAN SHAININ

AHDAF SOUEIF

CONGO
ÉTONNANTS VOYAGEURS, BRAZZAVILLE
13–17 FEBRUARY 2013

SHOULD LITERATURE BE POLITICAL?
STYLE VERSUS CONTENT
A NATIONAL LITERATURE
CENSORSHIP TODAY
THE FUTURE OF THE NOVEL

PARTICIPATING WRITERS

KHALED AL KHAMISSI

MARK BEHR

YAHIA BELASKRI

JEAN-MARIE BLAS DE ROBLES

IN KOLI JEAN BOFANE

SERGE BRAMLY

ANDRE BRINK

FLORENT COUAU-ZOTTI

OUSMANE DIARRA

EMMANUEL DONGALA (p.197)

ABDULRAZAK GURNAH

HELON HABILA (p.260)

HUBERT HADDAD

MICHEL LE BRIS

YVON LE MEN

HENRI LOPES

ALAIN MABANCKOU

NICQ MHLONGO

LÉONORA MIANO

NIMROD

PIA PETERSEN

EMMELIE PROPHETE

BOUALEM SANSAL

FELWINE SARR

SAMI TCHAK

TCHICHELE TCHIVELA

TARUN TEJPAL

DOMINIC THOMAS

TURKEY
YAŞAR UNIVERSITY, İZMIR
27–28 FEBRUARY 2013

A NATIONAL LITERATURE
THE FUTURE OF THE NOVEL

PARTICIPATING WRITERS

INCI ARAL

SEBNEM ISIGUZEL

PANOS KARNEZIS

SEMA KAYGUSUZ

DENISE MINA

MURAT UYURKULAK

CHINA
THE BOOKWORM LITERARY FESTIVAL, BEIJING
8–22 MARCH 2013

STYLE VERSUS CONTENT
THE FUTURE OF THE NOVEL

PARTICIPATING WRITERS

SOPHIE COOKE (p.302)	KEITH GRAY	ZHU WEN
LI ER (p.85)	A.D. MILLER	ZHANG YUERAN

BELGIUM
SCOTTISH GOVERNMENT EU OFFICE, BRUSSELS
21 MARCH 2013

A NATIONAL LITERATURE

PARTICIPATING WRITERS

STELLA DUFFY	**RACHIDA LAMRABET** (p.234)	CHRISTOPHER MEREDITH
KAPKA KASSABOVA (p.279)	GEARÓID MAC LOCHLAINN	ARTHUR RIORDAN

TRINIDAD
NGC BOCAS LIT FEST
27–28 APRIL 2013

A NATIONAL LITERATURE
SHOULD LITERATURE BE POLITICAL?

PARTICIPATING WRITERS

VAHNI CAPILDEO	HANNAH LOWE	MARINA WARNER
IFEONA FULANI	PANKAJ MISHRA	IRVINE WELSH
MARLON JAMES (p.272)	COURTTIA NEWLAND	
EARL LOVELACE	**OLIVE SENIOR** (p.147)	

FRANCE

ÉTONNANTS VOYAGEURS, ST MALO
18–20 MAY 2013

SHOULD LITERATURE BE POLITICAL?
STYLE VERSUS CONTENT
A NATIONAL LITERATURE
CENSORSHIP TODAY
THE FUTURE OF THE NOVEL

PARTICIPATING WRITERS

UWEM AKPAN

VASSILIS ALEXAKIS

SEFI ATTA

AYERDHAL

MURRAY BAIL

AZOUZ BEGAG

MARK BEHR

YAHIA BELASKRI

JONAS T. BENGTSSON

MBAREK BEYROUK

JEAN-MARIE BLAS DE ROBLÈS

SERGE BRAMLY

SERGE BRAMLY

CLÉMENT CALIARI

SORJ CHALANDON

BERNARD CHAMBAZ

BRUCE CLARKE

VELIBOR ČOLIĆ

MARYSE CONDÉ

JOHN CONNOLLY

JUSTIN CRONIN

GENEVIÈVE DAMAS

MAYLIS DE KERANGAL

DIDIER DECOIN

PATRICK DEVILLE

ARIANE DREYFUS

MATHIAS ÉNARD

DIANA EVANS

PERCIVAL EVERETT

JÉRÔME FERRARI

BEN FOUNTAIN

PETE FROMM

DAMON GALGUT

HOLLY GODDARD JONES

HAKAN GÜNDAY

HELON HABILA

HUBERT HADDAD (p.319)

ARNALDUR INDRIÐASON

GASPARD-MARIE JANVIER

JEAN-PAUL KAUFFMANN

HENRY KENOL

YANICK LAHENS

GILLES LAPOUGE

BJÖRN LARSSON

MICHEL LE BRIS (p.72)

HENRI LOPES

ALAIN MABANCKOU

IAN MACDONALD

KOPANO MATLWA

DEON MEYER

NIQ MHLONGO

LÉONORA MIANO

KGEBETLI MOELE

SCHOLASTIQUE MUKASONGA

TOBIE NATHAN

ANNE NIVAT

JANIS OTSIEMI

ELLIOT PERLMAN

YANN QUEFFELEC

ATIQ RAHIMI (p.139)

PATRICK RAMBAUD

JEAN ROUAUD

PAOLO RUMIZ

INSA SANE

BOUALEM SANSAL (p.170)

NOO SARO-WIWA

PINAR SELEK

DIMITRIS STEFANAKIS

NICK STONE

SAMI TCHAK

JEAN TEULÉ

KIM THÚY

LYONEL TROUILLOT

DAVID VANN

GARY VICTOR

OLIVIER WEBER

KENNETH WHITE

PORTUGAL
LISBON BOOK FAIR
25 MAY 2013

SHOULD LITERATURE BE POLITICAL?
THE FUTURE OF THE NOVEL

PARTICIPATING WRITERS

DULCE MARIA CARDOSO	DENISE MINA	JOÃO TORDO
MATHIAS ÉNARD	RUTE PINHEIRO COELHO	
ROSA LIKSOM	**JOSÉ RODRIGUES DOS SANTOS**	

MALAYSIA
#WORD: THE COOLER LUMPUR FESTIVAL,
KUALA LUMPUR
21–23 JUNE 2013

SHOULD LITERATURE BE POLITICAL?
A NATIONAL LITERATURE
CENSORSHIP TODAY

PARTICIPATING WRITERS

ALFIAN BIN SA'AT	SUZANNE JOINSON	NICOLA MORGAN
BERNICE CHAULY	SHARAAD KUTTAN	A SAMAD SAID
LOURD DE VEYRA	DI LI	HUZIR SULAIMAN
SHAMINI FLINT	MARINA MAHATHIR	**MA THIDA**
CHUAH GUAT ENG	BENJAMIN MARKOVITS	EZRA ZAID

SCOTLAND
EDINBURGH INTERNATIONAL BOOK FESTIVAL
17 AUGUST 2013

Edinburgh World Writers' Conference wrap up event: What can we learn about the future of fiction from the Writers' Conference discussions?

PARTICIPATING WRITERS

SEMA KAYGUSUZ   HARI KUNZRU   CHINA MIÉVILLE

AUSTRALIA
MELBOURNE WRITERS FESTIVAL
23 AUGUST – 1 SEPTEMBER 2013

SHOULD LITERATURE BE POLITICAL?
STYLE VERSUS CONTENT
A NATIONAL LITERATURE
CENSORSHIP TODAY
THE FUTURE OF THE NOVEL

PARTICIPATING WRITERS

ALI ALIZADEH	LISA GORTON	LAURA JEAN MCKAY
ROGER AVERILL	**KIRSTY GUNN** (p.310)	KIRSTY MURRAY
LARISSA BEHRENDT (p.206)	LEANNE HALL	PADDY O'REILLY
TONY BIRCH	JOHN HARDING	ALICE PUNG
BETHANIE BLANCHARD	JEREMY HARDING	FRANCESCA RENDLE-SHORT
KEVIN BROPHY	MELINDA HARVEY	GLYN ROBERTS
JOHN BURNSIDE	MJ HYLAND	ANNABEL SMITH
MEL CAMPBELL	JOHANNES JAKOB	JEFF SPARROW
TOM CHO	SARAH JANSEN	CARRIE TIFFANY
ALI COBBY ECKERMAN	TONI JORDAN	SAM TWYFORD-MOORE
TEJU COLE (p.50)	ANNA KRIEN	JULIENNE VAN LOON
ALISON CROGGON	MARGO LANAGAN	CHRIS WALLACE-CRABBE
CHRISTY DENA	NAM LE	LILI WILKINSON
JUNOT DÍAZ	**AMANDA LOHREY** (p.128)	DAMON YOUNG
AMY ESPESETH	ANDREW MCDONALD	OUYANG YU
PETER GOLDSWORTHY	LIAM MCILVANEY	ARNOLD ZABLE

INTRODUCTION

'It's a way of converting work into play,' David Lodge wrote of the industrial conference in his 1984 novel *Small World*, 'combining professionalism with tourism, and all at someone else's expense.' Novelists and poets, even more than Lodge's literary academics, suffer the broad assumption that their work is more or less play to begin with – so what stands to be learned from a public conference of writers?

When the inaugural International Writers' Conference was staged in 1962, as part of the Edinburgh International Festival of Music and Drama, the notion of writers debating in front of an audience, birthed by publisher John Calder and bookshop owner Jim Haynes, was new. Indeed, the arts festival itself was a youthful endeavour, with Edinburgh's now-august August jamboree a mere teenager still. The Writers' Conference served to connect the counter-culture, where Calder's and Haynes' interests largely lay, with mainstream publishing; to invigorate Scottish literature, then widely regarded as a somewhat parochial and limited concern; and to add literature to the art forms that stood to be shaken up and publicised within Edinburgh's growing summer spectacle.

There was no separate Book Festival at that time; this would not be established until 1983. By the time of the original Conference's fiftieth anniversary, and its revival, in 2012, the Edinburgh International Book Festival had established itself as the world's biggest amid many, many celebrations of writers and writing around the world. This was not, of course, the only change to the landscape against which the invited writers – a great many of whom were not born when the original event took place – spoke and debated.

The onset of more progressive and/or permissive times has lessened the impact of certain personal stances and declarations, rendering some of the grand shocks of 1962 (such as the 'people jumping up to confess they were homosexuals' – breathily reported by delegate Mary McCarthy) a little quaint. While the difficulties attached to being what the dominant intellectual paradigm still assumes one is not – homosexual; female; of working-class origin; of immigrant or minority ethnicity; any combination of the above – have hardly vanished without trace from the literary world, most would agree that greater general awareness of a spectrum of life experiences makes the public affirmation of such identities on the part of writers not so much a matter of controversy as a matter of course. Yet other shifts seem to have fostered increased caution and conservatism. The writers of the 2012 and 2013 conferences seem more groomed and gentle entities: eccentricities are less pronounced, offence more easily taken and more carefully not given, disagreements less bloody or at least less public in their expression.

One might give thanks for increased politeness and tolerance; grieve for brighter-burning personalities; or note that an insecure intellectual culture, geared away from the career scholar, and towards the adaptable and carefully considered Media Personality, has scant patience with truly spontaneous or tempestuous characters. Or one might contend that the availability of social media encourages sneakier attacks than were possible in 1962. During one keynote, I sat beside an author who I was interested to observe was tweeting rather bitterly about the speaker on the podium, but did not challenge him in the room. Whichever way you slice it, it's an interesting conundrum that writers should come across as less combative and less opinionated in an age that exposes them to ever harsher and more public criticism. The ease with which anonymous online attacks can be launched makes it a brutal climate in which to be a figure of any public standing; a still more brutal one if your stock-in-trade is art or entertainment; and a less, not more forgiving one if you express pain or problems through your work. If Twitter and its vast, noisily democratic ilk are unrefined by definition, the supposedly more rarefied confines of comment sections on a 'quality' publication's website offer little more defence against philistinism and cruelty. 'The man was an out and out ass,' posted a commenter on a Guardian review of D.T. Max's biography of David Foster Wallace in September 2012, 'who wrote pretensious [sic] overrated rubbish.' And 'Brilliant minds don't commit suicide, only plonkers do that,' weighed in another contributor to the thread. 'So how about a new headline, "The highs and lows of a bloke who ultimately wasn't man enough to hack it".' That Foster Wallace should attract such ferocious criticism posthumously (and that's just a taste) rather serves to illustrate why a sensitive radar such as he had trouble weathering the world in which he found himself. Living writers can expect no gentler treatment in recognition of their being around to read it. 'Sure to be an utter piece of sh•t, like all Smith's stinkers,' someone confidently predicted beneath a review of Zadie Smith's *NW* on the same newspaper's website.

Mean-spirited reviews are nothing new, of course, and books and authors have survived them with aplomb. Wasn't *Moby Dick* panned, *Wuthering Heights* called 'a compound of vulgar depravity and unnatural horrors', *Middlemarch* dismissed (as 'indifferent') by no less than Henry James? And don't Zadie Smith and the estate of David Foster Wallace persist in flourishing in spite of their detractors? Writers have never not been sensitive, and never not been attacked. But the permanent release valve that is the internet – the forum it offers for the expulsion of all manner of personal bile, under the cover of an impersonal username; and for amateur artists to sell their wares without the intervention of commercial gatekeepers – has a tendency to expose over and over again a widespread and deep suspicion of the very craft of writing. Anyone could do it, surely, given the leisure. No-one should do it; what's it for? Is it even a craft, if we can't explain what we need it for? Who, in short, do these people think they are?

Add to this sinister online atmosphere market conditions that threaten what slim livelihood a writer's life ever offered; a cash-strapped educational system that attaches greater importance to vocational training than to broad-based cultural learning; and technological advances that have unseated, if not the act of reading, at least the iconic status of the *book* – and perhaps it's little wonder that today's writers come across as a nervier breed than the rakish iconoclasts of 1962. Libraries, promoters and protectors of books and reading on both practical and symbolic levels, are increasingly endangered in most territories. Home libraries are impractical for a generation that expects to move home frequently, and rendered unnecessary if not obsolete in any case by the advent of the e-reader. While an e-book library is still a library, there's a flimsiness to it – and not just because it exists in code and not on paper. It's *legally* insubstantial. E-book ownership, notoriously, is currently a slippery matter, with content thus far having proved subject to change or withdrawal by the companies from which it's bought. The market urges us into temporary relationships with cultural artefacts, and therefore, arguably, with their creators. Buying a

£1.99 e-book is a minor investment, so jettisoning it – and any future bond with its writer – is no wrench. A friend who recently published her first novel was thrilled by unexpectedly rapid and voluminous online sales, but stung by the harshness of some of the reviews that swiftly followed. Easy come, easy go; easily picked up, literature is easily rejected.

There's a contradiction, however. We can enumerate all around us symptoms of writers and writing – fiction writing in particular – being taken less seriously; granted less cultural weight, and less social significance. But in spite of all of this, gossiping about books and writers remains popular; book prizes are big news; book festivals burgeon; and the fantasy of *being* a published writer hasn't lost its seductiveness. Among the organisations that now run writing courses or full-scale 'academies' are the aforementioned *Guardian*, the publishing house Faber and Faber, the literary agency Curtis Brown, and the Southbank Centre. One can of course conjecture as to the true motivation for such enterprises (rigorous hunt for new talent, or rigorous hunt for ready cash?) – but the fact that there's a market for them, as for the countless creative writing courses flourishing at higher education establishments old and new, shows that the alchemy of turning life into fiction retains its fascination as a life pursuit. Perhaps it's the very tantalising closeness of writing to most people's capacities that engenders the sort of opprobrium meted out to successful practitioners like Smith and Foster Wallace. What makes them so special, that they can bridge the gap between *wanting* to do it, and doing it?

That's part of the public appeal of a writers' conference, of course – and more generally of a book festival such as Edinburgh. Attendees want to hear what such people think, and perhaps challenge them – but also just to observe them, hear what they sound like, assess their being and bearing. If this sounds a little more like a zoo than a forum for intellectuals, perhaps that reflects the manner in which creative people tend to be regarded within a broad cultural context that we so often hear is geared more towards a fascination with celebrity itself than an interest in how it is earned. But while some of the authors who appeared at the World Writers' Conference manifestations around the world were certainly celebrities, and some household names, their audiences did not line up simply to gawp. Discussion ranged widely during the Conference, both in the rooms where it took place and in the surrounding cyberspace.

The latter connectedness – the availability of an event in one city to viewers and listeners many miles and hours distant – is an extraordinary advance, one unimaginable in 1962. It's also in some ways a contradiction of what a conference is, or used to be – that is to say, a physical coming together; a meeting of minds defined in part by its exclusivity, its shut-off hothouse atmosphere. Yet online participation certainly did not cancel out geographical specificity at the conferences: discussion was very differently angled, for instance, in territories whose recent or current political histories have strongly marked their literary cultures. A discussion on censorship means something different in Cape Town than in Toronto; a meditation on the future of the novel, as delegate Samar Yazbek noted from her native Syria during the Edinburgh leg of the conference, seems less urgent at a time of massacres. And in all the places to which the Writers' Conference found its way, the special intensity generated by having the bulk of the participants in one place at the same time – the charge that continues to cause live arts events to burgeon in popularity even as online communication renders them theoretically unnecessary – has been notable. The resulting year-long, world-spanning gathering of some of the finest living writers, and of their thoughts – the spontaneous and the planned, the raw and the polished, the weighty and the whimsical – was a once-in-a-generation undertaking.

THE FUTURE OF THE NOVEL

Modernity and machinery

by Hannah McGill ·

'I am trying to get the hang of this new fangled writing machine, but am not making a shining success of it,' typed Mark Twain to his brother Orion in 1874. 'The machine has several virtues. I believe it will print faster than I can write. It piles an awful stack of words on one page. It don't muss things or scatter ink blots around. Of course, it saves paper.'

Twain, an enthusiastic early adopter when it came to technology (and an inventor himself – he patented a self-gluing scrapbook, a shirt-tightening strap and a trivia game), was probably the first author to deliver a wholly typewritten manuscript: that of *Life on the Mississippi*, in 1883. It wasn't all his own manual labour: the early difficulties he reported to Orion seem to have endured, as he had professional typists do the fingerwork. Did the fact that he was dictating to a secretary, rather than forming words himself with a pen and ink, affect the style of his prose? Might dictating aloud have made Twain for instance, more conversational (*Life on the Mississippi* consists substantially of anecdotes from his own young days piloting steamships), or less focused (the book is widely critiqued as meandering and uneven)? The latter possibility would tally with certain observations that have been made about the work of his contemporary, Henry James. The pair had little else in common, and little mutual love lost (Twain is meant to have said of James that 'once you put one of his books down, you simply can't pick it up', while James's lofty counter-snipe was that Twain's appeal was 'to rudimentary minds'), but James also took up dictating his prose, thanks to worsening rheumatism in his right wrist, and the change in writing practice is seen by many as influential upon the development of his notoriously dense and circumlocutory late style. Another contemporary, Mary Augusta 'Mrs Humphry' Ward, commented, 'the diffuseness and over-elaboration which were the natural snares of his astonishing gifts were encouraged rather than checked by the new method'.

Twain dictated to a secretary, Mary Howden, who made manual notes and then typed them up; James delivered his elaborate sentences directly to a typist (and is reported to have become particularly attached to the percussion provided by the rattle of the keys of the Remington machine she used). Friedrich Nietzsche took up typing – with no intermediary – in 1882. Like James, Nietzsche was driven to give up handwriting by physical issues: failing vision, which gave him agonising headaches. He judged that the staccato rhythm of touch-typing had tightened his style. 'Our writing equipment takes part in the forming of our thoughts,' he wrote to a friend.

It was well into the next century before Truman Capote made the swipe at the Beats: 'It isn't writing at all, it's typing' – that remains a *de rigueur* footnote on Jack Kerouac's style, even though it's never been wholly clear what Capote meant by it. Was the charge that Kerouac was too spontaneous, or not spontaneous enough? Certainly he liked and favoured typing over handwriting, was unusually fast at it, and composed *On the Road* and *The Dharma Bums* on long scrolls of paper rather than separate sheets so as not to have to break his flow. But Capote's insult seems considerably less of one in days when his rival's method of committing a first draft directly to a keyboard is rather more common than his own process of pencil-writing two full drafts before typing two. One detects a not-inconsiderable degree of social snobbery in his comment: Capote hadn't laboured all his life to be accepted by the high-born and well-heeled just to see the limelight filched by blue-collar schlubs like Kerouac who lacked the refinement to eke out a longhand draft! What he made of the 'cut-up' technique favoured by Kerouac's associate William Burroughs – random strips of pre-printed matter cut out and assembled – goes unrecorded, although Burroughs made his feelings clear after the 1966 publication of *In Cold Blood*, with a letter telling Capote that he had 'written a dull unreadable book' and 'betrayed and sold out the talent that was granted you'. Kerouac himself had little time for cut-up: 'I wish [Burroughs]'d get back to those awfully funny stories of his,' he told the *Paris Review* in 1968. 'Cut-up is nothing new, in fact that steel-trap brain of mine does a lot of cutting up as it goes along ... as does everyone's brain while talking or thinking or writing.'

In the same interview Kerouac explains how typing saves him from the tyranny of self-correction, of trying to perfect his prose: 'I spent my entire youth writing slowly with revisions and endless rehashing speculation and deleting and got so I was writing one sentence a day and the sentence had no *feeling*. Goddamn it, *feeling* is what I like in art, not *craftiness* and the hiding of feelings.' And yet to many, it's the intervention of technology that implies craftiness, and blotchy old handwriting that serves to keep the process pure. Scratching a whole novel out in longhand still carries a certain puritanical cachet. Author interviews habitually detail their subjects' painstaking techniques. Joyce Carol Oates writes and rewrites her mammoth tomes by hand. So does Jackie Collins (she also has the manuscript bound in leather when she's done). Martin Amis recommends handwriting on the basis that, 'when you scratch out a word, it still exists there on the page. On the computer, when you delete a word it disappears forever …. Usually your first instinct is the right one.' James Ellroy, JK Rowling, even futurist and techno-dreamer William Gibson all attract interest for maintaining a commitment to longhand, even as handwriting becomes a rare sight rather than the singular mark of personality that it used to be.

Moving house recently, I came upon sackfuls of handwritten letters that I had received up to and during my student days from friends and boyfriends and family. The handwriting was piercingly familiar and still evocative of the individual's personality and physical manner. That's changed. I don't know what my friends' handwriting looks like now. I rarely see my partner's handwriting. Everyone's a font. Many are the Facebook font, Lucida Sans. As a student I was of the crossover generation that had one computer to a shared house, that usually submitted essays and always did exams in longhand, that knew how to use the grindingly slow dial-up internet, but didn't rely on it. But still, I've become accustomed enough to a life typed up on a screen that now if I write at length, I expect to be able to cut and paste whole paragraphs; to try sticking the beginning at the end; to substitute a name throughout.

The likes of Amis, Ellroy and Rowling have made a choice to keep handwriting , having grown up with it in co-existence with typewriting, and then home computers. Today's young writers, by contrast – unless they adopt a deliberately Luddite pose – will likely know writing foremost as typing, and typing first as typing on to a computer. And they might well have Facebook or Twitter open as they type, and crowd-source their research there, or execute it via quick dips into Google. And books written that way are liable – if not yet certain – to be read that way too: on screens, with distraction never far away.

To Walter Benjamin, the solitary nature of the endeavour was what distinguished the novel as a form. As he puts it in his essay *The Storyteller* (1945) – and in interesting contrast with the fashionable defence of all writers as storytellers and the book trade as an investment in storytelling above all – the novel 'neither comes from the oral tradition, nor goes into it. This distinguishes it from storytelling in particular. The storyteller takes what he tells from experience – his own or that reported by others. And he in turn makes it the experience of those who are listening to his tale. The novelist has isolated himself. The birthplace of the novel is the solitary individual, who ... is himself uncounselled, and cannot counsel others.'

Except that he (or she) can, if dictating, like Twain and James and like Milton before them. The receiver of the words is the first audience. However little an amanuensis might contribute (and Mary Howden was clear that she 'was not allowed to add so much as a comma' in Mark Twain's prose), the sharing of the manuscript between writer and scribe as it evolves stands in gentle contradiction of the image of the author as absolutely solitary creator, birthing an untouched, utterly subjective work. So too does an active relationship with an editor, with early readers, or with existing fans. Online chatrooms anxiously second-guessing the romantic destiny of the heroine of the Twilight series aren't the first manifestation of this interactivity. Fans, heeded or not, have long been forward in offering guidance to writers (Twain received particularly voluminous correspondence). Serialisation in magazines broke up the progress of Dickens's novels, allowing a gap for their content to be influenced by fluctuating sales or reader opinion. Julia McCord Chavez regards Dickens's serialisation as an early form of hypertext, which 'provides an opportunity for readers to experience reading as process and to share in the 'writerly' work of producing the text.' And Dickens further countered Benjamin's notion of the 'isolated' author by presenting his work in the form of performed public readings.

The birth of the typewriter, meanwhile, marks the commencement of the mechanisation of writing that would evolve with the word processor and the personal computer, and be expanded by experiments in automated writing in the form of machines, programmes, apps and supposedly success-generating plot formulae. **China Miéville** began his address to the Edinburgh conference by quoting the disapproving response of 1962 conference participant Lawrence Durrell to his encounter with a computer which could 'write sonnets if fed with the right material'. Subsequent experiments in artificial intelligence have generated many poems composed by computer programmes. The anthropomorphic urge that tempts us to credit robots with secret sensitivities can lend tremendous poignancy to these. Take these lines by Racter, a programme written by William Chamberlain and Thomas Etter which published a book of poetry and short prose in 1983:

> More than iron
> More than lead
> More than gold I need electricity
> I need it more than I need lamb or pork or lettuce or cucumber
> I need it for my dreams.

Novels are a tougher call for computers, although one invented by Alexander Propokovich did in 2008 take 72 hours to produce a version of Anna Karenina written in the style of Haruki Murakami. Much more standard, but also challenging to the notion of the creative autonomy of the writer, are the software packages, seminars and courses that train writers in strategies to make their books marketable. Story generators are popular as educational apps for children.

Do such labour-saving devices, in their ever-proliferating digital forms, really threaten the future organic creation of 'real' novels? And do new ways of reading inevitably engender limited forms of engagement with narrative? Or could such developments be means to develop and increase creativity and engagement, in both writers and readers? For some Conference participants, modern technology was not the waiting nemesis of the novel, but its best hope for survival. Miéville envisaged books as collective creative endeavours: open texts available online for amateur editing. French novelist **Mathias Énard**, speaking in Lisbon, wondered if the internet might bring forth 'an all-interactive, complex novel … which I wouldn't have to write, because the readers would write it …!'

As to reading, there is no shortage of interested parties who will assert, with equal parts certainty and regret, that long stories are simply against the modern mode of thinking. If the way in which the majority of us write has probably been altered by machinery, the way in which almost all of us read most certainly has; and it's a truism that our collective ability to focus has been irreparably impaired as a result. 'I'm not thinking the way I used to think,' fretted Nicholas Carr in a 2008 essay for *The Atlantic* entitled 'Is Google Making Us Stupid?' Immersing myself in a book or a lengthy article used to be easy .... Now my concentration often starts to drift after two or three pages. I get fidgety, lose the thread, begin looking for something else to do.' The world, Carr finds, provides the desired stupid-making distractions – and not just online. 'Television programs add text crawls and pop-up ads, and magazines and newspapers shorten their articles, introduce capsule summaries, and crowd their pages with easy-to-browse info-snippets .... Old media have little choice but to play by the new-media rules.' The result is that our soft and plastic brains are being altered, our cognitive pathways redrawn, in such a way that *no-one will ever read anything long ever again*. With apologies to Shakespeare: The oldest hath read most, we that are young/Shall never concentrate for half so long.

There is in this frequently voiced fear, of course, an element of the same things-are-getting-worse doom and gloomism that reliably infects the thinking of each generation as it edges closer to the grave – that has ex-punks condemn new music as 'just noise', children of the sexual revolution fret about short skirts and online porn and film buffs assert that cinema is absolutely, definitely now dead. Arguably this tendency has more to do with comfort than pessimism. Once the end of life creeps nearer than the beginning, and policemen and politicians start sprouting those baby faces, it can be gentler to imagine all that we loved going hopelessly to the dogs, than things getting more shiny, progressive and exciting once we're gone.

Speaking on the future of the novel at the World Writers' Conference in Turkey, **Inci Aral** discussed the hope that 'even today when we find ourselves bombarded by empty and meaningless visual images, we can still take refuge in good novels that contain that special element of the human spirit, and that 'as reading from the screen becomes more widespread the novel may still emerge victorious from the process.' The near future is, in this account of it, a stark choice, if not a fight to the death: insubstantial thrills from screen-based digital media, or spiritual solace and intellectual sustenance from real books printed on paper. By Aral's rationale, as in the dystopia described in Carr's essay, reading words off a screen has a radically different effect from reading them in a traditional book. 'We may well be reading more today than we did in the 1970s or 1980s,' Carr acknowledges in his essay '... but it's a different kind of reading.' And implicitly a *worse* kind: shallow, undemanding, obscurely but very definitely unwholesome. The comparison comes across as oddly moral, as once did the ire of vinyl buffs towards compact discs. It's not just a change in hardware: it's a loss of authenticity. Aral's stated fear is that in the all-electronic future, 'depth and content may suffer in the name of technique and the soul of the novel may be lost.'

And yet the list of qualities Aral ascribes to the book – 'portable, user-friendly, safe to use and you can even go to sleep with it in your hand' – also apply to the e-reader. So what is the soul of the novel? If it's not located in the writer's words, which we know can be replicated electronically, we must conclude that its soul is somehow contained in its form – is, in other words, made of paper. Maybe it's a component of that celebrated fragrance .... Romanticism regarding 'the smell of books' has gone from being a standard defence of the threatened medium, to a mockable hipster cliché. Somewhere between the two stages, a high-end perfumer, Geza Schoen, even created a scent intended to replicate it. (It was called Paper Passion and it retailed, during its brief novelty-item shelf life, for $98, with packaging by Karl Lagerfeld.) But the anxiety it conveys has something to do with permanence, with the perceived *weight* of printed characters versus the lightness of onscreen text. Kindles might have been carefully designed to appeal to the mildly technophobic – they can be dressed in cosy, tactile covers; they neither bleep nor forcibly connect to the internet; they emit a glow significantly less harsh than that from a laptop – but the print they display is nonetheless made up of pixels, not ink. To generations reared on print, those pixels powerfully convey that the content is insubstantial; delible; easy to alter; not really there. Implicit in the arguments of those who prize books printed on paper is the notion that books are real, like living things – while digital editions are sinister, overly perfect, like robots. Books, says Professor Faber in Ray Bradbury's *Fahrenheit 451*, 'show the pores in the face of life. The comfortable people want only the faces of the full moon, wax, faces without pores, hairless, expressionless.' E-books: creaseless, odourless, perfectible – poreless. *Unheimlich*, as Freudian terminology would have it: uncanny. In sentimental arguments about smell and tactility, the e-book is to the book as Freud's *doppelgänger* is to the human being: a theoretically indestructible defence against physical annihilation which by its very absence of organic vulnerability becomes creepy and untrustworthy.

But like the humanoid robots in the movies that unsettle us so when they malfunction, show their circuitry, or otherwise reveal that they are not so lifelike after all, e-books have limitations. Not to do with uncanny flawlessness, but with their simple functionality, their durability and their actual availability to be owned and kept. To protect rights-holders against the theoretically endless copy-and-paste reproduction made possible by digital formats, the text that's stored in the form of e-books is only hired by its purchasers. If paper can be burned – at 451 °F, as Ray Bradbury's account of a censorship-happy dystopia reminds us – e-book content can be recalled. It can also be altered. Should laws on censorship change, who's to say that the word 'nigger' couldn't be expunged from your e-copy of *Huckleberry Finn* (as it was from a recent revised edition), or your right to read *Lolita* or *American Psycho* or *Mein Kampf* or *The Anarchist Cookbook* withdrawn for your own good (as in each case various pressure groups, or in the final one the author himself, might prefer)?

Then there's the fact that Apple, Amazon and other distributors of e-books have made no commitment to maintain or protect a particular digital format. They're quite within their rights to cancel one, and leave an e-book collector with no access to his or her digital library. They might change their rules and start charging any old amount for access to their users' clouds of data; again, they haven't said that they won't. Or the companies themselves might cease to exist – in which case the rights of e-book owners to access the content they bought and paid for are a little obscure.

What drives the likes of Aral and Carr to worry, however, and to drumbeat for the survival of the traditional book over the rise of 'reading from a screen', would seem to be a less practical, more instinctive matter. Encased in statements such as theirs is a deep aversion to the perceived encroachment of a fast-moving, brightly-lit, disposable culture, one that thrives on novelty and discourages long-form composition, complexity of argument and the slow digestion of information. It's widely accepted that internet usage, social media and general technological saturation have decimated our attention spans (although the argument doesn't account for the length of Harry Potter books, the hours young people dedicate to acing intricate computer games, or, as Énard pointed out in Lisbon, publishers' ongoing preference for novels over short stories). The fear is that something once loved, and needed, and judged inherently improving and important – the long-form story on paper – has shed its relevance. And the fear creates the conviction that it should be saved; that it falls to a few defenders to *convince people they should want it back.*

Several Conference participants made the point that we have been here before: the death of the novel has been raised as an imminent inevitability since fairly close to its birth. Inci Aral acknowledged that 'the first worries about the [novel's] future surfaced as the era of Jane Austen, Stendhal and Flaubert drew to a close'. **Michel Le Bris**, speaking in St Malo, listed French thinkers from the time of transition between the nineteenth and twentieth century – Jules Romain, Ludovic Halévy, Edouard Rod, Jean Lorrain, Maurice Leblond, Lucien Maury, Camille Audigier, Louis Bertrand – who were united in offering a stark prognosis for the form. In Lorrain's version, the novel had been seen off by journalism; in Leblond's, by the impatient, novelty-crazed industrial age; Maury laid the blame with its own 'dryness of sentiment and moral scepticism'. The arguments, noted Le Bris 'are strangely familiar; they took place a century ago, but ring just as true today.'

Certainly they ring loudly. Threat and danger loomed large in many of the conference debates around the novel and its future. Speaking in Krasnoyarsk, **Konstantin Milchin** enumerated 'enemies' of the novel – 'new types of entertainment' that 'pull the attention of potential consumers away from the novel.' He identified a particular threat from television: documentaries and high-quality drama series. **Mathias Énard** in Lisbon echoed that movies and TV serials have 'taken a part of what the novel was'; Alexandre Dumas working today, he thought, would be writing for television. Which raises the interesting question: did we rely on books in part because we didn't have other forms, and should we accept that – even if modern technology hasn't somehow rewired our brains – the written word must cede to forms that now do some of its erstwhile jobs more efficiently than it can? Would people have clamoured so for the next instalment of *Little Dorrit* in print, if they had had the option of switching on a domestic screen and having it performed for them to a high standard? Have we the same need for poetic descriptions of the looks of unknown people and the atmospheres of unvisited places, when we have instantly shareable images, both still and moving – or for accounts of unheard conversations, when we can listen to endless recorded real ones? And if the evolution of communication methods does make the book less of a necessity, is resistance to its at least partial marginalisation a King Canute-style enterprise?

In his address on the future of the novel, given in Beijing, the Chinese novelist **Li Er** referenced Walter Benjamin's aforementioned *The Storyteller*, distilling its take on the modern world as a lament for a craft rendered obsolete by lack of demand. 'With the advent of capitalism and modern media ... the idea that novels have a duty to express individual experience has almost lost its reason to exist.' The danger, especially pertinent in a China in the throes of coming to terms with subjectivity and individual affirmation, is the development of a sophisticated, adaptive capitalist system that understands, absorbs and utilises that awareness of idiosyncrasy; one that 'can devour anything new, and is constantly draining the individual's subjectivity. Facing it is like facing a dinosaur of a system; it exists as a gigantic alienation of the self.' So subjective consciousness becomes another sales hook – like the ads that tell an undifferentiated mass 'You're unique', or the Coca Cola campaign that makes a certain percentage of people feel special by printing frequently occurring names on to bottles. In Michel Le Bris's opinion, the dizzying flow both of information and of populations between cultures and territories emphasises rather than negates the subjective self and its narrative. We find a world 'in which everyone, standing at a crossroads of multiple identities, will find themselves forced to invent a 'personal story' in order to make sense of themselves ... a dangerous world in which the imagination will be challenged ... a fascinating world in which creative fiction will play a central part.'

So novels, with their intensely private mode of consumption and their access to their characters' and readers' interiority – what Finland's **Rosa Liksom** in Lisbon called 'the intimate situation in which you meet the book' – can be seen as more viable than ever: they are bastions against the colonisation of the self. 'Fiction is once again centre stage', insisted Le Bris in his keynote. 'Evidently, it says something – otherwise we would be indifferent, but not so, we read, voraciously, we cannot be stopped, we are enthralled – *something which cannot be said in any other way.*'

But it can be presented, mounted, bound and printed in a multitude of ways. This momentous thing, this threatened thing, this novel: does it enthral us most effectively in its traditional paper form? Or is that the mere wistful projection of Luddites and nostalgists? We could consult the late Ray Bradbury, who said in 2000, 'Nothing a computer can do can compare to a book …. All the computer can give you is a manuscript. People don't want to read manuscripts. They want to read books. Books smell good. They look good. You can press it to your bosom. You can carry it in your pocket.' Or we could turn back to his creation Professor Faber, who tells Guy Montag in *Fahrenheit 451*, 'It's not books you need, it's some of the things that once were in books …. Books were only one type or receptacle where we stored a lot of things we were afraid we might forget. There is nothing magical in them at all. The magic is only in what books say, how they stitched the patches of the universe together into one garment for us.'

The autonovelator

by China Miéville
Keynote, Edinburgh, August 2012

'I have just … paid a depressing visit to an electronic computer which can write sonnets if fed with the right material,' said Lawrence Durrell, at the session fifty years ago of which this is an echo. 'I have a feeling that by Christmas it will have written its first novel, and possibly by next Christmas novel sets will be on sale at Woolworths and you will all be able to buy them, and write your own.'

Notionally, the horror here is something to do with the denigration of human creativity. But Durrell is aghast in particular that these novel sets will be on sale at Woolworths – the tragedy, perhaps, might have been a little lessened if they'd been exclusive to Waitrose.

It's not clear how scared he really was. Futures of anything tend to combine possibilities, desiderata, and dreaded outcomes, sometimes in one sentence. There's a feedback loop between soothsaying and the sooth said, analysis is bet and aspiration and warning. I want to plural, to discuss not the novel but novels, not the future, but futures. I'm an anguished optimist. None of the predictions here are impossible: some I even think are likely; most I broadly hope for; and one is a demand.

•

A first hope: the English-language publishing sphere starts tentatively to revel in that half-recognised distinctness of non-English-language novels, and with their vanguard of Scandinavian thrillers, small presses, centres and prizes for translation, continue to gnaw at the 3% problem [the estimated average percentage of books sold in the US that are works in translation], all striving against the still deeply inadequate but am-I-mad-to-think-improving-just-a-little profile of fiction translated into English.

And translation is now crowd-sourced, out of love. Obscure works of the Russian avant-garde and new translations of Bruno Schulz are available to anyone with access to a computer. One future is of glacially slowly decreasing parochialism. And those publishers of translated fiction are also conduits for suspicious-making foreign Modernism.

•

What is literature, and what do we want from it? The former is a key question, which I'm going to duck. What do we want from it? Many things. One is an expression of something otherwise inexpressible. An ineffability, by which you don't at all have to be a person of faith to have your breath taken away. Jewish mysticism warns of the *qliphoth* – husks, entropic shells of psychic muck and detritus that encrust and obscure the numinous. As you can tell, I'm turning my attention to English fiction.

Paulo Coelho's ill-judged Joyce-bashing has made him a butt of scorn at the Edinburgh conference (see Ali Smith p.290), but he's a safe target because, with books that multi-task a little too openly as self-help manuals, he's not so clubbable. Unlike, say, Ian McEwan, who not-that-differently declared against 'the dead hand of modernism', for all the world as if the dominant literary mode in post-war England was Steinian experimentation or some Albion Oulipo, against which young Turks hold out with limpidly observed interiority, decodable metaphors, strained middle-class relationships and eternal truths of the human condition (™).

All the usual caveats: yes, there are admirable novels written according to such norms, and conversely there have always been writers playing with form, et cetera. But two things remain key.

i) The culturally dominant strain of the English novel has for years been what Zadie Smith called 'lyrical realism': the remorseless prioritisation, with apologies for repeating my favourite heuristic, of recognition over estrangement.

ii) Today it is not quite qliphothic business as usual.

After the Booker Middlebrowmaggedon of 2011, the following year's judges were far too polite to draw attention to their task, which was to salvage something. But they didn't do badly. Longlists are performances, and while it's appropriate to cavil about our excluded favourites, the list sent various messages rather well. Including that the Booker is rapproching with that so-called dead hand.

There've been other wind-blown straws. The muted, palpable recent shame when Christine Brooke-Rose died, that this astonishing innovator was so overlooked in the country of her birth. Renewed interest in Ann Quin. Excitement at the online archive Ubuweb. With the internet has come proof that there are audiences way beyond the obvious.

•

I really, really don't want to talk about genre, because I always really want to, and nerd-whines are boring. But a détente between litfic and its others is real. It's a cliché to point out that generic tropes are infecting the mainstream, with a piling-up of various apocalypses by those guilty of literature. But on the other side, say, an extensive interview with Yinka Tutuola, son of the legendary Nigerian writer Amos Tutuola, about his father's work, is online not at any traditional outlet of the literati but at *Weird Fiction Review*, a fabulous site that emerges, with brilliance and polymath gusto, out of genre traditions.

It was a generic, science-fictional horror that oppressed Durrell, those fiction engines. He's not the only writer to have suffered this nightmare: the Automatic Novel Writing Machine crops up repeatedly in fiction as a sign of awful futurity. Given the fire, flood, uneasy dead and enormity on which one can draw, it's an underwhelmingly terrifying dystopia, a future in the despotic thrall of the autonovelator, but *après nous le déluge* – writers would far rather suffer planetary catastrophe than de-skilling, or a scab algorithm.

•

The machine is unbuilt. The past future of the novel did not lie in being digitally produced. As traumatically, it's being digitally distributed.

We are, at last, leaving phase one of the e-book discussion, during which people could ritually invoke the 'smell of paper' as a call to cultural barricades. Some anxieties are tenacious: how will people know what a splendid person I am without a pelt of the right visible books on my walls, without the pretty qliphoth husks? A hopeful future: that our grandchildren will consider our hankering for erudition-décor a little needy.

Early predictions for what digitality would do to the novel look pretty creaky, as the futures of the past always do. The hypertext novel? A few interesting experiments. The enhanced e-book, with soundtrack and animation? A banal abomination.

In fact what's becoming obvious – an intriguing counterpoint to the growth in experiment – is the tenacity of relatively traditional narrative-arc-shaped fiction. But you don't radically restructure how the novel's distributed and not have an impact on its form. Not only do we approach an era when absolutely no-one who really doesn't want to pay for a book will have to, but one in which the digital availability of the text alters the relationship between reader, writer, and book. The text won't be closed.

•

It never was, of course – think of the scrivener's edit, the monk's mashup – but it's going to be even less so. Anyone who wants to shove their hands into a book and grub about in its innards, add to and subtract from it, and pass it on, will, in this age of distributed text, be able to do so without much difficulty, and some are already starting.

One response might be a rearguard clamping down, as in the punitive model of so-called antipiracy action. About which here I'll only say – as someone very keen to continue to make a living from writing – that it's disingenuous, hypocritical, ineffectual, misunderstands the polyvalent causes and effects of online sharing, is moribund, and complicit with toxicity.

The Creators' Rights Alliance, with which my own trade union is associated, put out a manifesto that ends with a chilling injunction: '[A] fundamental part of this provision should involve education about intellectual property .... All schoolchildren should be encouraged in the habit of using the copyright symbol with their work, whether it be an essay or a musical composition.' The concept behind copyright is so simple that a child can understand it: 'I made it: it's mine.' A collection of artists and activists advocating the neoliberalisation of children's minds. That is scandalous and stupid. The text is open. This should – could – be our chance to remember that it was never just us who made it, and it was never just ours.

•

The problem with emphasising the authorial voice, and the novel's survival, even in its new forms, even with a permeable membrane between text and reader, is that it's hard to do so without sounding as if one's indulging a kind of ahistorical Olympian simpering at the specialness of writers. That the novel is as tenacious as a cockroach is morally neutral. We can hope for a good novel – created by whatever means – decry bad ones, and observe with a shrug that in total they endure.

To love literature doesn't mean we have to aggrandise it or those who create it. That aggrandisement is undermined by the permeable text. Be ready for guerrilla editors. Just as precocious 14-year-olds brilliantly – or craply – remix albums and put them up online, people are starting to provide their own cuts of novels. In the future, asked if you've read the latest Ali Smith or Ghada Karmi, the response might be not yes or no, but 'which mix', and why?

We'll be writing as part of a collective. As we always were. And so might anyone else be.

'You will all be able to buy them,' Durrell says of those novel-writing kits, addressing not the other writers, who didn't need them, but the public, 'and write your own.' That's a telling elision – he starts by kvetching about writing by machine, by no one, and segues instantly to doing so about writing by the public, by everyone. That's apocalypse. That, apparently, is a nightmare future.

The worst anxiety is not that the interfering public will ruin your work if they muck about with it, or that they'll write a terrible novel, but that they'll improve it, or write a great one. And once in a rare while, some of them will. How wonderful that will be.

You don't have to think that writing is lever-pulling, that anyone could have written *Jane Eyre* or *Notebook of a Return to my Native Land* to think that the model of writers as the Elect is at best wrong, at worst, a bit slanderous to everyone else. We piss and moan about the terrible quality of self-published books, as if slews of god-awful crap weren't professionally expensively published every year.

•

Of course there are contexts in which particular books become politically important, and writers who exhibit astonishing bravery in the face of oppression. For the most part we're not talking about that. What if most fiction – which, yes, we all do and should love – is at best moderately important? What if it's so vague and culturally dribblesome and so mediated by everything else, once the culture industry extrudes it through a writer-shaped nozzle, that our stentorious declarations about subversive literature are, mostly, kind of adorable?

Stand down. The blurring of boundaries between writers, books, and readers, self-publishing, the fanfication of fiction, doesn't mean some people won't be better than others at the whole writing thing, or unable to pay their rent that way – it should, though, undermine that patina of specialness. Most of us aren't that special, and the underlining of that is a good thing, the start of a great future. In which we can maybe focus more on the books. Which might even rarely be special.

One of the problems, we often hear, about online piracy, e-books and their ephemeral-seeming invisible files, is that they 'devalue writing', that our work is increasingly undervalued. Well, yes. Just like the work of nurses, teachers, public transport staff, cleaners, social workers, which has been undervalued a vast amount more for a whole lot longer. We live in a world that grossly and violently undervalues the great majority of people in it.

It's that hegemony of the market again. We've railed against it – as we should – throughout the Conference. There's a contingent relationship between book sales and literary merit, so we should totally break the pretence at a connection, because of our amplifying connection to everyone else, and orient future-ward with a demand.

What if novelists and poets were to get a salary, the wage of a skilled worker?

•

This would only be an exaggeration of the national stipends already offered by some countries for some writers. For the great majority of people who write, it would mean an improvement in their situation, an ability to write full-time. For a few it would mean an income cut, but you know what? It was a good run. And surely it's easily worth it to undermine the marketisation of literature for some kind of collectivity.

But who decides who qualifies as a writer? Does it take one sonnet? Of what quality? Ten novels? 50,000 readers? Ten, but the right readers? God knows we shouldn't trust the state to make that kind of decision. So we should democratise that boisterous debate, as widely and vigorously as possible. It needn't be the mere caprice of taste. Which changes. And people are perfectly capable of judging as relevant and important literature for which they don't personally care. Mistakes will be made, sure, but will they really be worse than the philistine thuggery of the market?

We couldn't bypass the state with this plan, though. So for the sake of literature, apart from any- and everything else, we'll have to take control of it, invert its priorities, democratise its structures, replace it with a system worth having.

So an unresentful sense of writers as people among people, and a fidelity to literature, require political and economic transformation. For futures for novels – and everything else. In the context of which futures, who knows what politics, what styles and which contents, what relationships to what reconceived communities, which struggles to express what inexpressibles, what stories and anti-stories we will all strive and honourably fail to write, and maybe even one day succeed?

The protean genre

The novel is adaptable – 'chimerical', one delegate to the Conference called it. That makes its future hard to predict, but it is also the very thing that will guarantee its survival. 'The novel has always been there, said **Hubert Haddad** in St Malo. 'It is a place where you ask the reader to be both credulous and critical. You ask the reader to go along with a story in which he has access to all forms of knowledge. It is not a genre, it is all genres at once. It can embrace or include all genres – including poetry, the dynamics of the theatre. The infinite scope of the novel is due to precisely that. It has been said that the novel is Proteus, and has infinite energy in the way that it stages the fable of civilisation.'

Sema Kaygusuz, speaking in İzmir, also took comfort in the novel's deep historical roots. 'The novel is not an invention, it is a discovery. Human beings discovered it in the Greek tragedies, in Boccaccio, in songs, in mythological stories. It is a very elastic form, but literature changes. Some forms of literature are going to die. In France for example, nobody wants to read short stories any more, and it's difficult to get them published. In Germany, it's the same with poetry. I would make a case for short stories becoming a major art form over the course of the next fifty years. I am always asking myself why I am reading any given book. And what I think is this: when I read, I am remembering what I know. Someone once asked Bach how he wrote his great music. He replied: "I don't know, I am just remembering it." I once saw a girl, in Anatolia, weaving cloth in an intricate very colourful pattern. I asked her who had taught her the design, and she said: "I just feel it in my belly." Our reading likewise taps into some deep knowledge that resides inside our unconscious.'

To the Russian delegates in Krasnoyarsk, this view would have seemed like a kind of Freud-tinged sentimentalism. They all concurred that the classic narrative novel as we know it today is a capitalist construct, a coinage of the Victorian bourgeoisie (see p.66). But **Tibor Fischer** had an answer for that argument, and it did not rest on any writerly gut instinct about humanity's storytelling heritage. 'Let's go back before the nineteenth century,' he said. 'I am re-reading Henry Fielding. His novel *Joseph Andrews* was published in 1742, a period when the term "novel" wasn't generally used, and people didn't really have an idea of what a novel should be. Fielding called his book a "history". Andrey [Astvatsaturov] has said that novels should be about incidents and essays and philosophy – and that is exactly what *Joseph Andrews* is. It's full of odd stories and diversions and authorial jokes, and you could mount a quite convincing argument that it is in fact a post-modern novel, because there is also meta-fiction. Richardson's Pamela – a fictional character – walks in and plays a role. So part of the problem is that there are certain expectations of the novel that date from the nineteenth century – and people do think that the novel was invented then – but no, we have examples from classical Greece and Rome that are pretty much the same thing as the novel. They are unlike, say, Balzac in that they may not have lengthy descriptions of furniture and décor, but the essential human relationships are all there.'

Inci Aral, in İzmir, was confident that the novel's reach could only increase. 'The powers of the novel to push the boundaries artistically or to engage in linguistic experimentation are vast. The author is free to do whatever he or she wishes between the covers of the book. The novel, which has no boundary other than its own narrative and aesthetic style never ceases to search for novelty. If it is to find new fields of existence in an electronic medium and an on-screen format then this will be alongside the existing printed form and will allow it to evolve in a new and altogether different manner. We cannot deny the fact that most readers today find themselves in front of a screen, and that the very practice of reading is declining in importance. It has been shown that in developed countries less than half of all adults read novels, and the number of readers, especially among the young, is rapidly falling. The situation is no doubt related to changing habits in the use of on-screen technology. The computer screen is used for entertainment, learning, leisure, shopping and self-expression, and is now a fundamental part of everyday life. Nevertheless the fact that most readers find themselves in front of a screen does not mean that they will cease to read. The drop-off in reader numbers should be ascribed to the struggle of paper versus screen and the pursuit of convenience. As reading from the screen becomes more widespread the novel may still emerge victorious from the process.'

Denise Mina, at the same session, provided examples of the ways in which the novel could adapt to outside pressures, could bend with the winds of change. 'Before the magazine, novelists needed a large number of wealthy subscribers in order to convince publishers to publish a book. People would pay for a book before it was written, the money would go to the publisher, and the subscribers would receive the book at the end of the process. the rise of monthly magazines that people could subscribe to meant that novelists such as Dickens and Poe could publish stories sequentially – every month a chapter that could later be gathered together into a book. That meant that they could make a living while they were writing, which was very radical. Another example: all novels published during the Second World War had to be 250 pages or fewer – because of paper rationing. It was in this period that Graham Greene produced his thrillers, which wouldn't have worked if they had been allowed to be longer. And one of the reasons that Orwell's works are so powerful is that they are very short. So these pragmatic constraints have an effect on style, and can produce quite radical shifts.' **Nathan Englander** in Edinburgh saw these shifts and external pressures as a literary form of natural selection, driving the novel as a species to adapt to new surroundings or perish. 'If it's going to die, let it die. I really am Darwinian on this point. The photograph did not kill the painting, and the moving picture did not kill the photograph; the talkie killed the silent film – except that this year a silent film won, like, twenty Oscars.' [*The Artist* (2011) was in fact nominated for ten, and won five].

Several delegates referred to a 'food chain' of publishing, meaning the dependent relationships within the fiction industry between writers, editors and readers, publishing houses, agents, bookshops, reviewers .... Fischer, citing Bakhtin, pointed out that the novel itself 'is an omnivore, and omnivores are good at survival. They can weather disaster. The novel won't die because its about a very basic impulse, storytelling, and it resides in the first and most essential form of communication, language. It will always have the ability to reinvent itself, to resurrect itself. **Michel Le Bris** used a similar predator metaphor. 'The novel feeds on its competitors,' he said. 'It is an extraordinarily plastic, flexible form compared to other art forms. So long at it can integrate and absorb techniques – from cinema and elsewhere – it will live.'

Jonathan Bastable (ed.)

After the Novelist

by Teju Cole
Keynote, Melbourne, August 2013

'A great writer is one who elongates the perspective of human sensibility,' Brodsky wrote. This is one understanding of what novels do: they take us to the limits of experience and of ourselves. For Brodsky, exemplars of such writing were Andrei Platonov and (he cites her memoirs) Nadezhda Mandelshtam. In the twentieth century, we can think of any number of writers who might fit Brodsky's criterion. Among those whose work is more troubled and strained, there are Camus, Woolf, Beckett, and Blanchot, just to name a few. But there are many others who also show us that human sensibility is more than we might have guessed. Our world is bigger because of Achebe, García-Márquez, Laxness, and Yourcenar. The diversity of these names indicates the obvious: excellence in the novel is not one-dimensional. It is a capacious form, one which allows for many kinds of victory.

But another kind of novel exists, one which Brodsky perhaps would not have recognised as elongating the perspective of human sensibility. When we talk about 'the novel,' are we referring to the examples cited above – literary novels of high achievement, diverse as they are – or are we talking about novels that are written as a product for the publishing market? It is true that the line between a purely commercial novel and an accomplished work of art is not completely clear. Some bestsellers are very well-written, and some magnificiently strange books sell well; but we cannot claim that they are indistinguishable. So, when we talk about the future of the novel, it is worth acknowledging that there are distinct ambitions, independent of style, in the works classified by the very term 'novel'. I would like to follow Brodsky and be concerned only with those works that elongate the perspective of human sensibility. I acknowledge the existence of the other kind, the kind that an author can write many of in one year, the kind that the reader hardly remembers reading, the kind that fits neatly into a genre and whose main purpose is to help the reader pass some hours on a plane: the survival or evolution of this more ubiquitous type of novel is not of particular interest to me.

Instead, I want to think about the health of that artificial line that goes from Rabelais to Flaubert to Joyce to Jelinek. What will become of this tradition of the novel which, as Randall Jarrell wrote, is 'a prose narrative of some length that has something wrong with it'? If there is more and more pressure from the other kind of novel, the neat and untroubled novel that has nothing wrong with it, how shall we sustain the novel that has something wrong with it?

But we are thinking about a tradition whose founders, Rabelais and Cervantes, did not consider themselves 'novelists.' What they did was write long (very long) prose full of productive defects. This, I think, might be where the novel will begin to return. There might be a homing instinct inside the novel that is carrying it back home to its wild origins.

The novel's great flourishing, market-wise, was in the nineteenth century, when *Pride and Prejudice* and *Effi Briest* and the French *roman d'analyse* entered fully into the life of the middle classes. It was a flourishing and it was also, of course, a poisoning, because one strand of the novel intensified what was human – ragged and flickering – about the form, but another strand became the crammed attic of all that was sentimental and settled. The early twentieth century kicked against this. We entered the era of the future of the novel: one answer to the question 'What is the future of the novel?' even now is still *Ulysses*. Another is *Mrs. Dalloway*. Yet another is *The Man Without Qualities*. It was in this era that the novel began to escape the novel again, with all kinds of inclusions that had not been seen since the early days, since Rabelais, Fielding and the other rough-mannered originators. The twentieth century modernist novel made itself a home for a long narrative about characters and their interactions, but it also allowed for their thoughts, their philosophical digressions, and their walks. The novel contained memoir, philosophy, law, letters, history, theology, yesterday's news, and, with full gusto and disorienting commitment in *Finnegans Wake*, even dreams and incomprehensibility.

It was electrifying, but we had gone too close to the edge. We had to retreat. And so – and of course I'm simplifying terribly – the Anglo-American novel in particular became quite a conservative thing (the French continued to fight the good fight). For every Faulkner in the US, there was a highly praised Pearl Buck and a deified Steinbeck. What could not be understood and enjoyed by everyone was considered with suspicion. We, particularly in America, entered the age of prizes and consensus. Experimentation remained alive, particularly as the novel found its way to cultures that had hitherto not written many novels, but the biggest names in Anglo-American publishing tended to be safe, the sort of names that did well on school curricula or found themselves quite happy in book clubs. The Pulitzer Prize for literature was unerringly middlebrow. This was the age of Austen and Dickens all over again, but with little of the sparkling quality of those popular but brainy novelists.

All the while, though, futurists of different stripes carried on their work, for the most part with less glare on their enterprise. Barth and Coover, Ondaatje and Naipaul, Frame and Murnane, Bender and Shields: many kept on sewing the suit of experimentalism in the shadows, influenced by their contemporaries in poetry. The Latin American boom and the Indian and African literatures it infected carried this work forward. *Tristram Shandy* migrated to Cartagena and to Bombay.

This was the work of the full-dressed post-*Ulysses* school (though no-one is post-*Ulysses*; we are all somehow still catching up to it). It is against this backdrop that we might try to understand what the internet in general, and Twitter in particular, mean for experimental prose. For isn't this, in all its narration and ungoverned excess, where we might now be going? Isn't Twitter the most vivid illustration since *Ulysses* of what full inclusion might mean? There are two hundred million people on Twitter. They are all writing, and all are writing under a formal constraint.

This leads one, almost, into a mystical formulation: on Twitter there is no 'novelist' but there is a novel: Twitter is the continuity of the published thoughts of all the people present on Twitter. It had a beginning, but it has no end. And each second, thousands of pages are added, millions of contributions per day. And each person who reads it, as Heraclitus might have promised, reads something different from everyone else. This is an inclusiveness, from an unexpected direction, that might begin to affect even the practice of the conventional published novel. It's hard to imagine that it wouldn't: most young novelists are themselves active on Twitter now. The atomised mode of information dispersal is more and more natural, and less and less 'experimental' or elite.

Consider this statement: 'Consciousness does not appear to itself chopped up in bits. Such words as "chain" or "train" do not describe it fitly as it presents itself in the first instance. It is nothing jointed; it flows. A "river" or a "stream" are the metaphors by which it is most naturally described. In talking of it hereafter, let us call it the stream of thought, of consciousness, or of subjective life.' This was written by William James' in 1890, in *The Principles of Psychology*. It was later taken as an apt coinage for the efforts of Joyce, Woolf, and Mansfield. The description fits, even more exactly, the experience of reading Twitter.

Though there are interesting individual experiments on Twitter, I am drawn to the original meaning of 'individual': that which is undivided. It is the undivided, undifferentiated cascade of thoughts streaming past the timeline that makes me suspect that Twitter is, indeed, elongating the perspective of human sensibility. I want to suggest, then, that Twitter is one of the futures of the novel. In a time of commercial publishing and excellent television, the novelist is smaller than ever before. But the novel itself, it seems, is suffering the opposite fate: it is getting bigger and bigger, and gradually swallowing the whole world.

Twitter storms

The discussion that followed **Teju Cole**'s keynote speech centred on his high hopes for Twitter – on whether its constant, never-ending torrent of nano-opinions and thoughtlets in some ways resembled a real-world version of Joyce's stream-of-consciousness technique. Could it be that the Twittersphere was the expression of a kind of global mind, an interior monologue of the type that (as many delegates to the Conference noted) the novel has always done uniquely well? And might the formal constraints of the tweet open the way to a new and challenging narrative genre? Cole was in discussion with **Christy Dena**, an Australian writer who specialises in storytelling through electronic media. 'You spoke about shared ideas, consciousness and flow,' she said to Cole. 'The novel is a medium in which the thoughts of a person can be delivered, and there is a parallel there with Twitter. Do you see that as the core function of the novel, part of its essence?'

'One of the similarities between the novel and Twitter is this transference of consciousness, said Cole. 'In a film, for example, everything has to be *shown*, however subtle the movie is in other ways. Music is quite abstract. In the case of a novel, you are sitting down and spending hours in the presence of the consciousness of another person, one that has been transferred into your own via language. It occurs to me that Twitter, unlike other forms of writing and other social media, has brought us closer to seeing what it might be like to have access to people's thoughts. The barrier is very low between having a thought and having it enter the minds of lots of other people all over the world.'

'It is removed from storytelling in the sense that people are not constructing a fictional world,' said Dena.

'Yes. From the very beginning the novel has been concerned with telling a coherent story that has boundaries – and this is one way in which

Twitter is not at all like a novel. There is a continuity between Cervantes and Ian McEwan, no matter how different they are. It is a peculiar thing to go back and look at a week of tweets when, say, you haven't been able to connect. You find everyone yabbering on about the very same concerns – last week's concerns. There is something very specifically historically grounded about it. If you look at Twitter from a week ago, then the concerns are utterly different. So despite the disorderliness, there are stories being told.' One might argue that any yellowing stack of old newspapers does that job just as well as a slightly neglected Twitter feed – and can make for equally diverting reading. Surely the thing that transmutes a more or less random assortment of facts and thoughts into a novel is their having been mediated through a single consciousness, through an intelligence that has its own individual way of marshalling the material and crafting the words? A novel, in other words, is by definition a thing that is consciously and deliberately *written by someone*. Isn't that what Cole meant when he said that the traditional novel, unlike Twitter, has coherence?

Dena suggested another way in which Twitter is unlike a story, namely, its spontaneity, its goldfish-like in-the-momentness. 'In your novel [*Open City*] you parallel the past and present of New York,' she said. 'But Twitter is a perpetual present.'

'Yes – it's maddening. And in a way, all the critical reception of Katherine Mansfield and Virginia Woolf and the Modernists was a longing to get closer and closer to what it might feel like to be in the minds of other persons – in a stream-like way. There was a longing, a desire to get at people's chattering thoughts. I am not even sure that this cascade of thoughts is a good thing. It's interesting, of course, but now all the unhappiness that exists in the world can be there every time you look at your phone.' This, in its nightmarishly technological guise, is exactly the 'squirrel's heartbeat' that George Eliot so feared, and that was cited by Ahdaf Soueif in her keynote speech on literature and politics (see p.104). For a writer, the greatest enemy of promise is no longer the pram in the hall, but the buzzing smartphone in the pocket.

At least it is for some. 'Do the expectations that people have for social media impinge on the time you have to write?' asked Dena. 'Not really,' said Cole. 'For me writing is thinking – and after that comes the bit where you sit down and transcribe your thoughts. That's the easy part. You have to defend the space where you do your thinking, but for me being online helps that process, because I want to know how other people think. I know that for others, online is a terrible distraction. As for the writing, how long does it take to write a 300-page novel, if all you had to do was type it. It could be done in a week. But it actually takes years to write one, so I don't think the raw time is a theft. The real question is: does the online dimension degrade your ability to think, or does it enhance it? I suspect that there is a slightly moralistic thing that happens with all new technology: if 'steamboats are ruining everything', then connectivity is the steamboat of our time. But actually connectivity is not ruining anything. I'm gathering ideas, I'm interested in the conversation, so when I'm on Twitter I'm working. I don't think Twitter kills the novel.'

'It's been said that one of the problems we have is complexity, that we cannot sustain the number of connections that we have.'

'Yes, and it's almost more than a person can bear. I find now that if I send out a tweet – and there must be some kind of internet law that describes this phenomenon – then it gets every possible response. People will correct my grammar and spelling, they will insult me enthusiastically without the least idea what they are talking about. I could tweet "I like daffodils.", and someone would tweet back "You're such a fucking idiot, who likes daffodils?' or "How can you tweet about flowers when there are people dying in Syria?" If there is anything that sometimes makes me want to take a step back from Twitter, it is that intensity and excess of response. Especially once you realise that what they are responding to is not your work, but a simplified idea of who you are. It is freeing. You can go through life thinking that all opinions are valid – until you encounter all opinions.'

'But that must change the way you write, because you are hearing what people think about your writing in a more direct way than was ever possible before.'

'I hate to admit it, but I think that's true. In the old days – five years ago – the voice in your head that you worried about was that of your parents and grandparents. You said to yourself: I can't write that sex scene; what if my mother reads it? Those were the inhibitive voices. Now we have a fuller sense of the variety of response. For the most part you can dismiss them, but they are there. The best advice I've ever had (and it's strange how the best advice can be so obvious and plain-spoken) was from a friend who said: no matter what you write now, there are lots of people who are going to hate it and let you know.'

Or they can join in – contribute rather than criticise. Dena raised the question of collaborative writing via Twitter and other digital channels. 'People talk about new media suddenly having created participation, but in fact the desire for participation has always been there,' she said. 'With Twitter we have the idea that everyone is doing the writing, but all of these desires in media interact. It is an ecology in which people respond to the novel, but there might be a movement in the other direction that would yield a new kind of solidified novel.' In this connection an audience member mentioned *The Lizzie Bennett Diaries*, a modern version of *Pride and Prejudice* told through 100 five-minute YouTube videos (the crucial marriage proposal scene was tagged #darcyday). Another participant brought up Jennifer Egan's *Black Box*, a short story told through a long series of tweets. 'It was interesting because she was working within the constraints of 140 characters. What is fascinating is that no two readings of it will be the same, because we each curate who we follow differently, so there are lots of other voices there in the storyline. I wonder if that is closer to the Joycean idea.'

The same speaker went on to say that she thought the story was somehow less interesting when re-printed in full in *The New Yorker*. Why might that be? Perhaps because the formal 140-word constraint becomes a meaningless gimmick on the page. Who's counting, after all? The printed version of Black Box also does away – inevitably – with the illusion of spontaneity, with the implied conceit that the tweets in the story were dashed off and posted inside a minute. And in fact Egan has said that she spent a year honing and polishing her long series of tweets, the first drafts of which were written by hand in a Japanese notebook. That particular notebook was perfect for the job because it happened to have three neat rectangles printed on every page – each of them like an empty 'New Tweet' window or (you might say) like the index cards on which Nabokov wrote his novels. At any rate, the process of writing a Twitter novel seems to have been ironically low-tech, and traditionally long-winded.

'Jennifer Egan is a wonderful novelist, but I didn't think her Twitter experiment worked,' responded Cole. 'I think it misunderstood what Twitter is good at. And we often find this. The funniest people on Twitter, for example, are not necessarily the professional stand-up comics. You need a different energy, a different wildness. I think there are people doing interesting narrative things on Twitter – but I don't think they are Pulitzer-prize-winning novelists. One of the reasons people founder when they are trying to tell a story on Twitter is that they forget that this stuff arrives in people's timelines suddenly, in the midst of everything else that they are doing. So it needs not only to work as a story, but each individual tweet has to work by itself, as a piece of language and a piece of narrative. It has to have a peculiar kind of completeness. Everyone knows that Brahms' Fourth Symphony is a masterpiece – but if you chopped it into three-minute slices and played them as pop songs, it would not work, because it is meant to be listened to over time. And yet there is such a thing as a perfect three-minute pop song, which can be just as moving and exciting in its way, but it is crafted to be that size and length.'

Dena provided an another example of Twitter fiction. 'A few years ago Jay Bushman – who was responsible for *The Lizzie Bennett Diaries* – created *War of the Worlds* on Twitter. The idea was that everyone knows what happens in that book, so he would tweet 'provocations' that anyone could pick up on. So other people might tweet: "I am in Melbourne and we can see UFOs overhead!" Everyone had the structure and they performed within it. That's been done successfully a few times, with different novels.' Of course, Orson Welles famously did precisely the same thing when he adapted *War of the Worlds* as a radio play in 1938 – that is, make the narrative material mimic the tropes and forms of the medium through which it was broadcast. The difference with the Twitter version is the global participation that Dena mentioned – but what then is the end product: a collaborative novel? A crowd-sourced art-happening? A hashtag ekphrasis?

A member of the Melbourne audience asked how the novel might look in twenty or thirty years' time. Dena thought books on paper would eventually become antiques, quaint objects that were once vitally useful and meaningful but not any more – like sugar shakers and cigarette cases. 'In the far, far future it will be something that people collect like vinyl records.' Cole at first took refuge in a pessimistic joke: 'I think you are going to be walking down the street and taking in information from your contact lenses with video and streaming text. And I think it's mostly going to be *Fifty Shades* kind of stuff. Whips and chains coming through your lenses while you sit in the kindergarten meeting with the other parents. Just a guess.'

Then, at the last, he grew a little wistful about his chosen genre, the essence of which he saw as indestructible. 'We have only had printed novels for 500 years. If they are gone in 50 years, that's OK. Because in any period the people with the whirlwind within them will find a way to express themselves. That is what survives, the forceful creativity which, like the DNA that uses our bodies to recreate itself, finds a way to proliferate. I'm not sure if we can make a judgment as to which is more desirable: the novel with its retrospective gaze, the book that you can always go back to; or, on the other hand, the incessant presentness of something like Twitter. Both are presenting human complexity to us in ways that can teach us a lot.

'My old-fashioned side sees a difference in that the novel is able to provide a kind of comfort. There is a solace that you get in the three days that it takes you to read a really good novel. Online cannot do that yet, not in the way that natural light falling on a printed page can. The novel can still be a place of tremendous slowness: you are spending time in the pages of a book, and an author is willing to honour your intelligence by being very slow, and dares to demand that you read 300 or 400 pages. That is precious. And it is hard to find online, where a link to a 1000-word article might well be tagged "long read". I think the novel will be fine, because something in us yearns for what is complex, for language used in a sophisticated way. That need is not going away.'

Jonathan Bastable (ed.)

Escape to the big time

by Georg Klein
Keynote, Berlin, September 2012

I want to begin by making a confession: I like it when novelists are dead. I find it pleasant to hold a novel in my hand and to know that its author is no longer among us. The spontaneous sympathy I then feel for both text and writer, is even a little bit more heartfelt if the book is out of print, if I had to get hold of it second hand from one of those dubious online dealers who offer as-new copies so cheaply that the cost of delivery exceeds the now no more than symbolic cost of the book itself.

I always read a novel which has become that cheap to the end. I feel an almost personal obligation to do so. I keep going to the very last page, even if it doesn't really grip me and push against my limits, even if I begin to fear that it was never, even when it was written, a good book. Then I put it in the wastepaper sack along with the newspapers of the last few days. It's a little like laying to rest a mummy which for far too long was displayed in a museum in an undignified way. The memory of this good deed is then the last future which, for a little while at least, we will share.

I know that this feeling has something to do with the way I imagine the past of the novel. If I don't shy away from a megalomaniac sense of vertigo, I am briefly able to imagine the totality of all the novels ever written: thousands, thousands upon thousands of novel manuscripts, of which many, presumably only a minority, but still a mighty host, have become books, lingering for a time in libraries or other memories until they too will disappear into nowhere.

The history of literature tries to control this vortex of time. Where there's a twisting maelstrom of production and destruction, it claims to recognise stable linearity: beginnings, development, opposition and gain, sometimes something new, better even, progress without end. The history of the novel, at least the history of the European novel, then turns into a tree whose growth we can supposedly reconstruct. This oak rises from the fertile soil of older narrative forms; at some point a separate sapling emerges from the epic thicket. The wood of the trunk grows stronger and harder; gradually the tree becomes aware of the tradition it forms, but also of unrealised possibilities. Grown stately and proud, it forks into powerful branches. Its youngest twigs reach further towards the light, towards new, not yet explored kinds of writing.

I like this illusion. I enjoy the idea that I could know what is old and what is new, that I understand how the new emerges from the old. Like every illusionary control of time it can help one to keep going, if one submits to it at the right moment. But there is also the fatally wrong moment: I remember a young woman author telling me about her collision with the history of the novel. She had written her first work of prose, a slim, autobiographical volume, in the finest enthusiasm of naïve creativity. Before she tackled a proper novel, she simply wanted to see just what had been written so far. She asked experienced readers for help and drew up a list. No more than a selection from the supposedly most important German-language novels of the twentieth century, twenty or thirty titles.

She began in chronological order. What had been conceived as an instructive game with time turned into a nightmare. She had entered the forest of literature in order to collect a few fine mushrooms in her basket. But she was forced to realise that a giant mushroom rhizome ran through the gentle grove from one end to the other. A network of dead fibres, but also of damp living ones. Not everything which strove towards the twilight there was in good condition. Much was maggot-eaten, there was much ugly rank vegetation, above all far too much iridescent beauty. In the young writer, however, the emotional surplus of yearning, anticipation and fear, the many-armed dream-catcher, which her future novel had been, shrank away into despondency and resignation.

A pity! With a little luck things could have turned out differently. From the experience of frightening greatness she drew the fatal conclusion that whatever there was inside her, driving her to write a novel, was embarrassingly small. The shock of greatness now prevented her from achieving what experienced readers spontaneously succeed in doing time and again: the fusion of one's own creative system with the structure of the text, the magnificent identification of a reading consciousness with the imagined world of the novel, the flight into a wonderful and vast expanse.

That could be called escapism. And there are spatial metaphors which suggest themselves to describe the experience. But someone who escapes into a novel, is also escaping from a particular time. Every habitual reader, the genre junkie just as much as the lover of subtle language games, senses and enjoys the fact that he is escaping that time which is constantly being presented to him as the really important, decisive one. This deceitfully dominant time format could perhaps be called 'small time' in contrast to the grand experience of time of the novel.

This small time has something to do with our everyday lives. And its dogmatic champions maintain that dealing with daily life prevents us squandering our always scarce hours on reading (never mind writing) novels. An old, threadbare reproach. But who can feel so certain of himself in this respect? A few weeks ago I was talking on the phone to an author; almost forty, his most recent novel was about to appear. I thought our conversation was going to be all about this happy, forthcoming event, when he abruptly asked me what kind of nursing-care insurance I had. At the moment he felt tormented by the thought that in the future, in thirty or thirty-five years he could be at the mercy of the infirmities of old age without appropriate support. His son would then find himself in the terribly awkward situation of having to take care of a poor, invalid writer, one perhaps even suffering from dementia.

A few days later I started reading his new novel. I can no longer say how many pages it took before I forgot the nursing-care insurance cover. But it was quite a few. On the unusually difficult way into the promise of time of the novel I felt that what prevented my immersion was a kind of future. It's not the presence of everyday life, its demands and duties that stand in the way of experiencing a novel. On the contrary: every genuine reader knows the special pleasure which comes from escaping into the time of the novel in the middle of everyday life, in the middle of the automatically prolonged present of getting things done, of errands. Not the sheer practical experience of the present, but a particular kind of future, a feeling of apprehension, a specific anxiety, indeed cowardice, appeared to me to be the time-enemy of the novel.

So I don't believe most people who claim that unfortunately they don't have any time to read novels, never mind write them, although in fact they feel strongly drawn to do one or the other or both. Out of a mistaken sense of consideration I don't say to them: it's only your small future that stops you dedicating yourself to the bigger time of the novel. The fact that you don't allow yourself to push against your own limits is a great pity, because it's precisely the experience of the novel that could help prevent your soul being soured by too much small future.

Four years ago the books editor of a newspaper asked me whether I would like to contribute to a series in the arts pages of the publication. Its title was 'The Future of Yesterday'. Short essay-like texts were supposed to discuss utopian novels of the past three hundred years. I was very taken by the idea, because I looked forward to re-acquainting myself with texts I had read for the first time decades before. Most of the titles that involuntarily came to mind were so-called science fiction novels from the second half of the twentieth century.

Fortunately the editor didn't expect me to consider whether they contained forecasts which had subsequently come true in technology, politics or society. Only the cheap know-it-all attitudes of those born too long after would throw themselves at these novels to explain that they told of gadgets, social orders and forms of rule which have not or perhaps even have become contemporary reality. Indeed, I didn't feel in the least that the technological, social or political environment around me would have been the future of these novels. I doubted that these authors, like members of some literary-military special unit equipped with telescopic sights and laser pointers, had been aiming at our twenty-first century.

Admittedly, as genre literature the majority of these books had in some formal aspects satisfied the expectations of genre readers. Probably the vain desire to predict something which could still come true in the lifetime of the author had played a limited part in the writing. But this prognostic ambition had evaporated from the space of reading, like some initially overpowering but then not very enduring perfume. How liberating to enter into the apocalyptic visions of these novels without the possible nuclear war between the Soviet Union and the former USA forcing itself into one's mind. How fascinatingly open to fantasise about a fictitious cyberspace and its obscure matrix without having to see this fictitious system and its world as representatives of yesterday's or today's internet. How good, not to be the posterity of these novels.

Relieved of all prognostic expectations they seemed to me to have gained in scope. And my reading profited in more than a futurological way from the character of our contemporary shared world; if I am not deceiving myself, then in recent decades a certain pressure of expectation has very much diminished. The novel no longer has to provide the guiding thread linking a historically tamed past with a critically comprehended present, a string of knots, by which one is then supposed to feel one's way forward into the already looming future.

I know there are phenomena which distract from this liberation of the novel. Even when I'm writing I often don't feel as free as the present-day novel actually is. The demons of small time know all about my diffidence and regularly lead me into temptation. It's not so long ago that an agency which looks after the media advancement, the public future of its clients, called me up. A very energetic young man got to the point right away. They had heard that my prose texts had an interesting closeness to science and technology. They had read random samples. I was the right man. An important client, a well known German scientist, the cutting edge of medical-biological progress in person, was looking for someone who could relate in an attractive way what his research team had discovered and which was about to cause a sensation. I should immediately look at the client's Wikipedia entry; the agency had brought it right up to date.

The Wikipedia article was very long, fairly well written and just easy enough so that with my chance biochemical and medical knowledge I was able to follow it. All cleverly and skilfully done. What could this established and eminent authority expect from me? The future was quickly told. Planned was a bestseller, that is, one with sales figures in the six-digit range. I asked for examples, and my caller had them at his fingertips. To my surprise these included not only popular non-fiction books but also mass-market fiction. As a professional, I would no doubt immediately appreciate that the future quite evidently lay in the fusion of up-to-date scientific topics with narrative forms of presentation. Time was short. It would be best if I could provide a written sample as soon as possible. An introductory chapter. The relevant material had already been prepared.

In the meantime I know what I should have replied: you're mistaken, I'm not an expert provider of narrative services. I am not an expert at all. I am a very dogged amateur in the field of experiencing big time. I don't believe in the continuous progress of science; I think that the natural sciences, especially medicine, are, just like literature, a maelstrom of production and annihilation. Consequently, in common with many authors, I love doctors as literary figures. I doubt whether the latest equipment and approaches are always better than yesterday's machines and abandoned procedures. I can certainly see that there is change. But I think that most of what we encounter as new is a surprising variation on and combination of older more or less well remembered or even quite forgotten elements. I enjoy the phenomenon of 'novelty' as an invigorating feeling, as hormonal agitation, but I am far from wanting to make a bony fetish of whatever's new. I would probably not buy the book that I'm supposed to write for you. And if I got it as a present and began to read it out of curiosity it would probably bore me to death. Of the many forms of future, of the expectations, longings, fears I have so far fallen victim to, the future you have in mind is among the most inhibiting. If it were to become dominant, this future-obsession would cannibalise everything that I find hopeful about writing.

Of course I didn't say any of that. It's not often that I make grand statements on the phone. I merely said: 'I'm really sorry. Thank you very much for thinking of me. But the imaginary scope of a possible novel has begun to absorb me. It will be called 'The Future of Mars' but will have almost nothing to do with what you imagine as the near future of 'science' and 'fiction'. We've simply got a small time problem here, a time problem among contemporaries. But you can certainly call me again in one and a half, in two or two and a half years!'

That time is up. That future is over. The nervous young man never called me again. I finished my novel in June; the book on which I was supposed to collaborate as a ghostwriter was considerably faster. It never became a bestseller. One can now buy copies online for 99 cents plus postage. I am afraid that the experience of big time can make one arrogant towards other forms of the experience of time. Perhaps I should order a copy and read it right to the end as slowly and devoutly as possible, and then also lay this narrative mummy to rest in an appropriately dignified manner.

Enemies of the novel

'The time for legends is over,' said **Mathias Énard** in Lisbon, quoting the lugubrious Austrian novelist Thomas Bernhard. 'Now it's time to talk about death.' And a surprising number of the delegates to the Conference expressed the view that their own craft was dead, or at the very least, doomed. 'Of course, the novel is not 3,000 years old and was not invented by any so-called Homer,' said **Konstantin Milchin** in Krasnoyarsk. 'The bourgeois genre that came together in the nineteenth century is a wide-ranging narrative tale concerning one or more individuals, along with their economically and socially defined fates, with their psychological troubles, and with situations that are recognisable to the reader. This is the same classical novel that continues to provide social comfort to a bourgeois public. That classical novel as a commercial undertaking, and as an artefact with a certain social function, certainly has a present and a somewhat circumscribed future. It lives on because, strange as it may seem, our contemporary culture is in many ways still stuck in the nineteenth century. But the novel as an aesthetic undertaking has neither a present nor a future. Its death throes were Beckett and the French *nouveau roman*, and also Nabokov. It's over.'

'I agree that the novel has died,' added **Andrey Astvatsaturov**. 'I know that we have regularly tried to bury it – a hundred years ago, then in the 1960s. I think the Edinburgh discussion of 1962 came just at the right moment for the death of the novel. The *nouveau roman*, which scored a line, so to speak, under the novel, was then just appearing. Those were novels in which all the obvious and most importants characteristics of the novel were absent. I would say that there was an attempt to give the novel back its power and its relevance during what you might call the second wave of modernism. I have in mind John Updike, John Gardner, William Styron.

But I believe we are now in the posthumous era of the novel, in the post-apocalyptic period of the novel. Yes, novels get written – all of us here write novels – but even on a dead body the hair and the nails continue to grow; a corpse continues to have the appearance of a living person for a little while.'

Kirill Kobrin's view was that the mighty and turbulent novel of old had merely faded into pettiness and insignificance – but he couched this thought in terms that somehow managed to sound even more pessimistic than his fellow Russians' talk of death and corpses. 'I think it is possible to define the difference between what is now called the novel on the one hand, and what was understood by the novel in the nineteenth century,' he said. 'It is the difference between a gladiatorial contest and a modern game of football. A gladiatorial bout – which is what I am comparing with the nineteenth-century novel – is both a spectacular show and also a matter of life and death for those involved; the modern novel is like a professional game of football in that it has a vast audience of people who are happy to punch each others' faces in or even kill each other, but the sportsmen never do more than break an opponent's leg, and that usually by accident. So the modern novel is like the Premier League – lots of people are interested in it but, believe me, compared with gladiatorial combat it is not much to look at.'

If the novel had gone the way of Cock Robin, who or what can be said to have played the part of the sparrow, with his bow and arrow? Two possible culprits were mentioned in every forum where the discussion took place: the internet – both for its effect on the publishing industry, and for the transformation it has supposedly wrought in readers' habits; and the high-quality TV drama serial, which was accused of moving in on territory that once belonged to the novel alone. 'The future of the novel is in a way the future of opponents to the novel,' said **Serge Bramly** in St Malo. 'I believe in what can be called dialogue, or conflict. In both situations, the enemy sets the tone and allows us to move forward. **Michel Le Bris** was talking about the nineteenth century, the golden age of the novel, when we had people like Dumas and Hugo. But it took both of them a long time to come to the novel as a form. Both started out as dramatists; theatre was a noble art and the novel was vulgar. There have been many prophets of the death of the novel. Some said that journalism would do it. When I was young, people said that television would do it. Cinema was for a long time seen as the scourge of the novel. But in each instance, the enemies of the novel provided an opportunity for the novel to reinvent itself, to change its shape and transfigure itself. The cinema is no longer a serious enemy of the novel – because it is all about special effects aimed at fourteen-year-olds. TV series such as *The Wire* are the true enemy of the novel, because it takes about the same time to watch as a book takes to read, you get involved in the plot and become attached to the characters.' But Bramly refused to be downhearted. 'This is a time of revival for the novel, thanks to this new enemy. It is through fighting the TV series that we get stronger – or else we die, like verse did because it gave up. The main advantage of the new technology is that it is a new opponent, a new enemy that makes the fight for the novel more interesting.'

Hari Kunzru, speaking in Edinburgh, also thought that the written novel would get past *The Wire*. 'I know a whole bunch of anti-novel types who claim that the new dominance of the HBO-type multi-part drama has hollowed out the space that was previously occupied by the novel. The argument goes that *The Wire* is rather like Balzac, a panoptical view of a culture from top to bottom. And I think there is something in that: these are visual narratives that have space, they have the leisure of expanding themselves, and they have the serial format that makes them reminiscent of nineteenth-century novels. But that is the *nineteenth century*. There are things that short stories and prose fiction can do that visual narratives cannot, because of the surface nature of the visual. In prose fiction you can do interiority, you can switch perspective easily, you can go from the global to the micro. All these things are tools that are very natural to prose fiction – and very useful in a complex world where things are only explicable across these scales. This is something that fiction writers still have over the visual crowd.'

The internet seemed to many a more dangerous and long-term opponent of the novel, and of the printed page both in general and in particular. 'The chief enemy of the novelist is the internet, not just because it's free but because it's very entertaining,' said **Tibor Fischer.** 'I teach nineteen year-olds and, in general, they don't read – although it has to be said English Literature students for some reason seem to be the most reluctant readers. We're losing the mass readership, we're losing the money and there's no way back.' So the consumer base was crumbling away, but the means of production – the economy of books – was also under attack. 'One reason new books are bought is because old ones get pulped. They are destroyed in fires and floods. They get eaten by dogs, or gnawed at by mould. And if a paperback is really popular it can rarely go through a dozen pairs of hands before it disintegrates. E-books don't get dog-eared, or eaten by dogs. E-books are practically immortal.'

For **Li Er**, speaking in Beijing (see keynote, p.85), the problem with the internet was not so much to do with the economics of book-making, but with the effect that a permanently plugged-in lifestyle has on the human psyche. For him, the encounter between the novel and the net was nothing short of shattering; it was a vase hurled against a brick wall. 'I feel that my life in China is fragmented. Modern life is interesting, because TV, newspapers, Weibo [a Chinese social network] and other media invade our lives totally. We have many questions, also many answers, but we cannot pay attention to one question for very long. We quickly lose interest and stop thinking, and the result is a kind of disintegration of life. When I answer my phone in a taxi, or read mails on a bus, or think a hundred thoughts or have ideas while waiting on the subway platform, these things take me out of the integral flow of time. We have to find an integrated way to reflect the fragmentation, to reflect the desire for integration while portraying life's fragments. I feel strongly that the stories are disappearing. I think modern writers are not telling stories; they are writing about how the stories are disappearing. The integration has gone, and I am deeply dissatisfied. The value of individals, the sense of self, happiness – they are all gone. I don't want to express the fragmented life, because I am against it. I am looking for another way to ameliorate the self. In this world, under this political system, that takes a lot of effort.'

Li Er told the following little parable to illustrate his point. 'Say you are a reading a newspaper article; say it is about a musician, the son of a famous singer, who has been convicted as a criminal. The newspaper story always provides a swift answer – otherwise it is not useful. Literature never provides a swift answer; literature is a long question. Literature not only gives you the facts about the criminal – when he won piano competitions, and so forth – it tells you why he became a criminal despite his very good education. In the course of this long slow questioning process, readers look into their own minds. This can only be done if there is no swift answer. Its absence makes the space for introspection, for getting to the root of the story.' Like other delegates who feared for the future of storytelling, Li Er expressed a hope, a vague feeling that, paradoxically, the novel might be able to reconstitute itself by turning the shards and offcuts of life into a new kind of story, a sort of narrative mosaic. 'We all think that now we have Twitter we will cease to need novels, or to care for emotions that can't be expressed in 140 characters. But an interesting thing is happening: here in China we publish 4,000 full-length novels each year, and the demand for them is increasing. Here's how I explain it: only full-length novels can offer us the many experiences, the fragments that make up a new integration. We are using fragments against the fragmentation, to create the illusion of integration on the page. We may find that novels grow longer and longer.'

That outcome would please **Ilya Boyashev,** who as chairperson in Krasnoyarsk had wistfully asked the panel: 'Will the novel always be the classic 300-page brick? Or has that big novel had its time? Because perhaps the era has gone when a person could retire to the comfort of a study, light the fire, and sit down with *War and Peace* or *The Forsyte Saga*.' Milchin replied that 'the traditional novel will however remain; but as an elite, exclusive entertainment – like good whisky.' He described the digital publishing revolution as 'the new electronic samizdat', and suggested that 'a new kind of novel might even be built upon the wreck of the old world, one that will be a mixture of text, video, and music.' Astvatsaturov added that the main threat to 'this now slightly historic genre' was the blogosphere, and he foresaw a new kaleidoscopic form of writing. 'I think the novel will be broken up into little scenes, short episodes, spicy little philosophical essays. I myself write novels of a sort, but they are novels in the form of short-story sequences – which is not my idea; Sherwood Anderson invented it. That is the kind of roomy, fissiparous novel that we can look forward to, something consisting of pictures, scenes and episodes.'

Both these visions sounded very like the splintered future that so worried Li Er. And they bring to mind something that **Teju Cole** said in Melbourne (see p.52) when he was asked if he felt that 'Twitter is closer to the form of a short poem [than to a novel], if what you are describing is the future of an immense short-poem anthology?' He replied: 'Certainly Twitter represents a kind of golden age of the fragment. Out of the 200 million people on there, there are going to be some who have a great feel for the form and for language. Occasionally when you are looking at your feed you think: wow, what a sentence. And some one could certainly make an anthology of them.'

Is that at all hopeful or enticing, though, the prospect of the plucking the occasional good one-liner from an infinite haystack of tweets and retweets? At the end of the Krasnoyarsk debate **Alex Preston**, summing up, quoted a line from *Northanger Abbey*: 'Oh! It is only a novel ... some work in which the greatest powers of the mind are displayed, in which the most thorough knowledge of human nature, the happiest delineation of its varieties, the liveliest effusions of wit and humour, are conveyed to the world in the best-chosen language.' Can Twitter, or a multimedia collage, or the bloated blogosphere, provide a satisfying subsitute for a novel that does what Jane Austen's character describes?

In Beijing, the short-story writer and film director **Zhu Wen** seemed exasperated with Li Er's pessimistic view on the prospects for the novel. And at the very end of the debate he gnomically suggested that there was nothing for it but to take the long view. 'I like the Chinese proverb that says: seas change to mulberry fields and mulberry fields to seas,' he said. 'It comes from a story of a very old man who was asked how old he was. The old man said: "I don't know; I only know that I have seen the seas change to mulberry fields, and then change back again".'

Jonathan Bastable (ed.)

A new age of fiction

by Michel Le Bris
Keynote, St Malo, May 2013

What is the future for the novel? A very dark one, and perhaps none at all, a view expressed with grave concern by the most highly regarded critics at a time when we all sense that we are entering, with the new century, a period of momentous change. How could we fail to perceive that the new era brings with it a new sensibility and fundamental changes in our mental bearings? Standing on the threshold of a new century .... Fear not: I speak of course to the dying days of the nineteenth century and the start of the troubling twentieth century. In 1891, Jules Romain had prophesied the 'end of the novel form'. The same year Ludovic Halévy agreed, 'All novel genres have been exhausted'. Edouard Rod then added, 'The novel has no future'. In 1905 Jean Lorrain observed, 'The French novel is dead; killed by journalism.' Maurice Leblond, the very same year, qualified the verdict, saying 'the novel was in its death throes', 'a victim of these industrial times when the launch of a book is not dramatically different from, say, the launch of a new cocktail, or quinine drink'. Or, as Lucien Maury was to claim in 1907, it had fallen victim to 'Parisianism; snobbism, a mix of cruel and light irony, dryness of sentiment and moral scepticism'.

In short, as Camille Audigier railed in 1911, we have had enough of these 'adulterous *mondaines* and swooning neurasthenics', enough of this 'agitation and theatricality', chimed in Louis Bertrand in 1912. It seemed as if there was nothing left to rejoice over. André Gide, when asked by a major newspaper in 1913 to name his ten favourite French novels, wondered if French letters could even lay claim to the novel as a form.

This long preamble is in fact intended to urge us all to take an optimistic view: all of this took place a century ago, and we are still here.

We continue to ponder, question and argue just as passionately as we did then, often in the same terms. So much so that one could hold that the novel form thrives in times of crisis, and that concern over its future is a sign of its good health ....

Indeed it was then that some new voices emerged. Marcel Schwob, discovering the work of RL Stevenson 'in the flickering light of a railroad lamp', found what might be expected of the times: an adventure novel that wove together the 'crisis of the inner and outer worlds'. Camille Mauclair saw in it *The Novel of Tomorrow*, free from social determinism à la Zola and individual psychology à la Barrès; André Gide discovered Conrad and undertook to translate *Typhoon*; in 1913 Jacques Rivière published his spectacular *Adventure Novel* in three installments in NRF, in the form of a manifesto. Then came Plon's 'Feux croisés' collection, Stock's 'Cosmopolitan Cabinet' and 'Scandinavian Library'. So that just when many were lamenting the novel as a lost cause, French readers were able to discover, in rapid succession, the likes of Dostoyevsky, Melville, Thomas Mann, Rilke, Hamsun, Kafka, Henry James, Kipling, James Joyce, Pirandello, George Eliot, Thomas Hardy, Conrad – in other words, proof of the amazing ability of fiction to relate to a world in the very process of becoming. A new generation of French writers followed, many of them travel writers, keen to take to the road.

One might wonder if it is not precisely in periods of crisis and profound change that fiction deploys its full power. Suffice it to think of Conrad's *Heart of Darkness*, or *Journey to the End of the Night* by Céline. The debates and controversies are strangely familiar; they took place a century ago, but ring just as true today. So there are grounds for optimism.

But what precisely can we be optimistic about? If the talk is about the internet, digitisation or the programmed obsolescence of paper, it is always predicated on the assumption that the globalised market leads to fatal outcomes. There are writers who, having initiated these debates in other festivals, have become bogged down in them. I know that the digital revolution will have an impact on literary forms through the new opportunities it creates – in terms of images, sound, links, interactive media just to name a few – not to mention the huge potential it holds for places such as Africa, where books struggle to survive.

As we know, new literary forms are emerging, notwithstanding the medium of production, whether paper or digital; these are made up of a blending of previously separate genres – fiction, storytelling, essays –in a shifting and dynamic balance, as if the ability to switch between genres compensated for the ever-present risk of the others failing to deliver. Back in 1992, when I was director of the Voyageurs imprint at Payot publishing house, we published John MacPhee, the pioneer of a new genre that would become known as 'creative nonfiction', and that has finally, it seems, been discovered in France. There was an extensive session dedicated to creative non-fiction at an earlier session of this Conference. This, I believe, shows just how important these developments are. However, and this might come as a surprise, as important as they may be, I believe they are secondary, in that they come after what is essential. What I mean by essential is the ability to perceive what is at stake in novel writing, therefore, to understand why the novel form is more necessary today than ever before.

In 1990, when I created the Étonnants Voyageurs Festival, which owes its name to a well-known Baudelaire poem, it was survival instinct on my part. I opened a space in which I, as a writer, could breathe freely, standing in resolute opposition to the literary fashions that were then ruling over the French literary scene: both an avant-garde ideology that postulated that literature had but one object, itself – thus reducing it to nothing but formal play, a play on words; and also the other fashion of marvelling at the contemplation of one's own navel as the one and only centre of the world. As for me, I wanted to assert that never has literature been as strong, as alive and as necessary as when it has taken on relating to the world.

A world was disappearing, this I felt with great intensity, as my generation had dreamed of 'doing away with the old world'. I lived very intensely through the lovely days of May 1968 in Paris. The shock waves of this movement, that took various forms and acquired a global dimension, had shaken the whole edifice, toppling the ideologies that the reigning thinking gurus claimed covered 'the whole range of thought'. It carried our most trusted reference points and most of our certainties away – save for one that led to the birth of Étonnants Voyageurs: that only artists and writers can delve into the unknown and give it a voice. It was ever thus. The pundits had failed to foresee the events of May 1968 – remember the infamous words of the most famous editorialist from *Le Monde*, 'France is bored', a pronouncement made just thirteen days before the start of the events – yet the movement had already been in the works for a decade, through music, comics, science fiction and everything we call 'counter-culture'. All the worthy pundits, be they specialists in politics, economy, and sociology *et al* had been deaf and blind to it, as they are again today. Pundits are by definition specialists of what is already known, and are thus the least competent in perceiving novelty and breaks. Better to listen to Bob Dylan that to read editorials in *Le Monde* if one wanted to understand the rising tide of the 1960s! The only specialists of the unknown that I am aware of are precisely artists and writers. As a result, they are needed with a renewed and special urgency in this period of momentous change of ours. Thus it is that the novel form is critical to our times.

Possibly even more than one imagines. For the change we are undergoing is completely singular. We have thought for centuries in terms of stable categories: nation-states, territories, borders, foreign/domestic oppositions, families, communities, identities but also concepts. It may well be that the world to come very quickly forces us to ditch stable categories and to risk ourselves into moving thought, in other words, as the Indian philosopher Arjun Appadurai puts it in *Modernity at Large*, forces us into thinking in terms of flows rather than structures. Flows of population, whether voluntary or imposed, greater than ever the world has ever known, flows of capital, flows of images, flows of sounds, flows of information: we must acknowledge the fact that they have overwhelmed all the structures which up to now attempted to contain or regulate them. They are followed by fantastic cultural collisions: a veritable maelstrom in which an old world expires while a new one is being born, the outlines of which we can hardly perceive, even though we know it will force us to rethink our mental coordinates. It is becoming vital for both our individual and collective imaginations to get back to centre stage, in terms of the power of creation.

We are entering a world in which it is not an exaggeration to say that someone born into one culture will be led to live in another, or that a second-generation immigrant will be torn apart between two worlds or two cultures. In fact this can occur within one's own country, thanks to the acceleration of transfers of rural populations with traditional cultures to tradition-crushing, family-rending megalopolises, which in their turn are also sources of new social behaviours and new cultures; in short, a world in which imaginary, flowing, perpetually renewed plural communities will be born, will constantly change and will disappear. But it is also a world in which everyone, standing at a crossroads of multiple identities, will find themselves forced to invent a 'personal story' in order to make sense of themselves, which will make a coherent whole of this multiplicity.

It is a dangerous world in which the imagination will be challenged at the risk of hankering after nostalgic roots, be they real or fantasised, after illusory homelands; all the more murderous as they are disconnected from reality, after dreamed-of undivided communities in which we can be 'among ourselves', delivered from the tragedy of history, when one wants to reject the new world with all one's might – which, not far from us, is what they call ethnic cleansing or delusional identity wishes or genocidal mania.

But it is also a fascinating world in which creative fiction will play a central part, something that Arjun Appadurai appears to overlook in his essay, perhaps because of his perspective as a sociologist. For what is literature if not the creation of worlds, the crisscrossing of multiple voices, the questioning, in its very movement, of the certainties of identity? Of course, it is form, but contrary to conceptual thought, it is open, and therefore at the origin of 'togetherness'. It stands at the crossroads of uniqueness and multiplicity and stubbornly tries to take up the gamble of nomadic thought. It is, in action, the very thought of flow. It explores a flowing space in which the inside and the outside become interchangeable and in which the self can deconstruct and reconstruct itself. Thus literature – and particularly the novel – stand more than ever at the core of what the world to come holds at stake.

Fiction is once again centre stage. It is striking that the social sciences and literature are tackling similar issues, after a period during which these disciplines attempted to displace literature, to take its place and leave it behind bars. Do we learn less from Conrad and Stevenson about the tropics than we do from Malinowski or about man in society from Proust and Chateaubriand than from Lévi-Strauss? Why do writers do a better job of telling us about the world than recognised anthropologists? Alan Bensa and François Pouillon, both anthropologists, raise this question in their collective work titled *Terrains d'écrivains* (*Lands of Writers*). Sylvie Laurent, a historian fascinated by the TV series *The Wire*, writing for the magazine *Esprit*, asks: 'What if fiction were closer to the truth than the social sciences?' An idea apparently appealing to sociologists, since David Simon, the author of the series, gets invited to lecture at Harvard. Why do psychoanalysts, whose knowledge is often tinged with arrogance, quote so liberally from literary works, although they are not writers? This is the question that the psychoanalyst Pierre Bayard asks in his book *Peut-on appliquer la littérature à la psychanalyse? (Can literature be applied to psychoanalysis?)* It is almost as if literature holds a form of knowledge that psychoanalysis is eternally searching for but unable to reach – the very topic of another recent book on Freud and writers. In a book that just came out, fifteen young historians ponder the question 'What are historians thinking about?', working under the guidance of Christophe Granger. Well, about literature, of course, 'to the point of obsession', expresses with dismay a critic from *Le Monde*. It has taken on an obsessional dimension: through various colloquia – 'History and Literature' in Lyon, at the Collège de France, at the Ecole des Hautes Etudes, at the CNRS (National Centre for Scientific Research) – while the journal *Sciences humaines* devoted a special issue to 'Literature, window on the world'. Not to mention all the philosophers who have reflected on the power of literature, such as Pierre Cassou-Noguès, who takes it quite far, positing that philosophy *is* fiction. Why is everybody all of a sudden so intent on the power of literature?

The fact that the social sciences, thrown into crisis as a result of the general state of upheaval in the world, are looking to the powers of literature is especially meaningful. We should heed this, as it shows that the arrogant theories that allowed the social sciences to exist self-referentially, excluding the outside world, are truly dead. And this brings us back to literature's ability to relate the world. I have no complaint: this has been my position since the Festival was created, and this is what led me to espouse the concept of world literature in 1993. This is what led, in 2008, to the drafting, along with Jean Rouaud, Alain Mabanckou, Anna Moï, and Abdourahman Waberi, of a manifesto, signed by forty-four writers, for a Francophone world literature. This is what I have fought for since my first book came out in 1977, *L'homme aux semelles de vent* (*The Man with Soles of Wind*). This is what I have been fighting for as far back as I can remember ....

It is not all about signs or systems of signs, contrary to what the gurus of structuralism tried so forcefully to drum into us. *The unutterable exists.* And literature exists precisely because the unutterable exists, as does humanity, with its acceptance of the other. If everything could be uttered – if everything were transparent, translatable, and exchangeable – everything would already have been told, and nobody would make a fuss about it. But the fact is: we have never stopped, wherever, whenever, in all places, in all cultures, from the beginning of times, to tell stories, to write stories. Such obstinacy makes one suppose that there must be some imperious necessity to this compulsion to approach the unutterable, to make it rise to the surface, to take us to the core of its mystery. We are, to quote Nancy Huston's beautiful expression, 'a storytelling species'.

How strange is fiction. It is not truth, obviously. But neither is it untruth. Evidently, it says something – otherwise we would be indifferent. But not so: we read, voraciously, we cannot be stopped, we are enthralled – *something which cannot be said in any other way*. Its figurative meaning cannot be reduced to literal meaning. If it could, fiction would be but an ornament, kid's play, a waste of time. But we hold it as essential. When we finish reading a great novel, do we not have the feeling that it was delivering something unique about the world and about human beings? Perhaps even more: the feeling that it allows the perception of the unknown world to come, it gives it a face, it makes it inhabitable. It makes us discover the other in our selves.

Fiction is not truth. Neither is it untruth. Thus, it forces us to suggest there is another way of knowledge than the discursive: that of imagination. It forces us to think in terms of *creative imagination*. Science is deployed in the space of sameness, indeed it rests on the assumption that from a founding rule one can replicate experience perfectly. But how can we think of 'the Other', without reducing it to the likeness of ourselves, to 'the Same'? The other is unknowable, but otherness can be met and embraced, and in so doing we discover the otherness within ourselves. And this we do through our imagination and the shifting interplay of fiction, and that is momentous indeed. This is where the secret of our becoming human can be found; from here springs and grows our ability to 'be together', an infinitely richer path than the one established by a rule or law, for this is the very essence of common rules accepted by all.

If a work written several centuries ago in another culture can still move me, when the times that saw it come to life are long gone, and its context – of which I know nothing – has been abolished, it must mean that there is something in it which cannot be reduced to the conditions of its enunciation, something that is capable of overcoming death and the passing of time, and beyond the narrow confines of cultures, is capable of talking still to our present. Has it not been said that a true work of art can be recognised in that it has 'passed the test of time'? But if there is transcendence in a work of art, it becomes obvious that it is due to a dimension of transcendence in its creator, due to a power in him – and therefore in his readers, that is to say in every man – that crosses over time and culture. And the power of literature is to continuously bring us back to this dimension within us that we tend to forget, caught up as we are in everyday life.

Perhaps our questioning about literature will appear futile to today's great minds: they would have us believe that the time is now for 'serious matters'. In their shadow theatres, they have attempted to bring back to life the old illusory recipes and tired slogans. For our part, let us not be afraid to assert that the 'human poem' we carry within ourselves and the richness of fiction is what brings us back to the essential in these chaotic times: this greatness in each one of us which producing and consuming have not yet exhausted; a power of creation, a verticality that is the very essence of being human. Our need for the novel is as imperious and real as it has ever been!

We believe that no thought of the new times, no policy, and no philosophy will be worth anything if it is not built on an idea which is bigger than mankind and which artists and poets invariably take us back to. In 1981 in an essay titled *Le Paradis Perdu* (*The Lost Paradise*), I wagered that 'out of the ruins of the Theoretical Age a new Age of Fiction will be reborn'. These words may not have been heard, but thirty years later I do not believe that I was wrong in making such a statement.

Reasons to be hopeful

While some delegates to the Conference were burying the novel with almost gleeful relish, others were thinking, as Mark Twain said of himself, that rumours of its death were greatly exaggerated.

One reason for optimism was – as **Michel Le Bris** reiterated in his keynote – the knowledge that we had been here before. 'Each generation believes it is observing the death of the novel,' said **Denise Mina** in İzmir. 'I think every generation believes it is observing the death of everything, because we cannot believe that the world will continue after we've gone. What is in fact happening is that the novel is changing. It is turning into something that we do not necessarily recognise, because it is not the thing that we grew up loving. But all art forms are in a constant state of flux, and the novel has never been static. I am thinking about the moral panic over Impressionism, then Fauvism – the fear that all art was dying. Many of the changes that we are seeing in the novel now are not stylistic, but pragmatic. They parallel changes in methods of generation that we see now. In time, we will see stylistic changes caused by the internet, because the means of production inevitably affects change. If we were to come back in a hundred years we might not recognise the novel, but to that future generation the novel as they know it will look like all there has ever been. And they too will see the death of the form.'

And as **Kirsty Gunn** reminded delegates, the 1962 Edinburgh conference was one of the occasions on which the novel was read its last rites. 'When I spoke at the end of the last session of 2013, I quoted those wonderful lines of Stephen Spender that were published in Angela Bartie and Eleanor Bell's book [*International Writers' Conference Revisited: Edinburgh 1962*]. "I am not saying this maliciously at all," Spender said, refuting ideas that had been put about by Alexander Trocchi and others that the novel was finished with. "But everything that has been said was said in 1905. It led to a completely dead end." He went on to make a call for belief in the future of the novel, for its health and wellbeing. "The history of modern literature since 1914–1920 or so is the attempt to recover from this point of view," he said: fragmentation would glue itself up together and become the new.

'I'm too young to remember the original Edinburgh Writers' Conference,' remarked **Tibor Fischer** in Krasnoyarsk. 'But I can just recall the late-1960s when there was much talk of the death of the book and the death of the novel. This talk went on through the 1970s, through the 1980s, 1990s and the "noughties" – and here we are. The book, the paper book, will not die, and the novel won't die either. The paper book may well become a rarity, but like vinyl, it will survive because. if for no other reason, there's no point in reading Proust or Joyce if you can't leave a copy lying around ostentatiously so that your friends know you're reading them. The future of the novel is safe. Though of course, it will never have again the primacy it enjoyed in the late-nineteenth and early-twentieth century, when it was the premier artistic vehicle.'

Many delegates took note of the recent rise of the 'box set', which satisfies a hunger for narrative without requiring consumers to sit down and *read*. **Inci Aral**, however thought that written form still had an edge. 'The world of the novel is still so rich and alluring that it beats the dominating visual image hands down. We are going through a complicated period in which some values are being lost. But, despite everything, the novel and individual psychology continue to retain their significance. Writers are still awarded recognition and respect. There is still enormous interest in creative writing centres and courses. Writing a novel remains to be many people's greatest dream. We are surrounded by surprising new narratives, constructs and new languages.'

AD Miller, speaking in Beijing, was one of those who thought that *storytelling* was the essence of the novel – and if TV or Netflix commandeered part of that job, if that is what it took for storytelling to survive, then well and good. 'I think it is fundamentally not the case that people have lost their appetite for stories. Anyone who has a child knows that there is a kind of innate fascination with narratives – narratives that allow us to explore other people's lives – and that this is a kind of hard-wired instinct in people. In the adult universe, there is encouraging evidence from television. **Li Er** mentioned Bakhtin's view of the novel as a polyphonic, many-voiced artefact, but top-end TV drama tells many really good novelistic stories. 'In series such as *The Sopranos* or *The Wire*, you have exactly the kind of thing that Bakhtin envisaged: multi-stranded, complicated stories involving different social registers, characters from different walks of life. These are hugely popular, so there is still an appetite for these kinds of stories, but perhaps it has migrated.'

Alen Mattich, speaking in Toronto, wondered if humanity's story-hunger might go back deeper and further even than childhood, if it might be bred in the bone. 'Until the geneticists change us, we are stuck with stories,' he said. 'People like life to be contained in some simple, straightforward narratives. In my day job I write about economics and markets, and in economics there is a phenomenon called "noise", the things that happen randomly and aren't part of a trend or pattern. But nobody wants to be told that the things that happen are merely random – so you spin a story. As a journalist you spend your whole time trying to explain why things today are the way they are – though you know that 95 % of the time it is just noise. Yet randomness doesn't suit people, they don't like to be told: it just happened. Editors, in particular, hate that. So you talk to people in the markets. Some have one idea; another group has a different idea that will often be exactly contradictory. But you make some sort of story out of it and it satisfies people. They don't necessarily believe it, but they like the story. The people in the markets know that the story will turn out to be nonsense, but even the ones who have been doing it for decades feel a little bit better knowing that there is a story behind things.'

But what about the deleterious effect of the internet, bemoaned by so many delegates? Here too, some expressed a hope that the digital revolution was not having quite the baleful effect that others feared. 'One theme of Li's Er talk was the impact of technology on fiction,' said Miller. 'Technology has several ramifications. One is about how people consume books, but another is about how novels can hope to capture the experience of living in the twenty-first century. As I understand it, part of Li's worry is that mass media in the post-modern age tends to homogenise consciousness, whereas in Britain there is a different, maybe even opposite anxiety, which is that everyday experience has become so fractured by the internet and the media that the novel as a form is no longer the right way to capture or describe that experience – in particular the traditional realistic novel. The novel is an artefact that began with capitalism, urbanisation, mass literacy. It is a form that emerged from huge changes, and in its history has swallowed huge changes – in democracy, in gender relations ... the novel is capacious enough to include all these transformations. So my question is: are the changes that we are living through now, though seismic, are they really so different in kind from (for example) industrialisation – a great theme of novels in the past? Has consciousness really changed in a more fundamental way? I am optimistic that the answer is no, and that the novel is a generous enough form to represent and address these changes. In fact how people live in the globalised, post-modern world is potentially a very fertile subject for novelists. It's an opportunity more than it is a threat.'

In Lisbon, **João Tordo** questioned the widely expressed view that the short takes of the internet and Twitter had eroded readers' attention span, destroying their intellectual stamina and rendering them incapable of reading a full-length novel. On the contrary, 'people like to read long things, and little by little they are creeping back to the slow pleasures of the book.' Fellow panelist **Mathias Énard** instantly coined a term for this flight from shallowness and brevity – 'Tolstoy syndrome' – and **Denise Mina** described what the syndrome might feel like from a reader's point of view. 'I think there is something really unique about the shape of the novel in the same way that there is something unique about the shape of a sonnet. Usually it is two sit-down reads. A novel is like a double baptism. You are immersed, you come out, and then you are immersed again. It is a compulsion to engage with narrative and with language.'

At the concluding meeting in Edinburgh, **China Miéville** was asked about the internet self-publishing explosion, if its vast mushroom cloud of wordage on the web would change the novel in regrettable ways. 'The problem is the signal-to-noise ratio, sifting out what's worth reading,' he replied. 'And that can only get worse. But I am less worried about it than some people, because for several hundred years it has been impossible to read more than a tiny fraction of all the books that are worth reading. One thing to bear in mind is how fast all this moves. I may be in a minority, but I think that talk of self-publishing leading to the death of the traditional publisher is already on the wane, and has receded enormously from where it was a year ago. The discussion is happening at an incredibly accelerated rate. So I feel quite Darwinian about this. By Darwinian I mean that I feel fairly sure, when it all shakes down, that there will be good things to read.'

And good things to write about. Gunn, in her summary of the

Conference year, quoted Nabokov. 'He said: "When people ask me if I'm interested in the future of the novel, I tell them that I am interested in the future of *my* novel." When I read that I laughed out loud! Throughout this most interesting initiative we writers have been describing not 'the novel', but *our* novel. There's nothing abstract whatsoever about the concept. Whether the novel is this kind of book or that, these kinds of words or those kinds of words .... Fiction to a fiction writer is nothing like an idea, a theory, an extension of the imagination. It's a made-up thing that is real. It's the stuff of our lives.'

Inci Aral, delivering her keynote speech in İzmir, agreed that the novel was vital and indispensable – not just to novelists, but to the health of the global culture. 'It is harder for a book-loving novelist to imagine the death of the novel than it is to imagine their own demise. Fortunately, there is no need for this. Whilst the world has been striding forwards from the Industrial era towards the modern day, the novel has managed to keep its place firmly on the agenda. This is even true during the last one hundred years and our digital age of ever-progressing technology. Even today when we find ourselves bombarded by empty and meaningless visual images, we can still take refuge in good novels that contain that special element of the human spirit. If such an influential art form were to be wiped out we would also have to give up hope for the other treasures and beautiful creations of humanity.'

Jonathan Bastable (ed.)

A shred of subjectivity

by Li Er
Keynote, Beijing, March 2013

The novel, as we know it today, though its origins are in myths, epic poems, fables, legends, is actually the product of capitalism and civic societies.

Georg Wilhelm Friedrich Hegel came straight out and said it: the novel is the civic class's epic poem, and it shows a realistic world using characteristics of the essay. In the 1930s, Mikhail Bakhtin further explored Hegel's point. Bakhtin talked about the novel as the epic poem's descendant and a burgeoning form, a new literary form that accompanied the development of the citizen society and the conflicts of capitalism. The novelistic form hadn't yet fixed itself, and was full of unlimited possibilities. Bakhtin emphasised the subjectivity of the individual: Dostoyevsky's fictional world is, to Bakhtin, the world of the individual. Each individual and each voice is accorded an equally important status; everyone has their say. There are as many voices as there are people.

But what's interesting is, almost during the same period, Walter Benjamin published a famous piece of criticism, *The Storyteller*. Benjamin's viewpoint was the opposite of Bakhtin's. He thought that in a highly developed society the value of the individual depreciates. He used a German proverb to explain: 'When someone goes on a trip, he has something to tell.' Storytellers, people who have returned from afar, have tales, different knowledge and values, and divergent experiences. The German proverb is almost the same as a Chinese one, which goes 'A monk from afar knows how to chant'. The fundamentals of the novel are created by relating different experiences. However, with the advent of capitalism and modern media, Benjamin believed that faraway horizons have been flattened, and differing experiences have cancelled each other out. How the faraway monk reads his scripture has all but been shown on television; on radio; on Weibo [the Chinese social-networking site]. In other words, the idea that novels have a duty to express individual experience has almost lost its reason to exist. This deeply saddened Benjamin. He went on to say that, with the development of the media, people no longer needed to learn about the world or enhance their accomplishments by reading works of literature. Bad news has become good news, and the worst news the best news. Thus people let an increasing amount of negative news into their lives, and only the worst and most evil will arouse our interest. When people aren't getting to know the world through literature but through the news, they become more superficial, and contemporary society becomes an 'uncivilised civilisation'.

Bakhtin and Benjamin's assessments of literature are obviously tied to the context of their lives: when Bakhtin was studying Dostoyevsky's novels and emphasising the individual, he had just returned from exile imposed by Stalin. And when Benjamin wrote *The Storyteller*, he was just beginning a life on the run from Hitler. In this sense, critics' assessment of novels and their history are closely connected to their own experiences. The implementation of their criticism could, however, strike through the limitations of their own beliefs. Bakhtin, a Marxist critic, had deep feelings for capitalist civilisation; similarly, Benjamin, another so-called Marxist critic, actually cherished the classical period. But what's more interesting is despite their opposing points of views they had this commonality: they both emphasised the value and the subjectivity of the individual.

Everyone knows that, compared to when Bakhtin and Benjamin were still alive, the current circumstances of Chinese society are more complicated. This complexity is more than my novelist colleagues in the west can imagine. We can say wholeheartedly that whatever crime and punishment Bakhtin saw in Dostoyevsky's novels is ubiquitous in China, while at the same time the influence of mass media now wholly permeates people's lives. Chinese people who live in the remote countryside receive information from the media practically simultaneously to people living in Beijing, London, or New York. Censorship in publishing and the media has, by and large, no effect on the reception of information. Chinese society has become a combination of pre-modern, modern, and post-modern societies. It's just like a sandwich.

The value of individual existence has never been as strong. But the power of the system, the power of capital, the power of industrialisation and technology, has formed a new system-level force that can devour anything new, and is constantly draining the individual's subjectivity. Facing it is like confronting a dinosaur of a system; it exists as a gigantic alienation of the self. People in these circumstances – or more specifically 'the Chinese people's circumstances' – might make you laugh out loud. I'm told that laughter is the highest wisdom of the human race. But this laughter, better yet, this sound of wisdom, might as well be a sigh of pity.

For Chinese novelists, the complex problem is this. Because of the affirmation of the individual's value, story, plot, the characters, the personalities, their actions, fate, the completeness of incidents, the law of causality – these classic narrative modes remain effective still. But on the other hand, when a person's subjectivity has been erased and is made to live with the realities I've described, these narrative modes are not real enough. The contemporary Chinese novelist, if he is a serious novelist, must then look for a new narrative method in order to establish a corresponding relationship between the novel and present social realities, and must respond as best as he can to the complexity of Chinese reality. These responses first of all arise out of my questioning of how to preserve my true self in contemporary society. What kind of method is there to use in order to preserve at least a shred of the individual's subjectivity? How to converse with others using personal experience is, I believe, the most crucial reason for the existence of the novel under our current heightened systematisation. In particular, this is the most potent motivation for continued self-regeneration in the novel form.

Questions of ownership

'I am amused that in a discussion about the future of the novel we have spent so much time talking about the future of the novelist, about whether novelists will make a living,' said **Alex Preston**, summing up the debate in Krasnoyarsk. Similar concerns arose in various forms all over the world – but this was not mere self-indulgence on the part of the assembled writers. The fretting about royalty cheques and pension plans usually cropped up in the context of a wider debate about how the internet is changing the structures of the publishing industry; the unwillingness of the public to pay for 'content' (whether that content is high art or a Wikipedia entry); and, perhaps most fundamentally, about copyright law – now falling so far behind the digital reality that it is like a bicycling policeman in hot pursuit of a stolen Lamborghini.

'The big publishers don't seem to have learned the lesson from the music industry,' said **Tibor Fischer**, 'If it's digital, you can kiss it goodbye. And it's ironic that as the access to a global market has become easier, it's become harder to make money. If I published a new novel today, it would be competing against, let's say, two million digital titles. In ten years, that will probably be twenty million. And even today, Amazon offers some bestselling books for twenty pence and many more for under a pound. Writing novels was never an easy path to wealth, but you always had a chance of a jackpot, and you also had a chance of a living wage. And while there's still a chance of a jackpot, the odds are much longer. Most established novelists are now in the same position as the poets in that they can no longer expect to make a living from their writing, or at least from their novels. Like musicians, they have to rely more on the live act, to make money now.' **AD Miller**, speaking in Beijing, conflated two perplexities: that the audience was dwindling, and that at the same time it was becoming ever more tight-fisted. 'There is this anxiety that before long no-one is going to have the appetite to read anything that is more than 140 characters long,' he said. 'And that if they do, they are certainly not going to be prepared to pay for it. That's a problem with the business model.'

Not prepared to pay for it .... For many of the delegates, the chronic breach of copyright and instantaneous piracy of their work represented a real threat not just to their own livings, but to the survival of the novel as an art form. During the first chapter of the Conference in Edinburgh, some delegates met in closed session to produce a 'Statement of Principle and Intent' which said in part that 'copyright which has historically been the basis for writers' income, is increasingly being infringed, something which threatens both the income generated by the individual literary work and its artistic integrity.' This was meant to be a banner to which all the assembled writers could rally, but **China Miéville**, for one, declined to sign it – to the dismay of some of his fellow writers. 'The statement talks about copyright having protected artistic integrity; that's a model which is broken and outdated,' he said in his defence after the Conference. 'You can make a strong case that copyright has been a profoundly philistine dynamic over the years. When it says that it protects the writers' incomes, I think that is highly questionable. My position is not a naïve libertarian one whereby you get rid of copyright, information is free and everyone makes loads of money. Nor do I think there aren't important and knotty questions of, for example, courtesy and fair recompense. My problem is with the punitive actions around it. There are undoubtedly times when the mass-scale pirating of a particular book has resulted in large scale losses for the author – I don't dispute that for a second. I can also name specific examples where the pirating of a particular book has given it a new lease of life and increased its sales. To posit that a non-paid-for download is stealing is in my view entirely wrong. It's a basic error: the idea that a million unpaid-for downloads are a million instances of theft is just nonsense because you have no idea how many of those people would have paid for it otherwise. Maybe 995,000 of them had no intention of looking at the book before they looked at it via download.'

Miéville returned to this theme in the 'bug fix' version of his keynote, delivered in Toronto. 'The blurring of boundaries between writers, books, and readers, self-publishing, the fanfication of fiction, the new collectivity – none of this means that some people won't be better at the writing thing than others, nor unable to pay their rent by doing it. Querying the existing model – opposing the rottweilers of copyright, who act as if they never made a mixtape for a friend or shared battered books in the playground – doesn't mean not wanting writers to be paid. So how? I don't know. I'm open-minded. I'm eager for a discussion, a calm, collaborative exploring of new options not predicated on suspicion or punishment of readers. The great majority of whom, like the great majority of writers, are honourable people, who know that if writers are never paid, they won't be able to write. We want to work something out.'

Miéville had suggested in his keynote address that it might be better if writers received a salary from the state (prompting **Inci Aral** to say in hers that 'for us in Turkey this is but a joke; while there exists a mentality that throws writers in prison, there can be no-one within the state who will fight the writer's corner.'). **Melvin Burgess** thought that the future might lie in the opposite direction – in disengagement from all the established (commercial) structures. 'I don't think the internet spells the end of the novelists and novels, but it might be the death knell for publishers,' he said. 'I have some books that I plan to publish myself: I will pay an editor to edit them, a PR person to promote them, and I will keep 75% of the royalties. I will be happy to wave goodbye to publishers. In a way, it will be like going back to the eighteenth century, when a writer would employ a printer to produce his book.' Taking this direction to its logical extremity, one might imagine the creative writer going the way of the thatcher and luthier: novelists could become traditional guildspeople, keeping their ancient craft from extinction by seling their wares and their skills into a niche market. Or perhaps literature was destined to become an industry more like fine art: novels will be produced in artificially limited runs like prints or etchings, perhaps in beautiful editions that a discerning public could be persuaded to pay good money for. Books would become desirable *objets d'art*. It worked for William Morris, after all, and it is already the way that some bilbiophiliacs and first-edition collectors see the old-fashioned print-on-paper artefact.

The erosion of copyright, meanwhile, opens up an altogether different future for the book, one in which there are no physical objects to speak of, because all texts are digitally available to everyone – and also open to be edited and altered by anyone. **Denise Mina**, speaking in İzmir, explored this possibility when she spoke about the rise of Creative Commons licensing for authored works. 'Creative Commons licensing is slipping in when you write for websites. Some short stories published on websites have this kind of license. It means that the operators of the website do not have to observe or enforce normal copyright, whereby the writer has control of the material and the writer's permission must be sought to use it. Creative Commons means that anyone can use it or download it – and *they can change it*. They can change your endings, your beginnings, your characters and your locations. They can fundamentally alter the politics of anything you write. I would hate that – but this could be one future. In this future, the final version of a novel would be the one decided on by the audience. This would be writing by committee. Now, before we throw our hands up in horror, let's remember that this is not a new thing. Here are the final four lines of an ancient Irish love poem:

> You have taken the east from me, you have taken the west from me.
> You have taken waters before me, and waters behind me.
> You have taken the moon, you have taken the sun from me.
> And my fear is great that you have taken God from me.

'That's from *Donal Óg*. This poem was passed from generation to generation for hundreds of years, and added to along the way. I had that poem above my desk for three years, and I read it every day. That is something very beautiful and poignant that has been written by committee, arrived at by people adding in and editing until they achieved a final version.'

But what about the economics of it? 'If we can't eat tomorrow, how are we supposed to write our next novel?' asked the Danish novelist **Janne Teller** in Edinburgh. **Ewan Morrison**, like Tibor Fischer, made a comparison with the music industry – but came to an almost opposite conclusion: 'I would support people like Dr Dre and Bono who defend copyright,' he said, taking issue with Miéville, 'because they believe that there won't be a future generation of musicians if everyone just gets to mash up their material for free and redistribute it.' Miéville responded in Toronto: 'Five minutes online and you meet that future generation, making music piratically, shoving things together, manipulating, and even finding new ways to make a living from it. Far from fearing it, we in fiction should be so lucky as to see that kind of creativity, the creation of new forms. Why are we not hankering for some book version of the mixtape? If some precocious young book-turk turns our stuff into something new we should have the grace to be grateful.

The original's still right there too. And theirs might even be brilliant. It might be better. This is how culture moves. I see Ewan's Dr Dre and raise him Public Enemy's Chuck D, who knows that without these so-called transgressions, culture would be vastly poorer. "How do you feel about other people remixing your tracks without permission?" asks *StayFree* magazine. "I think my feelings are obvious,' he replies. 'I think it's great".'

And as for the royalties, is that something a dedicated novelist should even consider? Perhaps there is nothing wrong with that old cliché, the struggling writer in his garret. 'Are we in it for the money? Really?' asked **Ali Smith** when the problems of making a living from fiction came up in Edinburgh. **Daniel Shepherd**, a young writer from New York, thought not. 'Are we businessmen or are we artists?' he asked the room. 'I don't care whether I sell one copy, or even whether my mother reads my book (I'm Jewish, of course she will). As artists we must give it everything. We are supposed to ejaculate on the page, spill blood on the page. We shouldn't be worrying about whether it's going to make us money.'

Jonathan Bastable (ed.)

Egypt rising

by Sahar el Mougy
Keynote, Cairo*, December 2012

In the last decade, the world as we have known it since the Second World War has changed, is still changing. We are actually in the very heart of this change now. The internet revolution is one facet of this. It is both a reflection of the ongoing strong current of change as well as one of its many causes. And in parallel with the internet revolution, waves of social upheaval have been gaining force in different parts of the world since 2004, culminating in the huge wave of protests of 2007 till the present moment. The two factors – the internet revolution and the social upheavals – raise questions related to the novel and to what extent the genre is affecting and being affected by the change.

I believe the internet has led to a multi-layered state of democratisation. It has led to an expansion of readership, with readers gaining access to free books online, the classics as well as the hacked. Culture is no longer accessed only by those who can pay for its products. Yet the democratisation of culture raises questions related to the publishing business: has this access enjoyed by the 'people' been as fortunate to the publishers? Is there a threat to their business? Will publishers have to think of ways of competing, or maybe minimising the damage?

The internet has also democratised writing and self-publishing. Since the year 2000, millions of people around the world have enjoyed the free space for self-expression offered by blogs and the pages of the social media. Some of those bloggers happened to be/turned out to be writers. They were young writers with hardly any access to the publishing world. But through the virtual space, they could write and with a press on the keyboard their writings were out there, readers reading and responding. Online self-publishing does not bring the writers money, yet their works are read, they are given feedback and offered a chance to engage with their peers.

In the case of Egypt, blogging has not been just an escape from, and a challenge to, the publishing business. More importantly, it has lead to some radical psychological change in the 1980s generation, which I call 'the Emergency-Law generation'. This is the generation which has been born to a multi-faceted marginalisation. They called themselves 'the Egyptian expatriates in Egypt' as shown in the slogan of the internet radio station Teet, whose mission statement reads: 'The Voice of the Egyptian Expatriates in Egypt'. Funny but true. Blogging eventually meant resistance, the cultural resistance of the oppressed as Bill Ashcroft puts it in *Post Colonial Transformations*, though the coloniser-colonised relationship has acquired new dimensions. Blogging has offered those writers a zone where they can deconstruct and reconstruct their sense of identity against the social and political mainstream. Lately, many Egyptian blogs have been popular enough to seduce publishers into publishing such works (novels, poetry collections and short stories).

The other element which I believe will impact on the novel in many ways is the social/political upheaval the world has been witnessing since 2004. From Iceland to Greece and Spain, from the Arab world to the UK, Russia and the US, ripples of anger against the failure of governance are growing. How will this new consciousness impact on the novel? While I do not have answers regarding world literature, I can attempt to trace some signs of change in Egypt. In parallel with the work of the civil opposition groups, the world of culture/writing has enjoyed a revival. New publishing houses have been founded, many of them introducing new voices. Quite a number of new novelists have emerged. Some of those writers came from the blogging world. More bookstores opened. Signing events took place, a newly introduced tradition which did not exist before 2004. Private book clubs, operating away from the cultural institutions which monopolised all cultural activities for decades, mushroomed. Meanwhile, *Writers and Artists for Change* was founded in June 2005, a branch of *Kefaya*, the mother movement to many off-shoots.

On September 5th, 2005, fifty-five Egyptian artists and theatre critics were burned to death in a fire that took place in a small performance hall in Beni Soueif. While attending a play in one of the theatre festivals, a candle used in the performance fell and a huge fire erupted. The attendees, mainly theatre critics, drama professors and artists, rushed to the two doors of the hall, but the doors were bolted from the outside! The fire brigade came late while ordinary people tried for thirty minutes to stop the fire. There were too few ambulances and the hospitals were in an appalling condition. The people who rushed to help transported the victims in their own cars and in taxis to the public hospital. Meanwhile, state security forces besieged the hospital and beat the relatives of the victims when they started complaining at the lack of aid. Many victims died in the fire, the others, who could have been saved, died in hospital. The tragedy came as yet another bitter reminder of the dilapidated state of the political regime. Writers and artists left their desks and protested for months on end against the Ministry of Culture and the corrupt regime which protected the minister for twenty-three years in office. Serious questions surfaced relating to the state's continuous efforts (since the 1970s) to 'tame' Egyptian writers.

In the meantime, a question relating to the content of the novels written by the writers of the last two decades poses itself. Children of the internet have been exposed to the world in a different way. The image has been part of their perception of the world. Will the content and style of such writings reflect this change as compared to the works of the previous generations? In certain cases, a happy marriage existed between narratives and the image, as in the case of the graphic novel. In some other cases, the novels were affected by the blogging medium in that they show a tendency to pull down the wall between writer and reader. There is always an addressee with whom the writer engages. I would borrow Maggie Gee's question here: will the novel develop into an oral saga? It very well might.

In some novels, the language and tools of the internet have been adopted and adapted within the narration. The formatting, for example, of emails, chats and fragmented conversations have inspired some novels. Some blogs have been converted, with minimal or no changes, into books. To what extent will the genre, already flexible and receptive of new elements, evolve or change? Could it be that what is happening represents the early seeds of a more radical change yet to materialise?

But one can already register some change in the content of the Egyptian novel, a change which coincided with the awakening which has been taking place since 2004. Many Egyptian novels stopped turning their back on the political. Unlike the works of the writers of the 1990s (myself included), which dealt with the subjective and the personal, some novels built bridges with the sociopolitical context. Looking back at the novels of the 1990s, one finds out that the writers gave their backs to the wider social and political context which marginalised them. The political scene was corrupt and unwelcoming of newcomers. Society was being infiltrated by the rigid Wahabi discourse. Where would they fit? Actually, they fitted nowhere. They did not see themselves as active agents in what was going on around them. The threads connecting them to the wider social/political context were too worn out to hang on to.

Rejecting the reality that was out there was both a need and a statement. The novelists explored their sense of estrangement, both on the level of the self-self or that of self-surrounding reality. The rejected self busied itself with its quest. There was a need to wrap one's self in the inner cocoon. I guess what took place in many novelists' minds then is that maybe the existentialist quest would bear fruit, unlike the engagement with the political. This was also a statement against the social mainstream which alienated the writers and pushed them to the faraway desert of indifference.

Significantly, some of those same writers (who enjoyed the cocoon in the 1990s) showed some degree of involvement with their context as revealed in their novels in the mid 2000s. For instance, in my 1999 novel *Daria*, the reader could hardly trace the timeframe of the story, which focuses on the protagonist's journey towards some degree of self-knowledge and her fight against patriarchal pressures. In 2007, I published *Noon,* which takes place in Cairo between 2001 and 2004. It begins with 9/11 and takes the reader to the fall of Saddam Hussein. Though it is not a political novel, it reveals a state of re-engagement. Now the journey of the self (of the four characters) could be located in a specific time, against a specific background which impacts on the characters in many ways. Many novels showed direct engagement. Then the revolution happened.

During the revolution, social media revealed a change in the position of Egyptian writers. It has made their voices louder when it comes to issues of change. Egyptian writers, who complained back in the 1990s of closed circles of readership, were both witnesses to social change as well as active agents in it. Their position changed from the marginal to the focal. During the Egyptian revolution, writers' tweets, Facebook statuses, article quotes and YouTube clips helped steer public opinion and raise debates. Their presence in the streets and on social media reflected the awakening of the people and simultaneously endorsed it. Ironically, such presence was highlighted because of the virtual space, which was no longer 'virtual'. The internet, rather than the media, became the treasure chest of the collective consciousness.

Now I believe the question of the collective consciousness has put writers in a difficult position. How will the novel capture a moment that is larger than life? One of the major successes of the revolution is the deconstruction of the image of the collective self, carefully etched by the dictator who has worked really hard to deform/defame it. We found out we are not 'lazy', 'submissive', 'indifferent' and 'ignorant' as they told us about ourselves. To the exact contrary, we are beautiful, compassionate, brave and wise. We have an insatiable craving for freedom and justice and dignity. And we are willing to pay the price for what we want. In the first eighteen days of the revolution, we were larger than life. Memory keeps a record of amazing moments which challenge the writer. Can he/she portray these moments of grandeur? How can writing capture and frame glory and bliss and the painful but joyous experience of rebirth?

Photography can do it. Poetry can do it, now. But the novel tells the novelist 'Wait, this is not the right time. Live the experience. Take photographs and make notes and enjoy the poetry. Join the marches and write articles if you wish. Sleep on it. One day you will revisit the squares and be able to write'.

The question of how the novel can keep up with such radical change of consciousness is open to infinite possibilities. When Egyptian novelists will write about the revolution is unknown to me. But I am certain that the Egyptian novel of the next decade will turn into a playground of experimentation and aesthetic adventures based on the principle that 'the sky is the limit'. Haven't we already seen it happen? And most certainly the novel will reflect new perceptions of reality and a reconstruction of the image of the collective self.

What is taking place in Egypt is no more than a single manifestation of a complex and multi-faceted change in world consciousness, a change which started in the early years of the millennium and is gaining force. I believe that novelists will be grappling in the next decades with such change, trying to understand and to foresee. They will have to think of new ways to write a new world that is being shaped at this very moment.

SHOULD LITERATURE BE POLITICAL?

Nailing the important stuff

by Hannah McGill

Can a work of literature affect political change? Should poets and fiction writers intend or expect their work to have impact on public opinion, on people's activism, or in the sphere of world events? Taking place against the backdrop of continued unrest in the wake of the Arab Spring – which resulted in the cancellation of the Cairo chapter – and the building debate around the 2014 Scottish independence referendum, the Edinburgh World Writers' Conference saw questions of writers' political standing and engagement thrown into sharp relief. Early in the Conference, during its inaugural Edinburgh leg, online delegate **Samar Yazbek** contributed to a discussion on the future of the novel from her native Syria, with the point that she was unable to consider this question 'separately from the massacres that are happening in my country'. The feeling in the room was one of having been brought up short; of a closing of the gap between writers living relatively comfortable lives and fretting over matters of status and terminology, and people confronting the threat of actual obliteration.

But can such a hierarchy of concerns be made to stand, or is it potentially dangerous to imply that matters of art and creativity are luxuries to be dealt with once the truly important stuff is all nailed down? Must a writer by definition consider his or her art form to be a matter of human necessity? Confronted with a similar question at the Conference's Melbourne chapter – 'Are we creating this debate instead of reading the literature that's being produced, or actually engaging with the politics that's happening in front of us right now?' asked an audience member – **Junot Díaz** argued passionately for the idea that engagement with and discussion of literature are a rare and important facet of a politicised life, that 'politics' are to be considered more broadly than in simple terms of activism or clear responses to definable issues. Someone's political awareness, he stressed, and the effect of art thereon, is 'impossible to trace, impossible to measure' – but the notion that art was somehow politically ineffectual or irrelevant struck him as 'a strange thing, given the passion that art evokes in people'. He also counselled against the assumption that the literature visible to any one of us constituted any sort of representative sample from which one could draw definitive conclusions: 'Have you read all of the literature in Urdu …?' An issue, of course, for all of the Conference debates, if not any debate about anything ever: one is limited by one's own experience of the subject. But even keeping in mind these evident stumbling blocks – no-one can peek into the mind of another to see how it might be affected by a particular cultural experience, and no-one can speak from the perspective of having read everything from everywhere – it proved awkward throughout the Conference sittings to define what 'politics' actually meant.

Ahdaf Soueif's keynote in Edinburgh sought the distinction between political engagement and the development of human empathy, and acknowledged its obscurity. Any writer, she noted, engages with politics by taking part in 'the great narrative of the world', and politics arguably permeate any story, since 'relationships are political.' Another delegate, **Alan Bissett**, noted that deliberate evasion of political issues was not a neutral stance: 'The absence of politics is itself political.' **Tamim Al-Barghouti**'s keynote for the cancelled Cairo leg identified the fact that non-political modes can be political in certain circumstances: 'A love poem by a Palestinian poet in standard Arabic may not seem like it's political, but it joins with thousands of other images, imaginings, reports and visions, to create a sense of Palestine in Egypt, Morocco, Lebanon, Syria.' And as **Ewan Morrison** pointed out in Edinburgh, allegory – the veiling of direct political comment in the service of making a political message all the more impactful – is one of literature's most pervasive and effective modes.

A number of conference delegates argued that writers are a check on society's thinking; natural dissidents engaged with thinking and questioning on behalf of all their readers and potential readers. 'The writer has a duty one way or another to play a political role,' said **John Burnside** in Edinburgh. 'Whether it's to give a model, such as 'I refuse to accept the bullshit that they're giving me. I'm going to investigate it for myself and find out what's really going on.' Or whether it's simply what a poet does, which is insist on the more sophisticated, subtle and meaningful use of language as a way of not capitulating to the kind of forces that make language simplistic, so they can control the market or control the way we think about things. I think that's what all writers do: they renew language. And that's a start, a fundamental, the biggest building block of them all.' Such deployment of creativity could, far from becoming an irrelevant indulgence, be all the more impactful in a time of crisis, argued **Njabulo Ndebele** in Cape Town. 'In difficult moments of transition, reductive simplification may trump complexity and nuance,' he said.

Yet it might be regarded as a tremendous post-modern cop-out – not to mention a reductive stance in terms of the risks taken by artists who take true personal risks against repressive regimes – to argue that any work of art becomes politically engaged simply by existing. If politics is everywhere and everything, doesn't it become meaningless to talk about it at all? It fell to **Amanda Lohrey** in Melbourne to sound a note of negativity regarding the capacity of the novel to 'make an effective political intervention'. Within a repressive regime, she argued, a novel might 'fortify the morale of activists on the ground, but it cannot do more than this to overthrow regimes'. One response, according to Lohrey, is what James Wood has termed 'hysterical realism': crowded, manic works in which meaning is deliberately obscured by irony, fragmentation and promiscuous referentiality. 'Nowadays anyone in possession of a laptop is thought to be a brilliance on the move, filling his or her novel with essaylets and great displays of knowledge,' noted Wood. 'The result – in America at least – is novels of immense self-consciousness with no selves in them at all, curiously arrested and very "brilliant" books that know a thousand things but do not know a single human being.' **Sophie Cooke** made the point in Beijing, while discussing style versus content in literature: 'I think it's possible now to write something that's very ironic, that maybe doesn't contain anything very heartfelt – you can get away with a lot of pastiche and look very clever and metatextual, but move away from honest content.'

Yet aren't Wood's knowledge of human beings and Cooke's honesty in writing hopelessly subjective considerations? The knowledge of human beings that infused *The Catcher in the Rye* compelled one reader, Mark Chapman, to kill a celebrity whom he perceived to be one of the book's 'phonies'. *The Great Gatsby*'s sorrowful analysis of the folly of investing in surface glitter induced director Baz Luhrmann to create a film version of the book that revelled in surface glitter. Mary Harron's 2000 film of Bret Easton Ellis's *American Psycho* made feminist black comedy out of the novel most reviled by twentieth-century feminists. The novels of Jane Austen can be read as complacently complicit with a system in which a woman's value is judged by her marriageability, or as harshly and subversively critical thereof, depending on how her tone and intent are interpreted. And authorial intent itself is only the beginning of interpretation, for as the post-modernist habit of 'reading against the grain' teaches us, texts can take on lives of which their authors never dreamed, once loosed on the imaginations of readers. The ideology that an author might wish to project, any embedded ideology that seeps through without his or her willing it, and the ideology suggested to the reader, are all different and potentially co-existent factors in the political impact of a text. As Lohrey reminded us in her keynote, political literature is an inherently problematic concept, since 'in any text the writer's unconscious engages with the reader's and the outcomes are highly unpredictable'. Who is to say that a message will be received in the manner for which the writer designed it?

If the writers attending the Conference could be said to unite around one idea regarding the political effectuality of fiction, it was that a novel can stimulate change – albeit incrementally or invisibly – by engaging its reader's humanity and curiosity. Good fiction, suggested **Miriam Toews** in Toronto, 'is ambiguous. There are no answers, no pat solutions: it's little glimpses into the soul.' To **China Miéville**, such soul exposure meant that politics would out: 'If you are a politically concerned person and you want to write fiction, those concerns will be embedded in the fabric of the fiction.' And possibly, the very act of reading it could be transformative, regardless of the content. In Berlin, **Janne Teller** cited neuroscience in a discussion of the effects of reading fiction: novels, she observed, are unusual among other art forms in that they do not provoke immediate sensory reactions. The text on the page must be interpreted by the brain; the novel exists only when the reader transforms the words into images. The novel can, therefore, strengthen our capacities for empathy and humanity, by activating our imaginations and our emotions. 'The crux of the novel is love', she concluded.

Still, as **Melvin Burgess** put it in Krasnoyarsk, 'to be truly political you have to take a stance, a position.' Is it enough to contend, as many speakers on the subject did, that all writing is political, or that writers inevitably participate in politics because their books emerge from a specific context? Some writers at the Conference favoured a more direct interpretation of authorial activism, with Alan Gibbons arguing in Edinburgh that writers bear a responsibility to make their voices heard on issues that directly affect writers and readers – in his example, the mass closure of libraries in the UK – and **Xiaolu Guo** speaking in Berlin of the need for authors to offer voices to the silenced and the deceased. Sophie Cooke, in Berlin, pondered whether the very form of a novel might bear ideological weight: did an individualistic narrative focused on a single hero's consciousness inevitably do less to represent lived life than a collective form of narrative representing multiple viewpoints? As her fellow panellist **Tim Parks** noted, it is also important to consider the predominance of Western models of individual agency in the debate: 'There are parts of the world where they just don't think like this about life. The self is simply not seen in this way.'

But as several delegates said: isn't the aim of literature to get people – one self at a time – to see things a different way? And isn't that the point of politics too?

The great narrative of the world

by Ahdaf Soueif
Keynote, Edinburgh, August 2012

The writers' conference held at the Edinburgh festival fifty years ago discussed this proposition: 'Many believe that the novelist has the duty to further by his writing the causes in which he believes. Others think that literature must be above the problems of the day.'

The assumption is that the novelist is able to do one or the other. And I'm not sure this assumption is true. Can a novelist deliberately sit down to write a novel that furthers a cause? Well, yes, and it may be a good cause and a just cause, but what you get will not be a novel – it will be a political tract with a veneer of fiction. It's my experience that even when we think we're choosing the story, it is the story that chooses us.

George Eliot wrote: 'If we had a keen vision and feeling for all ordinary human life, it would be like hearing the grass grow and the squirrel's heart beat, and we should die of that roar which lies on the other side of silence.' Today there is no other side, and there is no silence. The internet, Twitter and YouTube have made sure of that. Yes, the noise may be removed from our immediate circle, but we know that it exists; we know that it will take two taps on the keyboard to bring our screen chiming to life with trafficked women, terrorised children and desperate men. We know men and women brave seas and deserts in search of a livelihood, we know half the world goes hungry and the planet is crazed with man's excess and that there is, particularly among the young, a great and urgent desire to change the system.

The question is: do you want to engage with this? Or do you want to escape it? Do you want to live your life in a bubble? Or do you want to be part of the great narrative of the world?

Is a novelist a literary activist? An activist is impelled by a cause and adopts it. Most people are content to live their lives within prescribed and personal boundaries. But one of the points of artists surely is that they live outside their skin. That they're connected. That they hurt with the hurt of their fellow humans. How, then, can they disengage? How can you – if your task, if your gift, is narrative – absent yourself from the great narrative of the world?

Should the novel be political? I don't believe in 'should' anywhere near art. At any moment there are a thousand stories to be told. Do we storytellers choose which one to tell? Or are we chosen and pressed by a story until we sit down and work on it and bring it forth into the world? Does the story come to us when we're ready to take it on? And isn't the only 'should' then that we should give the story its due?

I believe our duty is to our readers and to the story we've agreed to tell. Our duty is to keep our readers reading, to let them into a world they make their own, a world where they recognise their own questions and their own longings, where they find characters who become friends, and they feel such powerful empathy that they want to reach through the print and help or comfort them. That's the deal: the writer engages the reader's emotions, makes the reader care what happens next; and the reader engages with the world being presented.

Our duty is to tell the story that's come to us in the most effective way possible. But we don't choose the story: we're drawn in where the feeling is deepest. A work of fiction lives by empathy – the extending of my self into another's, the willingness to imagine myself in someone else's shoes. This itself is a political act: empathy is at the heart of much revolutionary action.

But the novelist, like the activist, is also a citizen of the world and bears the responsibility of this citizenship. The question is, then, can you honour your responsibility as a citizen of the world and fulfil your responsibility to your art? The question becomes critical in times of crisis.

Mahmoud Darwish, the late, great Palestinian poet, in his address to the opening event of the first Palestine festival of literature in 2008, wrote of the difficulty of being a Palestinian writer who 'has to use the word to resist the military occupation, and has to resist – on behalf of the word – the danger of the banal and the repetitive. How can he achieve literary freedom in such slavish conditions? And how can he preserve the literariness of literature in such brutal times? The questions are difficult.'

But we tease out answers. Darwish's answer, perhaps, was to absent himself from the centre of the crisis. That centre was, for him, his hometown of Haifa. So he kept an office in Ramallah but lived mostly in Amman. At that distance he could produce the work that was both true poetry and true to the situation. But what if you cannot or will not remove yourself from the situation? In Egypt, in the decade of slow, simmering discontent before the revolution [of 2011], novelists produced texts of critique, of dystopia, of nightmare. Now, we all seem to have given up – for the moment – on fiction.

Fiction will come again, I hope. And maybe I'll tell the story of Boulaq sands, less than a kilometre from my home, where the police killed Amr el-Bunni, and a community is being terrorised out of their homes to make way for a luxury development. Or maybe I'll tell the story of Samira Ibrahim, who put a stop to the military's virginity tests; or Ahmad Harara, shot in one eye on January 28th, and in the other in December; or Khaled Said's mother, who has adopted all the young revolutionaries in lieu of her murdered son, or ....

Attempts at fiction right now would be too simple. The immediate truth is too glaring to allow a more subtle truth to take form. For reality has to take time to be processed, to transform into fiction. So it's no use a story presenting itself, tempting, asking to be written, because another story will – in the next minute – come roaring over it, making the same demand. And you, the novelist, can't grab one of them and run away and lock yourself up with it and surrender to it and wait and work for the transformation to happen – because you, the citizen, need to be present, there, on the ground, marching, supporting, talking, instigating, articulating. Your talent – at the time of crisis – is to tell the stories as they are, to help them to achieve power as reality not as fiction.

Politics on the page

The proposition 'Should literature be political?' was a slippery one. It was understood in different ways – not just from country to country, but also within the course of the discussion at one location. Sometimes the talk was of writers being persecuted by oppressive regimes; at other times it turned to the undeconstructed social assumptions that lie hidden in the classics of English literature, or to the liberating message of what was labelled (tentatively or queasily) 'subaltern and post-colonial writing'. Occasionally the discussion was straightforwardly practical – a kind of workshop in which writers swapped tips for conveying political ideas through a written work of art.

But one particular variation on the theme was present from the very start, when the Egyptian novelist **Ahdaf Soueif** gave her keynote on the first day of the Conference in Edinburgh. And it surfaced wherever in the world the conversation went. It might be summed up in the terse question: 'Are writers political?' To put in a number of other ways: is writing a political activity? Should writers be involved in the politics of their place and time? And can literature, in the end, make the slightest difference to the course of events?

Three contributors framed the problem by making reference to the Hitler regime. 'There are times and contexts that are more political than others,' said **Benjamin Markovits** in Kuala Lumpur. 'There's a line in a poem by Brecht, written in the Nazi period, in which he says that a conversation about the weather is a crime at the moment because it involves not speaking about so many more important things.' In Cape Town, an audience member challenged 'the notion that literature necessarily ennobles people – I thought that died out with the Nazi party. Because you can have people who are prepared to take part in murder and massacre and yet see themselves as cultured because they listen to Mozart and read Goethe ...' – prompting this response from **Antjie**: 'You must remember that before the Nazis did what they did, they burned books.' Back in Edinburgh, the Turkish novelist **Elif Shafak** put this thought to Ahdaf Soueif: 'Is fiction a luxury at times like these? It's not a new question, of course. Theodor Adorno of the Frankfurt school asked it when he said: Can there be poetry after Auschwitz? Is poetry still meaningful in the light of such violence and cruelty?'

'I don't think it is a luxury,' said Soueif. 'I think it would be a wonderful contribution if someone could write a properly imagined novel – rather than a political tract disguised as a novel – about the Egyptian revolution. I just don't see how it can be done. I think it is a logistical problem: how can you be engaged with it, active on the ground, and at the same time removed enough to give a novel the attention and concentration that it needs? I just don't see how it is possible.'

'If I hear you right,' said Shafak, 'you are saying that while events take place, it is harder to find the time for fiction – but essays, commentary, these things are still possible. I think Doris Lessing said that fiction comes after the event.' (Amanda Lohrey later said exactly this in Melbourne – and was criticised for it. See p.128).

'No, it's not a matter of analysis' said Soueif. 'It is a matter of giving the mental and emotional space for patterns to form, for characters to be fully imagined and realised. I mean: you can go for days without producing a sentence, just going through the process of imagining that will eventually yield a sentence. I believe that if (God forbid) I were taken away today and put in a jail for a year – it would have to be a very comfortable jail with a desk and a desklamp and electricity – then I would produce the novel [of the Egyptian revolution]. But I'd need to be locked away, because I can't choose to absent myself from what is happening now.'

So is it not possible to create a novel that addresses the urgent issues of the day? That, surely is what the Russian titans did, or attempted to do. Dostoyevsky wrote about the nascent revolutionary movement; Turgenev explored that same theme, and also the iniquities of serfdom; Tolstoy's big novels are full of asides on the agrarian reform, the state of the peasantry, and his many other real-world obsessions. He certainly felt that these passages were what made the books worth reading, but (as Hemingway once pointed out) they are precisely the bits that most readers now leaf past so as to get back to the stories of the Annas and Natashas and rest of the vast cast of living, breathing human beings. Yet Tolstoy wasn't wrong. The publication of a novel by one of the great Russians was, at the time, a major political event. It is just that the political and social concerns that informed those books, that gave rise to the word-tempests, have entirely faded away. What's left behind is the eternal fascination of character and story; what's left is *literature*, unqualified by *political* or any other adjective. The Danish writer **Janne Teller**, in Edinburgh, hinted at this truth when she asked rhetorically why we still read Dostoyevsky, and elaborated her (rather Russian-sounding) metaphor of the overcoat. In St Malo, the Togolese novelist **Sami Tchak** made a remark that took for granted the eternal elements in the great novels: 'We are mistaken if we believe that literature should have a goal or an outcome,' he said. 'All great literature is tragic rather than hopeful. Tolstoy and Dostoyevsky bring us back to the human condition, to questions such as death. Literature may be political, but it can play no role in the destiny of nations.'

No-one took issue with this observation in St Malo, but elsewhere writers jumped up to argue for the usefulness and efficacy of political literature. 'As a writer I see myself as a representative of the cultural resistance, of cultural rebellion,' said **Earl Lovelace** in Trinidad. 'I agree,' said **Olive Senior**. 'Literature arises out of tumult, out of the times in which we live, and I wonder if prosperity and stability don't give rise to books that might be called navel-gazing.' **Pankaj Mishra**, taking part in the same discussion, enlarged on this theme. 'Writing *is* a form of resistance,' he said, 'especially if you come from a non-western, non-affluent society which hasn't produced a whole lot of modern literature of its own, in which you are constantly receiving literature produced elsewhere, and in which you can't find reflections of yourself. Writing in that context is an act of asserting one's own humanity, and a political intervention. But who is this question meant for? I would say it is more pertinent to writers in the Anglo-American world, where literature was for a very long time political – in the broad sense that writers were aware of conflict and violence beyond the domestic, of the existence and persistence of inequality. If you look at the canonical writers of America and Europe in the nineteenth and early-twentieth century, they were all intensely aware of these conflicts and how they impacted individual lives. But in the decades since the Second World War we have seen the rise of a studiedly apolitical literature, as if to be political was somehow to be less serious or to be insufficiently committed to the aesthetic of the novel.'

The Malaysian dramatist **Huzir Sulaiman**, though not a western writer, had a compelling answer for that. 'The thing about art, and this is my political credo, is that it should ask questions rather than provide answers,' he said in Kuala Lumpur. 'And when people look at political literature, I think they are often in search of an argument, something that is being advocated or fought for. Those are answers, but I am much more interested in things that open up the possibility for debate and discussion and disagreement – for critique and sometimes, very occasionally, for reinforcement of the status quo. My early plays tended to be classified as political. *Atomic Dryer* was a satire about the making of the Malaysian atomic bomb; *Election Day* was a play about friendship and betrayal set against the backdrop of the 1999 Malaysian general elections. But then my own interests as a writer moved inwards, to issues of psychology, of the family, of memory and history – which of course can also be political themes, but not in the sense of an overt critique of the state apparatus.'

Is it enough to say that the psychological can also be political? In Edinburgh, Elif Shafak took another quotation and punted it upfield towards the goalposts. The words were Chinua Achebe's. 'It is clear to me that an African creative writer who tries to avoid the big social and political issues of contemporary Africa will end up being completely irrelevant, like that absurd man in the proverb who leaves his burning house to pursue a rat fleeing from the flames.' **Ben Okri** immediately went chasing after the ball. 'If your house is burning, you put it out.' he said. 'You put the fire out, you don't write. After you have put out the fire and built a new house, then you can write about the fire that you put out. You don't write as a way of putting out the fire. The putting-out of the fire is personal, physical, individual activism. It's struggles, failures, conflicts – taking part as a citizen. Writing and literature – these are a completely separate activity that requires different skills and a timeframe. So literature can only be political if it is first of all literature, which is to say that it survives and continues to engage us way after the time that the novelist was writing in and writing about. In Nigeria many novels were published that were attempts to put the fire out. After five years we could no longer understand what those writers were talking about. Their novels became footnotes because they were political, but they were not literature.'

So according to Okri, a book can fail precisely because it engages with the present moment, with the proximate unfolding history. Or rather, a book must fail if that is all it does. Herein lies the difference between the stale novels he had in mind and the works of Tolstoy and Dostoyevsky, and even the avowedly political fiction of Orwell. The hellish totalitarianism that Orwell railed against is gone, and so in a sense the job his fiction was sent out to do is complete, his work is done. Yet we can still read *Nineteen Eighty-Four* and weep for Winston and Julia.

In Melbourne **Junot Díaz** was asked: 'Are you looking for converts when you write? Are you trying to persuade people?' He answered: 'No, never. If I wanted to convince and convert people, there are so many better and easier ways to do it than writing novels.' So why write novels, or indeed any kind of literature? What's the point? Antjie Krog had two final quotations that together made the case for all art that is wrought in words.

'Poets are the unacknowledged legislators of the world.'
(Percy Bysshe Shelley)

The poet ... is the arbiter of the diverse and he is the key. He is the equaliser of his age and land ...' (Walt Whitman)

Jonathan Bastable (ed.)

Weapons of struggle

by Njabulo Ndebele
Keynote, Cape Town, September 2012

The question 'Should literature be political?' is timeless, and best approached not with a view to finding definitive, timeless answers, but to opening our minds as to why we might be asking it yet again. In Africa, it was asked in the 1960s and 1970s during struggles against British, French, and Portuguese colonialism. In South Africa, particularly from the time of the 1976 youth uprising, it was posed again. Its urgency increased during the state of emergency in the mid-1980s when the apartheid regime escalated its repression. The drama of conflict at that time was clear: from a moral point of view, the state represented evil, oppressing black citizens, who joined with increasing numbers of sympathetic white South Africans in representing good.

No dramatic conflict could have been clearer and more defined. It had the clarity of a soap opera: strong bold lines of action and little subtlety. Mass protests, mass arrests and killings; mass poverty of the many; extreme wealth for the few; the enormous power of the state in defence of a small population of whites ranged against an enormous powerless labour reservoir of black people. In this situation, literature was to be one of the 'weapons of struggle'. Writers became known as 'cultural workers'. Poetry flourished, particularly in performance, where the evocative power of words and images combined with the physical language of the body to create an intense immediacy. And the end of it all was as heroically peaceful as the repression and resistance that brought it about had been violent. The formal handing over of the instruments of state to the new government of Mandela occurred with all the pageantry of spectacle: the swearing in of the new president and the fly-past of military aircraft with four helicopters bearing the new flag had thousands gasping and shedding a tear.

A film with a good ending. But there may have been a price!

During the state of emergency, when the question of whether literature should be political enjoyed some currency, it was asked as the struggles against violent oppression themselves took on some violent forms of expression. The complex reasons behind the quest for freedom, and the ethical values which justified that quest, seemed in danger of being reduced to nothing more than escalating acts of vengeance. The call to reflect on such questions invited some impatience, and even charges of betrayal. In difficult moments of transition, reductive simplification may trump complexity and nuance. It is as if moral complexity – a major source of literary value – is contrasted with political agency, whose capacity for reductive simplification may devalue the complicating tendencies of literature.

But non-political literature can be intensely political not so much in its postures as in the expressive value it earns through exploding simplification. In *The African Child*, first published in 1954, Camara Laye wrote about a boy growing up in a village in Guinea. In ever expanding circles of experience, he passes from the innocence of a village child to a world citizen living in France. In the evocation of a life ideologically degraded by colonialism, Laye – and later Chinua Achebe – delineated ways of life that had their sense of self: an identity that did not require justification. In a colonial environment, such a literary rendering of African life was a radical act of self-assertion.

Ousmane Sembene's *God's Bits of Wood*, published in 1960, tells of a strike by railway workers along the line between Bamako in Mali to Dakar in Senegal. Self-evidently heroic in character, it nevertheless does more than depict worker heroism. At the same time that the workers are engaged in a struggle symbolic of the wider anti-colonial project, we also see them in their entire human landscape, often times complicating, at other times demeaning, even when judged by their own actions. These two books reveal the continuum between political literature and literary politics. Both achieve transcendence through art that politicises and depoliticises all at once.

The risk of moral devaluation may increase even as legitimate political struggle gains momentum and draws closer to the humanistic goals for which it was waged. How are ethical and moral values to be rescued when children stand in a circle around a woman they have set alight after denouncing her as a collaborator, as happened in the 1980s? We urge closer attention to William Golding's *Lord of the Flies*, that most political of all non-political novels. Much later, it was established that the murdered woman was not a collaborator at all, the imagined offence which had brought her death. At a tragically painful moment we rediscover human folly and remember why we call for and endeavour to create fair political and legal processes to mitigate that folly.

There isn't a great deal in South Africa that can be called 'political literature' in the sense of a literature that dramatises political activism. We are more likely to see literature that 'politicises' by deepening of awareness, as in Camara Laye's book. Who, really, are the people who voted for democracy in 1994? Who and what have they become since then? Different answers are emerging. Many tell their stories through biography or autobiography, 'setting the record straight' through the 'facts' of their lives. Others, such as Kopano Matlwa in *Coconut*, challenge new prejudices held by some of South Africa's new citizens about other fellow citizens. So do Zuki Warner's characters in her *Men of the South*, some of whom grapple with their hidden sexualities. Car-jackers in Sifiso Mzobe's *Young Blood* have an intriguing human face. Their lives are subject to a code of conduct whose ethics disturbingly resemble those of 'normal society'.

Perhaps partly through literature in its deeply reflective politics, the politics of texture, we live in the time of literature that politicises as it depoliticises. I am thinking of a book: *Slow Violence and the Environmentalism of the Poor* by Rob Nixon. It is not a novel. But its compelling message makes a strong case for our times. The aim of this book is to make us aware of pervasive yet hidden acts of large scale ongoing violence whose impact will be devastating in the future: the violence of environmental degradation; of corruption; of the depreciation of morality through weak and uncultivated leadership. 'Assaults on a nation's environmental resources frequently entail not just the physical displacement of local communities, but their imaginative displacement as well ...' It is such 'imaginative displacement' that leads to public blindness.

To counter such contemporary tendencies, we need writing that explodes willed invisibility so that we can see with an awareness that recognises the dangerous present, and at the same time enables us to project our minds and our imaginations far into the future to prevent current trends from turning into tragedy in the long term. This kind of reflective capacity could very well be one of the fundamental values of modern society. It is the source of responsibility, compassion, tolerance, endurance, patience, and beauty. Africa has to cultivate it with an urgency that must permeate the entire political and social life of a continent increasingly impatient and desperate for renewal.

And so, why do we ask this question again, at this time? Should literature be political? Maybe we sense the need for a kind of reflective activism whose coherence only literature may render with some believable conviction. Maybe we yearn for renewal.

Game-changing books

If writing is a weapon of struggle, if fiction can change the world for the better, then which specific books have managed to pull off that amazing trick? Can they be identified by name, and is it possible to measure or quantify their effect?

In St Malo the Nigerian writer **Uwem Akpan** stood up and made this declaration. 'Today, Nigeria is mourning the death of Chinua Achebe, the great author of *Things Fall Apart*. That's a book that changed things. It changed the way that the western world looks at Africa, because it made people see that Africans have culture. That book began something. Should a writer be political in the sense of going out on the streets and mounting a protest? I'm not sure. Maybe it depends on the temperament of the writer. In my country, Wole Soyinka does that very well: he combines poetry, fiction, essays, documentaries – and he founded a political party. Should everybody do it? I don't think everybody has those gifts.'

With the possible exception of George Orwell, Achebe was the writer most often mentioned in connection with the political novel. In Kuala Lumpur, **Benjamin Markovits** said that *Things Fall Apart* was a personal favourite – but immediately linked his love for the book to its internal qualities, its portrayal of character and its storytelling. 'It's wonderful because it depicts something awful in ways that leave the reader uncertain,' he said. 'It's a story about the colonisation of an African tribe by western missionaries. Achebe spends two-thirds of the book painting a very difficult picture of what life in this tribe is like, focussing on one particular character who is an awful human being in lots of ways. He is a bully, he is petty, he breaks many of the laws of his own tribe, and he acts in a cowardly way when he gets involved in the killing of someone he has raised as his own son. And yet this is the guy – not anybody else – who sees soonest what is being done to his tribe when the missionaries come. And that seems to me an interesting decision: to make the hero of the book the least likeable member of the tribe. You are not sure at the end of the book where it leaves you. That's a real achievement.'

But has *Things Fall Apart* changed the world for the better? Can any novel do that, in fact? Markovits seemed less convinced than Akpan, but many of the writers at the Conference thought that literature ought at least to try. **Antjie Krog**, speaking in Cape Town, quoted Matthew Arnold and Dylan Thomas in defence of literature's ameliorating mission: 'Knowledge of literature is beneficial to critical thinking and moral health and should be an undertaking as serious and valuable as moneymaking or scientific advancement,' said Arnold; 'A good poem helps to change the shape and significance of the universe, helps to extend everyone's knowledge of himself and the world around him,' said Thomas. In St Malo an audience member cited Madame de Stael's dictum that 'literature is an art before it is a weapon' – and insisted that it must aim to become that weapon once it has achieved its artistic purpose.

Clément Caliari in St Malo went so far as to summon his fellow writers to the barricades. 'Today, when we are in the midst of the biggest economic crisis since the 1930s, where should writers be? Should politics take place only in parliaments, in the newspapers and on TV? Literature can demonstrate the possibility of doing politics in schools, in the workplace, on the streets, on a bus. Writers needn't be waving a manifesto, it can be more subtle than that, but I think it is a shame that they are not more politically active. We are always being given political solutions, but writers could, for example, be showing the effects of austerity and cuts in public finances, portraying the world that such policies might lead to. Most literature does not use that tool.'

Rute Pinheiro Coelho, in Lisbon, agreed. 'Every writer wants to awaken ideas in the mind of the public, to change the reader's mentality, and that is the case whether the message of the novel is political or not. The written word is a weapon of intervention. A novel that cannot evoke feeling is a failed work.' But does affecting a reader on an emotional level equate to political change? **Alison Croggan** in Melbourne wasn't convinced. 'Art always expresses desire of one kind or another, and it is very satisfying when that desire is articulated, when a book says what you have felt inside, but have never quite been able to say for yourself. Suddenly there it is, reflected somewhere else. But art doesn't directly do anything.' **Junot Díaz** in the same debate suggested that these small, invisible and individual changes of heart add up incrementally, that they amount to an invisible force that can eventually break cover and make a difference. 'Is art capable of helping us in making political interventions? I don't think anyone has made the argument that that's not possible.'

Several delegates gave instances to prove that it certainly was possible. Akpan's nod to Achebe was one such example. 'I believe that literature does carry hope,' added **Bernard Chambaz** in St Malo. 'I'd like to give you the example of Hugo's *Les Miserables*. When it was first published, workers would read a chapter communally in their lunchbreaks. They loved that book because it gave them a sense of dignity. And when they finished the book, the groups of workers would draw lots to decide who kept it. That surely, is an expression of political literature.'

Carlos Gamerro, in Edinburgh, told this strange tale, taken from recent Argentinian history: 'Rodolfo Walsh was one of our great political writers. He was killed on March 25th, 1977, the day after writing the first denunciation of the crimes of the dictatorship. He began as a writer of crime fiction in what you might call the analytical English tradition: a closed room, the sudden appearance of a corpse – nothing political. His second work, which was in a way a continuation of his detective stories, was an investigation into the murder of Peronists [in 1956] on the first anniversary of Peron's overthrow. He carried out the investigation himself, as a journalist, and it was published as a clandestine piece of non-fiction. It was a political book for sure, but ten years after it was published he said: "When I re-read it there are sentences that irk me. I know that I could write a much better book now." I thought that was fascinating: he was looking back on this secret book that he had to write in a state of urgency, and he wasn't worried about the evidence or the facts or justice, but about sentences and words. That is what I call a political writer, with the emphasis on the writing. And when he was writing that open letter to the junta he studied Cicero, because he wanted to imbue it with the cadences and the power of a public speech.'

In Cape Town, Antjie Krog told a rather different story about writers and big, visible politics. 'A play called *Die Pluimsaad Waai Ver* [*The Plume's Seed Blows Far*], by NP van Wyk Louw, the best poet Afrikaans produced, formed part of the Republic festivities in 1966. The Anglo-Boer War and tension within Afrikanerdom itself was van Wyk Louw's theme, and it was underpinned by his belief in loyal resistance that reminded a nation that it was better to perish than to survive through injustice. The play therefore opened with an old woman walking onto the stage, asking: What is a nation? The opening was attended by Prime Minister Hendrik Verwoerd. A few days later, on Republic Day at the Voortrekker monument, Verwoerd raised his disapproval of the play to three quarters of a million people – the biggest crowd ever to have assembled in the country until then. When will it happen, Verwoerd asked, that writers and poets step forward to sing the praises of our heroic achievements instead of asking waveringly: what is a nation? We want our writers to jubilate: this is our nation, this is how we made miracles .... He was loudly applauded and van Wyk Louw was deeply hurt. In the light of today, this interaction is something to envy. A head of state who goes to a serious play, commissioned by his Department of Art, and then engages with the text.'

When **Njabulo Ndebele** referred to this story, it was almost as if he was writing the scene as it might appear in a novel. In his telling, it ceased to be merely a political incident; it was suddenly a parable about one man's attempt to hang onto his integrity, his moral self, despite all the forces ranged against him: 'I am thinking of the situation where Dr Henrik Verwoerd goes to this performance, and responds to it. He might even enjoy the complexities and appreciate the nuances, and so forth. But when he stands on a political podium, the structure of power in which he finds himself may be so strong that it has the capacity to trump his own sense of that complexity. In other words, the more he speaks in opposition, in a willed ignorance, the more he may become aware of demeaning himself and lying to himself. He is not prepared to speak openly about the vulnerability he has experienced, because he sees complexity as a form of weakness.'

That's the way to do it – by getting deep inside someone's head, by imagining a character so intensely that, though fictional, he becomes real. And that is in fact the way it has always been done. **Atiq Rahimi**, summing up in St Malo, had this to say: 'With literature you can change worlds, not merely the World. This is the work of centuries. What would human consciousness now be without *The Bhagavad-Gita* or *The Iliad*? The impact of literature is not necessarily immediate or direct. Literature opens our eyes to the human condition by denouncing the wrongs – that's where the consciousness comes from.'

Jonathan Bastable (ed.)

The power and the story

by Melvin Burgess
Keynote, Krasnoyarsk, November 2012

Should novels involve politics? You have no choice. How do you escape politics? It is all around us. It defines our relationships with government, with our employers, it shapes the exchanges we have with our friends and our families. Politics helps define what we think and even how we feel. In these days of massive industrialisation, it is present in the water we drink and in the air we breathe.

We are social animals, and since politics is the study of the power dynamics in how we organise society, it's there right at the base of all culture, including literature of all kinds, whether it's novels, plays, poetry or advertisements. Even your shopping list has a political nature. Of all the arts literature is the one most concerned with human behaviour, human relationships, human character. You may as well argue that you can have novels without characters in them. It just doesn't add up.

That, however, does not make all writing political. To be political, which not all of us are, is a very different thing from being of politics, which we all are. I'd like to clearly differentiate between these two aspects of politics and novels. Let's look at the former first of all – the political novel. To be truly political, you have to take a stance, a position. This can be done in various ways. I'd like to quickly take a look at just some of them.

Firstly, there is the interpretation of events historically. History, as the saying goes, is always written by the winner. To that extent, fiction is not always to be found in novels; it can be found in the history books as well. But let's stick to more obvious fiction for now. One example of an English writer who did this, is Shakespeare. He was many things, but one thing he was not is radical. His most political role was to praise the Tudor royal family of the day. He wrote, for example, *Richard III*, a play specifically justifying the very dodgy assassination of the Plantagenet ruler by the usurper Henry Tudor. He was, in short, a very effective propagandist for the government of the day.

That is the first role – the writer as propagandist.

A second, but related role for writers politically, is to actually play a role in the formation of the idea behind nationhood itself. Shakespeare also fulfills this role for England. Goethe and Schiller do the same in Germany, Rabbie Burns in Scotland, Pushkin in Russia. All these writers helped to create a romantic myth, the fictitious character, of the nations they were a part of.

That's the second political role – nation building.

A third aspect, and a very important one today, is that of giving voice, in particular to the dispossessed. In the past as well as in the present, political elites have seen the value in suppressing the culture of people they see rule over, especially conquered peoples or minorities. Writers who have done this are Maxim Gorky – one of my personal favorites – Alexander Solzhenitsyn, and a great many modern novelists. A fourth aspect of politics in novel writing is satire – puncturing the myths of social groups, particularly elites. I could mention the Irish writer Jonathan Swift in this context.

Fifthly, an area of political activity that has inspired a huge amount of writing in the past fifty years is that of interpersonal politics. This is something that came out sexual politics, specifically, feminism: the study of power in relations between men and women. Margaret Atwood, Germaine Greer, Simone de Beauvoir are examples of this. The rise of feminism has not just given us a new understanding of the role of the sexes historically and socially, it's also given rise to a new way of analysing other groups. My own genre, writing for Young Adults – still a very recent phenomenon – is an example. YA writing is very much a grandchild of the feminist movement. It was feminism, for example, that pointed out how few books there were with strong, positive role models for and about woman. We can today say exactly the same for teenagers, who have such poor provision in terms of all media right around the world. There can only be one reason. Culturally, society doesn't want teenagers to have a voice. In this sense teenagers are perhaps a hundred years behind younger children, for whom literature began to be produced at least that long ago.

Finally, I'd like to mention those writers who have tried to tackle political issues in their rawest state – to write about the methods the state itself uses to hang on to power. This is not nearly such a common approach and the reason for it is, that novels do not easily lend themselves to it. Novels deal most easily in the personal – in character and in relationship – in what is thought, felt and experienced by individuals. This makes it very hard for them to deal directly with the bigger social issues. But it can be done. George Orwell is one example, using allegory and also science fiction.

Those are all examples of political literature. But being overtly political is not for all writers. As I said at the start, politics is all around us, but there is a big difference between being political, and being of politics. So in what way does politics show itself in novels that are not specifically political in nature? In the first place, of course, the politics of the day affect the characters and institutions we write about. That is true of all contemporary and historical novels. Tolstoy is all about social order. Dickens is all about class. If these writers were not politically aware, their novels would have been so much poorer – and the same is true of all of us. We cannot afford to be lazy about our knowledge of politics and how it affects people's day to day lives.

That's obvious. But what about other genres – science fiction, fantasy, books for children? How does politics show its face in this kind of work?

Let me give an example from fantasy – which of all genres you would imagine is the least political. Take Tolkien, *The Lord of the Rings*. I've heard various political commentaries on *The Lord of the Rings*, but to consider just one; the idea that Tolkien presents the concept of danger as always coming from without – that the ordinary, decent people in your community are not to be feared and always to be trusted. This is a political understanding even though it is actually about comfort reading – something you would think is as far removed as could be from politics. Tolkien is conflating safety with home – very successfully. I put it to you that if you want to write comfort fiction – and I have no argument with that – surely this is the sort of understanding you need to be aware of in your work, if you are to be fully in control of what you are writing.

Tolkien has spawned a host of imitators doing the same thing. Some of those imitators may be aware of how they are using his concept of home and safety – some of them will not. Which are the better writers? Which are more in control of their material? I put it to you that it is our job as writers to be aware as much as possible of the mechanics of our work, and in the ways those mechanics affect the reader. That is what being a writer is. That's our craft and our trade.

If we ignore politics we are allowing a vital element of our writing to pass out of our awareness and beyond our control. It's our job to bring all the elements of a story to life and we can only do this by being aware ourselves. Character, relationship, situation … politics. It is a part of what we do.

To finish then; because society is political, readers and writers are also political, as least in as much as we are formed by politics. To write and to be unaware of the political significance and meaning coming across in our books, is to be only half a writer. It is one of our tools. And anyone who tries to use a tool without understanding how it works is going to get their fingers cut sooner rather than later.

The Russian dimension

It is hard to think of a time or a place where the practice of writing has been more political, or more deadly, than twentieth-century Russia. No-one writing in the Russian language can put pen to paper without a thought for all the silenced predecessors. 'The great purges and trials of the years 1937 and 1938 altered the literary and artistic scene beyond all recognition,' wrote Isaiah Berlin from the British Embassy in Moscow in 1946. 'The number of writers and artists exiled or exterminated during this time ... was such that Russian literature and thought emerged in 1939 like an area devastated by war, with some splendid buildings still relatively intact, but standing solitary amid stretches of ruined and deserted country. Men of genius like Meyerhold the producer and Mandelshtam the poet, and of talent like Babel, Pilnyak, Yashvili, Tabidze, the then recently returned London émigré Prince DS Mirsky, the critic Averbakh (to take the best-known names alone) were "repressed", that is, killed or done away with in one way or another.'

'Of course, the relationship between literature and politics has always been a sore point for Russian society.' said **Irina Prokhorova** in Krasnoyarsk. 'For us it is question rooted in the twentieth century, when literature had to react to the dramatic events of that time. The hardest question is where the boundary lies: where literature ends and the political sphere begins, how a writer's work relates to the political reality. The reluctance of contemporary writers to be politically engaged flows out of the tragedy of the twentieth century.'

It was this long, dark shadow of Stalinism that Prokhorova had in mind. But for **Andrey Astvatstaturov** the paralysis in Russian letters was due not to the ghost of the Terror, but to a kind of post-Soviet cynicism which, he suggested, took hold in the woefully disappointing Yeltsin years. 'Here in Russia, the end of the 1980s and the beginning of the 1990s were marked by political activism, confrontation and a clash of ideals. It seemed that a time for literary-political engagement had come. But this animation quickly turned into a let-down, because pluralism and freedom of speech turned out to be a simple collision of economic interests; and because politicians who had seemed honest and truthful turned out to be glory-hunters and careerists. The main one reminded us of nothing more than a clown. Many of my fellow writers are politicised, and their texts would seem to be an eloquent refutation of my words. Zakhar Prilepin, for example, is the author of a political novel called *Sanka* in which the main character is a protester and a rebel. But I believe that the popularity of the novel is due to the fact that it's a good and beautiful aesthetic gesture, and that the majority of readers, although worshipping Zakhar, don't share his national-Bolshevik opinions. Even his *Letter to Comrade Stalin* could be seen as an aesthetic gesture. It's a pose rather than a position, and I doubt Zakhar really believes in what he has written.'

Kirill Kobrin, sitting on the Krasnoyarsk panel, commented drily that Astvatsaturov's speech 'fits neatly into the Russian literary tradition of asking "Who is to blame?" and then "What is to be done?"'. The British delegates appeared to be almost taken aback by the bleak and weary tone of the discourse. 'Everyone here sounds very traumatised by what you have described as "the cataclysm of the twentieth century".' said **Melvin Burgess**. Meanwhile, **Tibor Fischer** looked for common ground – and he found it, appropriately enough, east of London and west of Moscow. 'Part of the problem, as with any debate on this theme, is how you define politics. Irina made a important point: that there is a huge difference between the Russian tradition and the British. I can't think of a major Russian writer who at some point didn't have a scrape with the state or the authorities. I can only think of two English writers who were properly engaged with the politics of their time, and they are John Milton and George Orwell. There are lots of other writers – Charles Dickens, George Eliot – who had a social conscience, who were interested in society and how it works, but my view is that politics is dangerous because it is easy to lapse into sloganeering, and slogans belong on T-shirts, not in novels.

'To give a Russian example, I think most of us would agree that *Resurrection* is the least successful and least enjoyable of Tolstoy's major works, because so much of that book consists of Tolstoy preaching. A novel, fundamentally, should be about human nature, and that is going to impinge on politics from time to time. The best political work that I can think of in recent years is the TV sitcom *Yes, Minister*. It was all about ministries and how they work, but the humour sprang from the interaction between the main characters. Another example: when I was studying French at university in the 1970s, Jean-Paul Sartre was still considered an important figure, partly because he was still alive, but also because his political engagement made him very fashionable. At that time, Camus, who had died ten years earlier, was still read and respected, but he was seen as a minor player. Now the pendulum has swung the other way, and I don't come across many people who read Sartre's novels, whereas Camus has come to be regarded as one of the major figures of twentieth-century French literature. You could argue that there are political elements hovering in the background of *L'Étranger* (*The Outsider*), but essentially it is a book about a character, about human nature.'

Konstantin Milchin agreed with Fischer that there was a cultural/political gap between the Russian and British traditions. Maybe it was more of a chasm. 'I think in the world at large literature is certainly still political, but it is one-sided,' he said. 'An intellectual [in the west] is, with a few exceptions, Left-Liberal by definition. In Russia it is somewhat different – partly because writers have a different role here. The usual divisions of political power don't work, since historically we have had neither a functioning parliament nor a workable justice system, so it falls to the republic of authors to stand up for democratic principles, to express the discontent of the people. In countries such as England the people have other mechanisms for voicing their complaints, but here there has only been literature.'

Prokhorova tried to pin down the political function in literature by picking up on an example that Burgess had used in his address. 'When we speak of literature and politics we sometimes mix up two functions: the position of the writer as a human being on the one hand, and the literary text on the other – but they often lead separate ways. Tolkien, who was formed by the catastrophes of the twentieth century, chose a fantasy genre for his novels. In Tolkien's portrayal of the clash of good and evil, of the threat to Middle Earth, where does the politics begin and end? It can of course all be seen as an allegory of the terrible war that had just taken place in the real world – but how does the young generation read those texts? Does it perceive them as political, as Tolkien's contemporaries – the children of war – surely did? Is the political element still there in the text? Does it continue to define the text?' This set of questions was very close to the separate points that **Janne Teller** and **Ben Okri** had made in Edinburgh (see p.110): when it comes to worthwhile political literature, the narrative always trumps the politics.

But isn't it agreed that all writing is political? This assertion was made at least once everwhere that the theme was discussed. In Krasnoyarsk it was Burgess who articulated it. 'At the heart of it is the question: what is political involvement?' he said. 'One of the things that drove me mad at the Edinburgh Conference was the fact that everyone seemed to regard writing as some form of self-expression. It's an act of communication, an act in which we imaginatively explore the society around us in terms of relationships and character – and in terms of the individual, yes, but within society. We try to turn up insights, to recover understandings. And sometimes, imaginatively, you can arrive at understandings of people which are harder to reach through the study of real life. That's the fantastic thing that novels do: we hear the inner voice of people, their inner response to the world around them. Nightingales are of course exempt – but where there are power relationships between people, that is political.' Prokhorova added this rueful corollary: 'In the Soviet Union, politics was forcibly imposed on all writers, and choosing to write about nightingales was as much a political gesture as writing about the building of communism. So in a sense, not even nightingales are exempt.'

The great Russian Osip Mandelshtam had used the expression 'nightingale fever' to describe his own compulsion to write poetry. His friend Anna Akhmatova, meanwhile, said that poems visited her like bouts of sickness. Mandelshtam died of his febrile malady; Akhmatova survived to write *Requiem*, a wonderful poem – both lyric and epic – in which the wives and mothers of the Purge victims are likened to the grieving mother of Christ at the cross. In the foreword she describes how for seventeen months she stood in the prison queues of Leningrad, trying to get word to or from her jailed son. 'Somehow someone identified me. Then the blue-lipped woman behind me, who of course had never before heard my name, awoke from the glacial stupor that we all inhabited and spoke into my ear (we all whispered there). "Can you describe *this*?" I said: "I can." Then something like a smile flitted across what had once been her face.'

There you have it: the personal and the political, the insupportable burden of the outer world and the sorrowful depths of the interior, observed twitch of one woman's lips.

Jonathan Bastable (ed.)

The heart of a heartless world

by Amanda Lohrey
Keynote, Melbourne, August 2013

Can literature affect political change? The first half of the twentieth century was characterised by fierce debates about the relationship between politics and art, largely inspired by militant Left movements throughout Europe. One thinks of Bolshevik agitprop on the role of art to enlighten and inspire the masses by unmasking false consciousness and modelling possible utopias. My generation of Left artists was influenced by debates between European Marxists on the politics of representation and the most politically effective genres of realism. Among the most robust of these was the argument between German playwright and poet Bertolt Brecht and the distinguished Hungarian theorist George Lukacs. the strategic nature of all literary forms was encapsulated in a checklist of questions posed by Brecht: Who is this sentence of use to? Who does it claim to be of use to? What does it call for? What practical action corresponds to it? What sort of sentence results from it? What sort of sentences support it? In what situation is it spoken? By whom? *(Brecht on Theatre: The Development of an Aesthetic,* trans. John Willett, 1977)

In the post-1945 Cold War era debates on politics and aesthetics continued with decreasing potency of address and penetration, especially in the Anglo-American world where influential and often CIA-funded critics and academicians maintained the line that political fiction was mere propaganda. Literature transcended politics; it was about the fundamentals of love, death and the landscape. True poetry was a meditation on how light was reflected in a rockpool or the outline of a maidenhair fern at dusk. Political fiction or poetry was 'didactic' and it 'dated'. Meanwhile Left writers and critics continued to argue that writers should make it an integral part of their project to contest official histories, to interrogate the so-called master narratives of the culture and show how history and politics construct the personal. At the very least, such writing could give a voice to the voiceless so that the oppressed could recognise themselves in the work of art and gain strength from a mirroring effect that validated the experience of the marginalised. In addition, sales and critical acclaim could endow the writer with a prestige that he or she could wield on the campaign trail, as in the case of German novelist Günter Grass who campaigned actively over two decades for the Social Democratic Party of Germany.

Whichever side you are on, it is important to acknowledge that writing about politics is inherently problematical. Brecht's questions are a blunt address to the cognitive, but what of the unconscious? How sound are the rationalist assumptions that underlie the Left/liberal political project, namely that all people are inherently reasonable? Social utility is a Victorian notion that does not sit comfortably with post-Freudian perspectives on the riddle of human subjectivity. Art that aims to make a political intervention must grapple first with the unconscious, that substratum of desire, pleasure, fatalism and pain. This is a potential quicksand for the artist who is aiming to do more than write as a navigator of the psyche, who has specific goals of social utility in mind, namely converts. There is always a danger that an artist who paints a lurid picture of the apocalypse will seduce, not repel; consider audience response to the character of Colonel Kilgore in Francis Ford Coppola's *Apocalypse Now,* or Vito Corleone in *The Godfather.*

In his essay 'Right and Wrong Political Uses of Political Literature' (1997) Italo Calvino attacked the 'wrongheaded notion of the committed writer' and raised this question of the unconscious. 'We can never forget that what books communicate often remains unknown even to the author himself, that books often say something different from what they set out to say, that in any book there is a part that is the author's and the part that is a collective and anonymous work.' In other words, in any text the writer's unconscious engages with the reader's and the outcomes are highly unpredictable.

But there is a further factor at work here and it is a historical one. The second half of the twentieth century saw a decline in Left politics, the rise of affluence, consumerism and the mass media and the triumph of neoliberalism and globalised capitalism, promoted during the ideological counter-attack of the 1980s which saw the foundation of a number of business-financed Right-wing thinktanks in developed countries (see Alex Carey's *Taking the Risk Out of Democracy*, 1995). I think you can argue that these thinktanks have been far more influential than literary fiction in constructing public narratives of the political. They have, for example, successfully planted in the mainstream media a number of pundits and columnists whose vicious paranoid narratives continue to be retailed *ad nauseam*.

Some artists may strive to counter this, but who is listening? Artists are a product of their culture, as are their potential audiences. One of the insights of the Frankfurt School was to predict that when the utopian impulse in western culture was converted to consumerist mode and the project of a purely individual and psychological model of salvation, the artist who sought to make political interventions would become enfeebled. And so it has proved. Italian filmmaker Bernardo Bertolucci made two of the most remarkable political movies in the history of cinema, *The Conformist* (1970) and *1900* (1976) but when asked in 1988 why he had abandoned political cinema, Bertolucci replied: 'The cinema always depends on reality. I couldn't make *1900* today. Even though it was a historical story it corresponded to something in Italian society in the mid-70s .... It is very difficult today to talk about politics .... Or even to talk about what is Left and what is Right. Everything is mixed up in this soup called consumerism.'

Fredric Jameson has written of the power of systems to co-opt and defuse even the most potentially dangerous forms of political art by transforming them into cultural commodities, especially in the case of case of modernist art but also in the domain of fiction. In his scarifying critique of the postmodern novel, *The Postmodern Aura* (1985), Charles Newman writes of 'the redundancy of the adversary style' in an era in which avant-gardism becomes fashionable and a consumer passion for novelty creates 'an entire culture of short-term traders'. What is new and temporarily shocking soon passes into the banality of the over-exposed and in first world countries the 'problem' of art becomes not its repression but public indifference to it.

One could argue at this point for satire, for making your readership laugh and your opponent look ridiculous, but if we consider the fine tradition within North American literature of the anti-war novel (Joseph Heller's *Catch-22*, Kurt Vonnegut's *Slaughterhouse-Five*) the political outcomes are not encouraging. Widely acclaimed on publication, *Catch-22* sold millions of copies and is still taught in schools and universities. But has it inhibited any further US military adventurism? One of the criticisms of Heller's novel is that it deflates into a lame ending when its hero Yossarian deserts to Sweden. In his essay, 'The Deserters: The Contemporary Defeat of Fiction' Carl Oglesby, a radical student activist in the 60s and later a writer, castigates Heller for this tepid resolution. Why, asks Oglesby, doesn't Yossarian assassinate the villain of the novel, Colonel Cathcart? Instead of rebelling *within* history, Yossarian rebels *against* it in a narrative in which Sweden stands for the 'beyond' of history. The possibility of rebellion is foreclosed. What I find interesting here is that in the best novel about the Vietnam War, Tim O'Brien's *Going After Cacciato* (1978) the regular soldiers have indeed made this progression and do assassinate their officers; it's called fragging. But for them there is no escape either. Or rather, they escape into fantasy and the novel has no exit other than into a form of magical escapism and the pathos of men who can envisage no authentic political agency. Theirs is an even more extreme form of desertion than Yossarian's. And thus we progress from Vietnam to Iraq and a culture in which the writer, in Oglesby's words, is a figure of 'privileged impotence'. Unless, of course, like Arundhati Roy, she chooses to abandon fiction for polemical non-fiction and a role as a frontline political activist.

The end of the Cold War and the advent of the post-colonial moment to some degree reconfigured the critical and artistic terrain that prevailed up until the 1980s. Writers in Britain's ex-colonies produced a wave of novels about imperialism and its effects and these invariably won the Commonwealth Writers Prize which became a mirror of the post-colonial moment. In Latin America the Leftist writer Gabriel García Márquez made of magical realism a romantic form of political opposition, but one that for readers in the west was read mostly for its romance rather than its oppositional politics which, in any case, tended to be occluded by the 'magic'. The early works of Salman Rushdie promised a new form of storytelling based on a richly inventive bricolage of cultural reference and hybrid modes of rhetoric but in James Wood's recent and famously adversarial view, the genre eventually declined into a decadence which he provocatively labelled 'hysterical realism' (2000). Such novels, wrote Wood, 'accumulate meaning only to disperse it'. With their 'cartoonish' plotting and bizarre characters they create a manic surface, the effect of which is to deny the possibility of character development and hence of reader empathy ('no-one really exists'). Wood writes of a 'weightless excess' that is not genuinely experimental: 'the practical effect is a grammar of realism that challenges nobody and nothing'. Newman too has a great deal to say on this subject, citing its 'easily purchased surrealism, wilful randomness and cheap narrative collage', its 'logorrhoea', its decline into a 'routinised disturbance available to any middle-class terrorist'. The initial freshness of perception that Márquez and the early Rushdie introduced has proved to be short-lived.

Wood doesn't offer a political explanation of this but Jameson might characterise it as a form of postmodern panic or hysteria in the face of globalising capitalism's colonisation of every sphere and dimension of experience, its totalising character which can only be escaped through wilful indeterminacy and chaos, including in fiction. This, however, creates a form of weak narrative which offers weak resistance to strong or fundamentalist narratives. To this I would add the decline of the writer as sage or oracle, along with the decline of the potency of the serious literary novel in the hectic, multi-vocal world of television and the internet with their 'flood of secondary realities'. The novel is now a very small player in what Hans Magnus Enzensberger called the 'consciousness industry'.

What is left? Two things, I would suggest. Firstly, the revelatory power of the documentary and, secondly, the mythic power of the story. The novel as honest chronicle is still a means to documenting and celebrating, in Newman's words, 'the particularity of partial knowledge'. It can still bring news, it can still bring to our attention those areas of human experience that are passed over or denied in the mass media. But to have political influence it must be first be read, and read sympathetically, by a large audience – and that is another matter.

On the mythic plane, I would argue that the novel takes its place as one agent, along with cinema and television, within the Levi-Strauss model of the function of myth, namely to mediate between and resolve within narrative those contradictions that are not susceptible to resolution in everyday life. In other words, mythic storytelling offers substitute gratification within, and compensation for, a fraught reality. As such the primary function of narrative is the opposite of reformist; it is to console and pacify, to dissipate rage rather than to incite it, and to relieve the pain of the incomprehensible. To borrow from that prodigious reader Karl Marx, storytelling is the heart of a heartless world. Is it then the opiate of the masses? Probably.

The impotent text

'My argument in brief is that the novel has little power to make an effective political intervention,' said **Amanda Lohrey** in a summary of her keynote in Melbourne. 'The novel comes after the event; it is a chronicle of, or an argument with, the event – but does not shape it. Only in repressive societies can the novel achieve a form of symbolic power as a gesture of resistance which may help to fortify the morale of activists on the ground but it cannot do more than this to overthrow regimes. To quote Marcuse, art by itself can never achieve transformation but it can under certain circumstances "free the perception and sensibility needed for the transformation".'

It was a shame that Lohrey could not be present at the discussion that followed her paper, as it meant that she could not defend herself when all the other panellists took issue with her. Leading the charge was **Junot Díaz**, who said that her thesis was mostly '*ipso dixit* – because I say so'. It struck him as 'a series of unsustainable, weird generalisations about what constitutes literature and what constitutes politics, and an enormous confidence that everyone reads books and interprets them in exactly the same way. It was profoundly deterministic, and that's not the truth of it. We all know that everyone reads books differently, and one of the things that makes literature fascinating is that it is able to countenance multiple simultaneous arguments. We have no idea how art interfaces with people, and how that fuels larger political change; this is a great mystery that Lohrey seemed unwilling to recognise. We cannot be sure that literature does not play an enormous role in political change, because we have no control sample. We'd have to find a society where all art is removed, and then see what happens politically. We console ourselves by imagining that we know what the hell this is, that we have full access and omnipotent knowledge of the way this all works. We have rarely assessed how individual transformations make possible the larger political change that we so overvalue.'

Díaz went on to cite an example of his literary-political interface in action. 'What about the effect that *Uncle Tom's Cabin* had on the anti-slavery movement? A lot of the great political change is not top-down. Slavery gets undone because of a set of granular, molecular changes in people's psychic relationship to the concept. So 99 % of the actors in such a movement wouldn't even be considered actors in Lohrey's economy. Many great changes come about through quotidian, invisible resistance which is hard for our blunt instruments to measure. Art eludes all of our metrics. So the question is: how does literature provide the spaces for individuals to reconstitute themselves? I could set up dozens of economies where art seems to have no role, and Lohrey's argument seemed to fail to account for what art most often exhibits, which is a trickster-like quality.'

Amanda Lohrey might have questioned whether it is perceptive or fruitful to talk about art and literature in the language of the science textbook and the IT manual (Díaz is professor of creative writing at the Massachussetts Institute of Technology). She might also have wondered if it is disingenuous to complain that her thesis had not been subject to rigorous lab-testing. Literary criticism can only be a matter of spotting patterns and drawing conclusions from one's reading of the events and the texts. These things are not subject to experimentation and measuring – Díaz's metrics. Any statement about the past, however well researched and supported, is necessarily a personal opinion. If one had to be able to quantify a writer's intention and a reader's response in the same way that you measure a lab rat's reaction to a physical stimulus, then there would be no biography, no history books, no writing about writing. Even Díaz's own contention that *Uncle Tom's Cabin* gave a boost to the anti-slavery movement would become an unprovable *ipso dixit*. As an audience member said later in the debate: 'A big problem with political writing is that the audience self-selects. By definition, most people aren't going to agree with the premise of a writer who is trying to change their opinion, and so are unlikely to buy or consume that writing.' In other words: who is to say what proportion of the readers of *Uncle Tom's Cabin* were already opposed to slavery before they read it: 20%? 98%? What proportion of pro-slavery readers switched to an anti-slavery stance as a result of reading the book? We cannot know, but in Díaz's economy, these are the statistics that matter.

Alison Croggan's objection to Lohrey's argument was on the grounds that it demanded too much of the written word: 'It's asking that literature cause the revolution and overthrow capitalism all by itself.' Jeremy Harding thought the address was overly partisan: 'These are the terms of the Bolshevik party. This is a narrowly Left-wing view of the role of art in society. I think Amanda is saying something about the way that quite traditional Left-wing movements conceived of art. It was utopian, and in Amanda's work there is a sense of work abandoned. It was utopian for the Bolsheviks too: Mayakovsky thought that his work could actually get up and go to the factory and be a model worker.' Well, Mayakovsky might have expressed in an imaginative way his belief that the work of a poet was important to the grand new project of building communism, as important in its way as the sweaty labour of a stoker or a foundryman. But it was only a joyous little metaphor, and his situation was in any case unusual in that he was a first-class writer who enthusiastically supported the government of the day, a new-minted kind of authority that seemed itself to be a creative force in the world. Mayakovsky was 'the drummer-boy of the Revolution', and that status gave him an illusion of power and effectiveness that writers rarely experience. When he became disillusioned with the Soviet regime and his role in it, he went to his study and shot himself through the heart ....

A better and rather intriguing illustration of the political clout of fiction was provided by the Australian writer Lili Wilkinson. 'I don't have an imperial metric, but I have an example,' she said. 'It comes from Harry Potter. There is an online community called the Harry Potter Alliance, consisting of tens of thousands of people, mostly students and teenagers. They like to identify what the real world dark arts are – genocide and homophobia and bullying, and so on – and they ask the question: what would Dumbledore do? Then they do it. So, a couple of years ago they sent seven aeroplanes' worth of supplies to earthquake victims in Haiti; they have enrolled ten thousand young Americans to vote; and they are running a campaign to get the Harry-Potter-branded chocolate frogs to be made of free-trade chocolate. So teenagers, who are a largely disenfranchised group within democracies because they don't vote or are not yet allowed to vote, are finding alternate pathways towards political engagement through literature that is not explicitly political.'

'This is the power of reading,' commented Junot Díaz. 'I want to change who we give authority to. It's less the writer, and more people's incredibly creative relationship to the work that allows them to look at Harry Potter and say: this is going to be a lens through which I understand our political and social moment. George Bush is Voldemort – yes, there you go.' He later added that the power of reading exerts itself not only on the person holding the book in their hands. 'They circulate in our communities,' he said. 'Say you and I don't read books that speak in favour of the Far Right, that doesn't mean that those books have no purchase on us, because we have people in our lives that those books mean a lot to. Books don't necessarily live only inside the person who reads them. And that is part of the great value of art: it has an invisible influence, what physicists would call "spooky effects".'

It may not have been a spooky effect – but strangely, all the support for Lohrey's rather downbeat view of the power of literature was voiced in debates that took place beforehand or elsewhere. In Edinburgh, on the opening day of the global conversation, **Ewan Morrison** had by some weird synchronicity cited Herbert Marcuse, as Lohrey would a year later on the opposite side of the world. 'Marcuse coined the term "repressive tolerance",' he said, 'meaning that society encourages us to verbalise how we feel. We get to shout about the government – what they do and who they bomb – and then nothing happens. We express it, but there are no repercussions. So I think we have to look at the failures. In the 1960s there was a very language-based mode of critiquing the world. For example, we thought that William Burrough's cut-up technique was exposing and undermining the bourgeois constructs of society. We thought within separatist essentialist feminism that writing the female body was destroying patriarchal language. Within Scottish nationalism we believed that speaking our own vernacular was subverting the British global dominance. Those projects failed. And in the past two years there has been a super-abundance of books about Wall Street traders. Has this in any way affected what has gone on in global politics? No. It's been an act of repressive tolerance. It's been the failure of the novel to do anything political. The novel is overstretched in trying to deal with it.'

Dimitris Stefanakis, speaking from the floor in St Malo, was unequivocal. 'There was once a naïve theory that it is possible to change the world through literature,' he said. 'I think we now know that this is a lie. You cannot change or improve the world through literature. I think that for the moment, all we can do is to continue to write and to express what is personal. We can say that all novels have a political aspect, but the literary intent must come first.' **Andrey Astvatsaturov**, speaking in Krasnoyarsk, was a good deal more pessimistic. 'There is no politics at the moment,' he said. 'Political literature is impossible in current conditions. There is only a corporate system, which operates by its own rules. It needs no personalties, only wardens, who have no will: managers, conformists. Literature is a membrane that resonates with public opinion and culture. In the contemporary world political literature is simply inappropriate. Ideologies (liberalism, socialism, communism, Stalinism) are games of language that can't be made to create an illusion of reality. There is no subject either. Character is an object, a mere construct of influences. Politics is a performance, a backroom deal of the corporations. The game, the pose, and the aesthetic gesture are all that's possible. The challenge of our age is to stay lonely.'

    John Burnside in Edinburgh sounded a pragmatic and more buoyant note when he questioned the word 'political', saying: 'I believe with Emerson that every state is corrupt. Therefore our duty is to resist always by trying to sneak something which is *dissident* past the market.' Junot Díaz, at the end of the fractious discussion in Melbourne, found some optimism in the long view: 'Literary culture has never been static,' he said. 'Genres rise and genres fall. Today the novel is predominant but perhaps tomorrow it will be spoken word, or poetry. Who is to say and – more vexing – who can ever know? For me what matters is that we defend literary culture as vigorously as we can. Literary culture has been a consistent defence against tyranny, against solitude, against despair, against the wanton cruelty, stupidity and senselessness of our species. The form matters to me less than the desire to see literary culture, which I love so deeply, survive and perhaps one day become more than just a minority interest.'

Jonathan Bastable (ed.)

Words as a pledge

by Atiq Rahimi
Keynote, St Malo, May 2013

'A writer isn't a writer,' said the French thinker Gilles Deleuze. 'He is a politician, a machine, an experiment.'

Should literature be political? Let's ask ourselves the question once again, as if it were the first time. Let's forget for a moment that before us, and since the eighteenth century, writers have asked themselves the same question time and time again, at the risk of losing themselves in it or of happily finding an answer. Let's ask ourselves then, because as Maurice Blanchot would put it: 'Questions are the desire of thoughts.' And he adds: 'But answers are their sorrow!'

So as to avoid making this question, which has marked the history of literature, a sorrowful one, I would like to start my speech with a tale. This is part of my original culture: I tell stories to avoid giving an answer (Maurice Blanchot wouldn't be full of sorrow if he were Afghani!). In a major book of Persian literature called *Memorial of the Saints*, written in the thirteenth century, the great poet Farid Uddin Attar explains that one day, a young disciple asked his master what the power of wise men was. 'Speech', the master answered, 'speech!' Then the master showed his disciple the mountain at the foot of which he lived as a hermit, and said: 'When a wise man orders this mountain to move, it moves.' And at that precise moment, the mountain started shaking. The master scolded it: 'I've not asked you to move! I just wanted to show him an example!'

On the surface, of course this tale shows what has been mankind's dream since time immemorial: to create, to change, to move, to destroy, to rebuild the world with words. Just with words! Who hasn't dreamed of being able to say one day: 'Let there be light!' and to see light appear? 'Any man is God when he dreams' said Hölderlin. Yet beyond this mystical and fanciful quest, there is something in that tale which makes me wonder about the link between the power and speech of wise men, intellectuals and writers.

First, about asking a mountain to move and getting it to move: I interpret this allegorically (and perhaps naïvely) as a pragmatic aspect of language, its transitive function. And I don't just mean in our daily conversations, but also in a literary text. Then, about the fact that the wise man just gives an 'example', and that the example becomes a commandment: that opens a debate on the notion of *exemplarity* and *metalanguage* in literature.

Everyone undoubtedly remembers the following title, which is magical in French, *Quand dire c'est faire* [*When To Say Is To Do*], and which in English is ironic, *How to Do Things with Words*, by John Langshaw Austin. When speaking of *performative utterance*, this English philosopher means a series of sentences which aren't simply a string of words that explain a state or a situation .... They become the very act they describe. Once uttered, they can change a life or a community's life dramatically. For instance, 'I now pronounce you man and wife' used by a mayor. Or 'War is declared' used by a statesman who, just by uttering these words, throws his people into the great madness and terror it involves .... A few centuries ago, in Amsterdam's synagogue, a sermon banished Spinoza from the Jewish community and condemned him to silence. And more recently, a fatwa forced Salman Rushdie into concealment ....

Believers say that the universe is created by the very words of God. And even if we don't believe it, we still witness the way the words attributed to God lead men to action, whether on the path of wisdom or the madness of suicide attacks .... But you might ask: is this the doing of the power of words ... or of the words of power? JL Austin said it well: for a performative utterance to be 'fortunate' as he put it himself, in other words feasible, you need the right set of circumstances. You can't just have anyone pronounce any couple man and wife! First and foremost, the person who unites the two beings must have some legitimacy and some power. Then, the couple must fulfill certain conditions and so on.

And to get a mountain to move, you have to gain some wisdom first. In order to cry out 'I accuse', you have to be Zola first. And to be Zola, you have to have written *Nana, Germinal, The Beast Within* .... 'It is splendid to be a great writer,' said Flaubert, 'To put men into the frying pan of your words and make them pop like chestnuts. There must be a delirious pride in the feeling that you are bringing the full weight of your ideas to bear on mankind. But for that you must have something to say.' When the writer has something to say, does it follow that he changes anything in the world? Sartre would reply yes, because for him, *saying things means wanting to change them; talking or writing means acting on the world.*

Bright minds will probably ask: if writers wield such power with their speech, why is the world torn in a thousand pieces? Why is there so much tyranny? So much war? So much injustice? Where do we find ourselves after *Germinal*, after *War and Peace*, after *A Farewell to Arms*, after *The Plague* …? What is literature up to? Alas, another question that sentences literature to uncertainty. 'Clearly, if Marx had followed his dreams of youth and written the most beautiful novel in the world, he would have held the world spellbound, but he wouldn't have moved it. You therefore have to write *Capital* and not *War and Peace*. You don't describe Caesar's murder, you have to be Brutus …. Making such links, such comparisons, might seem absurd to onlookers. But when art is weighed against action, immediate and pressing, action can only consider art as wrong, and art can only concur.' Maurice Blanchot said these words. And he is not wrong.

Even Sartre, a keen supporter of politically engaged literature, said in a fit of despair: 'When a child is dying, *Nausea* seems very lightweight!' Or Hölderlin: 'What are poets good for in times of trouble?' But before sinking into unfathomable despair, let's reassure poets: You are here precisely to tell us what poets are good for in times of trouble. Because by telling us that, poets name, define and recall the nature of our lives in these 'times of trouble'. These lines are from Shams, master of Rumi, a mystic Persian of the thirteenth century:

> We are not able to talk,
> If only we could listen!
> We must say all!
> And listen to all!
> But,
> Our ears are sealed
> Our lips are sealed
> Our hearts are sealed.

This cry has echoed for centuries to denounce the permanent and implacable censorship that is breathed into the heart of writers, in Iran just as well as in Afghanistan (my country of origin), where in actual fact words defy tyranny. In those countries, the existential problem isn't 'to be or not to be …' but to say or not to say, that is the question. Thus, any act becomes political. Even silence. Even lies. I remember that when the Soviets were in Afghanistan, a brilliant saying from Poland was used by intellectuals, and it went: 'If you want to survive, don't think. If you think, don't talk. If you talk, don't write. If you write, don't sign it. If you sign it, don't be surprised!'

Unfortunately, this still goes for my native country, even if the new post-Taliban constitution allows freedom of the press. But the problem lies elsewhere; it lies in each of us, because *our hearts are sealed*. In the south of Afghanistan, Pashtun women have a poetic tradition called *landay*. These are short anonymous poems, which reveal a lot, like for instance:

Lay your lips on mine,
But leave my tongue free, that I may tell you I love you

Imagine what would happen to that woman if she signed this!

This is how, by describing the conditions of mankind or by revealing humanity's desires and dreams, a literary text can above all become a cry, an *act of proclamation*. It 'gives a syntax to the cry', as Deleuze would put it. It is a performative utterance. And even if that cry doesn't waken slumbering spirits, at least it might trouble their sleep! Such an act isn't a provocation, but a pro-vocation! In that sense, politics isn't the will, the fear or the duty of the writer. It is in the ink of its writing. Writers aren't 'engaged' in history, they are 'embarked' on it – as Camus said, using Pascal's wording.

Now, let's talk about the other aspect of the literary experience, its *exemplarity*. 'Man's world is the planet of inexperience,' said Kundera. 'Inexperience is a quality of the human condition. We are born one time only; we never start a new life equipped with the experience we've gained from a previous one.' It is because this world is a *planet of inexperience* that literature has a meaning. Given that we don't live a permanent experience, literature helps us conceive the life of others (of those who lived before our time, or those who live at the same time as we do but elsewhere), as a pointer, perhaps even a *mimetic desire*, as René Girard put it. We live and so we think with and through other people's experiences, just as others live with and through our writing as an existential, sentimental, political, metaphysical experience ... Salman Rushdie said: 'It is literature which for me opened the mysterious and decisive doors of imagination and understanding. To see the way others see. To think the way others think. And above all, to feel.' Diderot said: 'reading novels makes us better people, not only because fictions illustrate abstract principles, or because characters show us what behaviours to adopt or avoid, but also because it turns the empathy felt by the reader into an experience of the other, therefore an altruistic experience.'

In that sense, an experience isn't just 'personal experience', it isn't just past; it isn't a 'study', a scientific experiment carried out to check or justify knowledge data, which would make it a future-oriented act. It is the proof of our existence here and now. It is the act of meditating on what we live. It is living the world as the world lives us. It is an 'inner experience' for Georges Bataille and an 'original experience' for Maurice Blanchot: it is 'being in touch with the ontological being, renewing the self through that contact – a challenge, which remains undetermined'. Writing is an experience with *language, i.e. with oneself* (Carlos Luscano). It is an experience which helps me see the world within myself, so I can deconstruct it in order to understand it, and then rebuild it as I wish. By changing the world bit by bit, one day, we will change the world.

So, should we still doubt the political dimension of literature? First, I'd say YES! We must doubt it because as Paul Valéry says: 'Politics means wanting to conquer and to retain power; it therefore involves an action of constraint or of illusion over minds which are the essence of all power.' The political mind always ends up forced into forgery. It introduces a forged intellectual currency onto the market; it introduces forged historical notions; it builds specious reasoning arguments; in a word, it does anything it can to keep its authority, its so-called moral authority.'

And then, I'd say NO, because literature is a fight against all political systems. It is the power of words against the words of power. Thus, the definition of politics in writing.

On ambiguity

by Benjamin Markovits

At the beginning of the discussion that took place in Kuala Lumpur, **Benjamin Markovits** made a lengthy opening statement about the mechanisms of politics within the novel. Here it is in full:

'I thought I'd start by trying to change the question,' said Markovits. 'If the question is "Should literature be political?", then there is a useful one word answer: no. I have the freedom of the writer at heart, and so want to leave space for the writers who want to write non-political literature. If we change the question to "Is all literature political in some way or another?", then I'd be happy to say yes. I think both fiction and politics are an attempt to sell a worldview. But I think there is a difference between the kind of view of the world that a politician wants to sell, and the one a novelist wants to sell you.

'Let me ask a couple of different questions. If literature is political, is it good for the politics? And if literature is political, is it good for the literature? To answer that I have a story to tell – but first let me say this: –

'I teach creative writing, and on one of the courses we look at five novels. We read *The Aspern Papers* by Henry James; *The Bell Jar* by Sylvia Plath; *Pnin* by Vladimir Nabokov; *Things Fall Apart* by Chinua Achebe; and *Wonder Boys* by Michael Chabon. It occurs to me that though these books are superficially very different from each other they have certain things in common. Firstly, they have some kind of structural asymmetry. If a book has too much structure it feels like a *made thing,* we become suspicious of it, it becomes something plotted. If a book has no structure it feels like chaos. So the books that we think of as the highest literature have something structured about them and something asymmetric. Secondly, all these books have an ironic relationship between form and content – most obviously when there is a narrator whose views the reader is not supposed to trust. This is deeper, because we want not to know exactly what literature means. If we know too much what an author is trying to tell us then, in Keats' phrase, "We hate literature ['poetry', in the original quotation] that has a palpable design upon us – and if we do not agree, seems to put its hands in its breeches pocket." If it's trying to sell us something too obviously then we don't want to buy. Thirdly, all these books have a commitment to moral ambiguity. Things are mixed up in them. There is the wonderful line of Robert Browning's that Graham Greene quotes, and that I give too often to my students: "My interest is on the dangerous edge of things: the honest thief, the tender murderer, the superstitious atheist."

'You can see why, from a fiction writer's point of view, these are interesting people. And you realise that literature has a bias towards certain kinds of problems and solutions. We want things to be complicated and unclear. From a political point of view, that is not always useful, because politicians want to make things clear and to solve problems. Robert Frost once said to CP Snow: "If I thought that by my writing about the poor they would become less poor, then I wouldn't do it." He's being a bit of a jerk there, and we don't have to take him that seriously, but clearly his interest in the poor is a detached one.

'So here's the story that answers my earlier questions. I used to teach English at a very privileged school in New England, and after I left I wrote a novel that was set on the campus. In this novel I imagine a washed-up, childless high-school teacher who becomes obsessed with one of his young students. His own marriage has become sexless, and there's a very bright girl in his class, and he starts thinking about her in ways that make him both unhappy and happy. She renews his sense of ambition for life. And as the story progresses we also see what's happening from her point of view, but it's a more or less sympathetic portrayal of this teacher who wants to sleep with one of his students. Ten years later a story broke about an endemic culture of sexual abuse at this school, in which a number of teachers (before my time) were grooming students and crossing the boundary of appropriate behaviour. I then got a lot of emails from friends asking: did you see what was going on? Is that why you wrote this character? The answer was no, and actually that if you look at any school too closely you will find some uncomfortable facts about the relationships between teachers and students.

'But the story also made me think that I was committed to the idea that my portrayal of the man should be sympathetic. It might be that I was missing the point, that from a political point of view I should have seen that what he was doing was simply wrong, that my job should have been to condemn him. But I don't think that would have produced literature. I don't tell that story to suggest that literature should be above such considerations. We should be suspicious of literature, of its wanting to make everything ambiguous and more complicated than you think. On the other hand, that's the writing game – and if you don't play it you will end up with work that is less interesting.'

The big 'P' and the little 'p'

by Olive Senior
Keynote, Trinidad, April 2013

First, I have to take issue with the question 'Should literature be political?', which has the fussiness of Granny about it. It suggests an anxiety about written literature, the notion that literary production is something precious and should be protected somehow from the unwashed hordes who are political animals because they foment revolutions and overturn thrones. Mark you, the unwashed hordes have created literature too, though it's been called folklore and folksongs. And now, woe, technology has opened the door to everyone calling him- or herself a 'writer'.

Let us start by defining what is meant by our use of 'literature' here and – even more important – what we mean by 'politics'. I will use 'literature' here NOT in its broadest sense of embracing all literary production. I am using it in reference to works of the creative imagination – fiction, poetry, drama, in whatever form these are expressed since technology now opens up so many worlds beyond the artefact we normally call a book. So our concern here is with *content*.

We should treat works of the creative imagination as different from other forms of literary production. This distinction enables us to see and acknowledge that the writer who wants to make a statement has a wide choice of genres and that each genre has its place. Many writers, like myself, have engaged in a variety of these genres. But we must be clear in our own minds as to what we are doing. Non-creative literature operates according to a conscious mandate. Creative literature does not. Fabrication by a journalist is regarded as betrayal. Fabrication is what a fiction writer does.

Politics. Anxiety arises from our narrow use of the term. We tend to think of politics exclusively in terms of partisan politics, electoral politics, political leadership and so on, with strife and confrontation implied, so a lot of people will try to disengage by saying: 'I am not concerned with politics'. The bottom line is that the word 'politics' conjures up partisanship, divisiveness and a low threshold of scoring dirty points against an opponent.

But politics in its very first definition relates to the art of government. We might refer to that as 'Big P', because I want to make the case that Big P, the larger politics of the nation, inescapably shapes us in a trickle-down effect from the cradle to the grave. Politics determines the price of bread or the availability of guns or whether one lives in splendour or the squalor of a refugee camp. Closer to home, it might be a Caribbean mother having to choose between bread today and school fees tomorrow. Big P shapes the world into which we are born, our daily environment, and leads to what we might call 'small p' politics; that is, all those decisions of personal governance that we are forced to make, both externally and unconsciously, every moment of our lives.

We are all enmeshed in politics because we are all citizens of somewhere – even writers – and we cannot escape being shaped by political decisions, big and small. So instead of asking the question 'Should literature be political', I would rephrase it as a statement: *Literature is political* because we the creators of literature are political animals; it is part of accepting our responsibility of being human, of being citizens of the world.

Does this mean that I am advocating that literature as I have narrowly defined it should be in the service of Politics? Absolutely not. This is where creative writers must part company with those writers who operate out of a mandate that is overt and prescriptive. Consumers of each genre usually know what to expect. And 'creative literature' works best if we do NOT know what to expect. Literature in this narrow sense is, above all, a product of *imagination*. The gift of the creative industries is to present the unexpected, to show the world in a different light.

Every author has a worldview that reflects a political stance and shapes what we do, even unconsciously. For example, as a child, I grew up in a world where I never saw myself or the people around me visually portrayed in the children's books I read (though I took great pleasure in reading them). As a writer of children's books now, I would say that I am simply concerned with telling a story that a child anywhere in the world that might want to read. But, I have to confess, I am very much concerned that the illustrations should reflect and express a multicultural world, for that is what I live in. Is that political? Can any of us escape the political? I would say no. Even romantic literature plunges us into the realm of political economy: does the potential suitor have a job?

The raw material of writers is the entire world that we live in; a world that continuously shapes us as we in turn shape it, through our poetry or fiction. The writer is someone who has no choice but to be engaged with society, which means political engagement. Nothing escapes the snare of the political, big P or small p – it is about the price of bread, the paycheck you bring home, how you interact with neighbours or whom you choose to romance. You can rebel against the latter or hew your own path, but your choice will be shaped by political concerns, and those have always included religion, race or ethnicity, sex and gender. Today, perhaps, more than ever.

So what makes literature different then from the other arts of writing – journalism, history, political science, advertising or party propaganda? To me, that is the crux of the matter. The difference lies not in *what* we write but in the *how*. It is the difference between a journalist writing a story about, say, the shortage of public housing and the novelist inventing a character and a credible situation to demonstrate the impact of that situation perhaps down several generations, or how it leads ultimately to a revolution, or a suicide. It is taking the facts of the matter and then stitching them into a plot or a poem that illuminates it beyond the everyday experience.

The good thing is that in doing so, the creative writer has enormous resources that the fact-based writer has not. Literature is an art. It is about transformation. It is about taking one thing and making something else of it, changed but recognisable. So, politics might be the subject matter, but only as raw material. Literature does not need to employ polemics or confrontation. Nor is it about telling readers what they already know, but enabling them to contemplate what they didn't know they knew. It is not a question of avoiding issues but of being crafty in portraying them.

Literature is, above all, storytelling. And, as Chinua Achebe has said, storytelling is a threat. Storytellers, poets, writers, have always found ways of confronting tyranny, especially in spaces where such actions are dangerous and deadly. Throughout the ages, writers have developed and employed myriad literary devices and explored the fullest limits of language through satire, magical realism, fantasy, fable and so on. Writers over the ages have found ways of talking about issues – like politics – without seeming to talk about them. The function is not to present the world as it is, but to present it in a new light through the narrative power of art. Literature does not ask: 'What is it about?' It asks: 'How do we tell it to make it real?'

So, since I have to answer the question: 'Should literature be political?' I will say, yes, but not in an explicit way. The purpose of literature is not to represent but to re-present, to hold up that mirror in a light that enables us to see reality both reflected and refracted. And that applies to politics or any subject that we choose, or in the best case scenario, in the subject that chooses us. As writers we live lives that are not navel-gazing but conscious, fully engaged with the world.

My favourite quotation is Gauguin's statement: 'Art is either plagiarism or revolution.' So let me end by taking issue with the title of this debate, especially with the prescriptive *should*. Should the subject matter of literature be prescribed by anyone? I say no. So let's end by revolting against those who would apply the word 'should' to art. Even in a question. To young writers I say: Ignore prescriptions. Don't be left behind. Write on!

When is a book political?

Wherever discussion took place on the question 'Should literature be political?', there were multifarious attempts to set boundaries and clarify terms. The process began as a kind of notional land clearance, intended to open a intellectual space in which the conversation could take place, but ended up being more like sandbagging in a rising flood – a desperate communal attempt to keep the the discussion from being overwhelmed by definitions and phraseology.

This was everywhere a two-phase operation. The first task consisted in finding an answer to the question: what do we mean by politics? The second task was to decide which books can rightly be considered political. Interestingly, writers from countries with a history of political oppression tended to define politics and political literature more narrowly. 'This topic was probably much more relevant to the Conference of 1962 than it is today,' said **Andrey Astvatsaturov** in Krasnoyarsk. 'because the 1960s were a revolutionary and turbulent time age, a time of writers' political engagement.' He also cited the 1930s as a traumatically political era – when, in his opinion 'writers and intellectuals were confronted with a painful choice, but one they couldn't avoid making. Two opposing forces were active: Nazism and Communism, Hitler and Stalin. The destiny of the world was being shaped, and in that situation you had to decide on your political view, and you had to engage. Even if you were not happy with either political force, you had to decide which camp to join. With little enthusiasm, conservatives concluded that the Führer was the lesser moral evil; while liberals and the Left-wing supported the USSR and Stalin.'

Astvatsaturov concluded that 'there is no politics at the moment; only a corporate system.' But **Melvin Burgess**, taking part in the same debate, took the opposite view. 'Perhaps it is true that the huge upheavals that occurred between Left and Right, between totalitarianism and democracy, have left us feeling as if politics no longer exists. But it does exist, only in different forms. Because politics isn't just about ideology, it's also about roles and power within society. So your relationship with your employer is political, as is your relationship with your boyfriend or girlfriend or your children.'

Most of the writers at the Conference tended towards Burgess's broader formulation. The Portuguese delegate **José Rodrigues dos Santos**, speaking in Lisbon, said that 'politics is not necessarily something that involves political parties, but rather an activity related to the management of societies. Decisions and actions that affect us all are politics, but also ideas and concepts. Actually, it's the latter that provide the blueprint for the former.' Turning his attention to the second question, he asked 'Can Agatha Christie's *The Murder of Roger Ackroyd*, a simple crime investigation, somehow be a political novel? The book does present us with a message: thou shall not kill. It is a sheer political message, created for social management.' Warming to his theme, Dos Santos suggested that the market is full of books that are political thought they are not at all serious. 'Is Dan Brown's *The Da Vinci Code* a political book? How can we say it isn't, if it deals in a critical way with issues such as who Jesus Christ really was, how his legend was shaped for political purposes, the role of women in the religious system of power ...'.

Ahdaf Soueif made a similar but more subtle point in the discussion that followed her keynote address in Edinburgh. The political message of a novel may be only implied, it may be hidden in the architecture, so to speak; or it may lie in unquestioned assumptions that only come to light when the architecture of the story is deconstructed: 'Some people would limit the definition of a political novel to things like *The West Wing*. I would say that Eliot's *Middlemarch* is a political novel in that it deals with the limitations placed on women at the time and the tragic outcome of that for the main character. It deals with the gradual shift of power from the landowners towards the lawyers and financiers. Ultimately you could even say that escapist fiction such as Mills and Boon is political in the resolute absence of world politics, but also in the relationships: the man is always richer and taller and older than the woman, for example.'

The black British writer **Courttia Newland**, speaking in Trinidad, made an analogous observation when he said that he was aware as a child that 'even Peter and Jane are political' – because those early-reading books failed to portray people who looked like him. In his own books, he added: 'I was at first trying to correct the stereotypes that are put into the cultural arena about people like myself. The publishing industry has an idea of black British people that is just about criminality. I wrote about those people and tried to humanise them, but in later books I moved away from that, to say that there are other kinds of people within that world: detectives, lovers, dreamers ...'.

Most of the writers at the Conference would have agreed that Newland's was a political project. In 'phase two' of the conversation, speakers offered many examples of novels that were (successfully or not) political works. **Shamani Flint**, speaking in Kuala Lumpur, said that 'the first book that I realised was political, as I grew up, was *To Kill A Mockingbird*. I think that was when I saw that writing can change people's opinions, that it can provide information that allows you to rethink a point of view. **Benjamin Markovits** named Chinua Achebe's *Things Fall Apart* (see p.144). In the same discussion the Vietnamese writer **Di Li** cited *Animal Farm* – saying that, while it might seem almost a cliché to cite it, that book had only recently been published in her country. George Orwell cropped up often – and not always in entirely approving terms. 'His work was almost destroyed by the attempt to convey a political message,' said the Greek writer **Dimitris Stefanakis** in St Malo – thinking, perhaps, of the unsatifactory AFTERWORD on Newspeak in *Nineteen Eighty Four*. 'In literature political thought should be elusive. Shakespeare's plays are just as political as Orwell's novels, for instance. *Anna Karenina* is a political text that denounces injustice in the family and the social position of women – but Tolstoy, unlike Orwell, has literary concerns to the fore.'

Orwell also figured in the political hall of fame compiled by Dos Santos: 'We can name many fine novels that do have a clear political message,' he said. 'Flaubert's *Madame Bovary* questions the social anathema of nineteenth-century female adultery; George Orwell's *Nineteen Eighty Four* or *Animal Farm* are powerful critical metaphors for communist totalitarian dictatorships; Eça de Queirós' *O Crime do Padre Amaro* gives us a strong critique of the Catholic Church's hypocrisy towards priests' celibacy; and John Steinbeck's *The Grapes of Wrath* shows us the misery spread by unregulated capitalism in the wake of the Great Depression.'

In Edinburgh, **Alan Bissett** had a heroes' gallery of his own, which overlapped with Dos Santos'. 'Literature is always political; it is simply a question of where politics comes in the mix,' said Bissett. I think there is a place for novels where politics comes very high in the list, where ambiguity and irony and even psychological depth are secondary to the politics. That would be *Animal Farm*, *The Ragged-Trousered Philanthropists*, *One Day in the Life of Ivan Denisovich*, *The Grapes of Wrath* – all books where it is very clear what the writer's message is. That shouldn't be the only type of novel that is written, but certainly that kind of novel should not be devalued.' The question is, though, would we still be reading those books if their political message was all they had to offer? As Stefanakis had suggested, probably not: there surely has to be more to a political novel than politics.

Léonora Miano, speaking in Brazzaville, put a different spin on the conversation by suggesting that political literature has less to do with the content of specific books than with the commitment of the individual novelist. 'Should writers be *engagé*? In trying to answer this question, my conclusion is a simple one: being *engagé* is a commitment to a life of writing; it means embracing writing as a way of life and a way of relating to other people. When the world is collapsing and the sound and the fury of armed conflict is all about us, choosing to focus on sensuality can be seen as a political statement. This is what Mahmoud Darwish accomplishes in his poetry. This is what the songs of slaves accomplish – and these are oral documents. Literature of the oral and the written traditions is our legacy, we peoples of the earth. The answer to the question "Should literature be political?" is not to be found in the content of written works. All literature is political. It is a voice like no other. The voice that speaks in the first person, the "I", is political, liable to be censured in certain latitudes. To write is to dare to create. And the artistic impulse is itself a political manifesto.'

Jonathan Bastable (ed.)

The state fell, the poem ruled

by Tamim Al-Barghouti
Keynote, Cairo*, December 2012

Poetry is a form of language, which itself is the product of a given community. The history of a community is a combination of its current state, as well as its past and future. This history records the community's times of war and peace, and is itself a conflict between the way a community sees itself and the way it is seen by others. Poetry, though, is itself a means of regaining control over how we name things. A poet might for example choose to call death 'martyrdom', or anger 'love', or fire 'a tree', or the sun 'a gazelle'. I call my country Palestine; my opponents call it Israel. I refer to the rebellion of my people as a resistance; my opponents call it terrorism. I call those who are killed by airstrikes martyrs; my opponents either say, 'they had it coming' or 'that's collateral damage'. I agree with those who say that poets usually try to steer clear of topics like these, and I swear to you I've tried to steer clear of the airstrikes, but they won't leave me alone. We tried writing about what's on the inside, but it didn't take us long to discover that even in our hearts, there are tanks and jets and children under siege, grandmothers stranded at border posts, families with no hope of reunion – or at least not until the global balance of power shifts somehow.

We decided to try our hand at singing and we realised that if we imitated those who invaded and occupied our lands and learnt to sing opera, our rulers would borrow money to build a monumental opera house for us to sing in, except no-one we knew would turn up. Then when the ruler found he couldn't afford the interest on the loans he'd taken out to build the building, the whole country would be taken over, occupied. But then when it's time to recite our folk epics like *The Saga of Bani Hilal*, or *The Hero of Hashim*, they get recited in coffee-houses and village squares.

Millions of people know the lyrics to these epics by heart, but no-one pays any attention when one of the famous epic-reciters dies and if you want to know why a reciter of epics has to sit on a wooden chair in a coffee-house while the audience at the opera house luxuriate in cushioned seats, remember what Ibn Khaldun said: 'The oppressed love nothing more than imitating their oppressors.' This brings us back to the shifting balance of power – and to politics – whether we like it or not.

I was born in 1977. I hadn't yet turned five months old when the Egyptian authorities ordered my father to leave Egypt. Anwar Sadat had decided to make peace with Israel so he ordered everyone in Egypt associated with the PLO (Palestinian Liberation Organisation) to get out, and he ordered the closure of the PLO media bureau where my father worked. My father finally settled – after stints in Baghdad and Beirut – in Budapest, and the only time our family could be together was during summer holidays. At my Hungarian kindergarten, the teacher insisted that my name, Tamim, was the Arabic version of the name Tamás (Hungarian for Thomas) or other European varieties of the same, and my parents were unable to convince her that the name Tamim is actually the name of an old Arab tribe and not a derivation of Thomas or Tamás. Later when I was old enough to read, I learnt that Tamás, or Thomas, is the Greek version – adopted via Latin into other European languages – of the Hebrew name T'oma. T'oma in Hebrew means twin. By definition, one cannot be a twin unless one has a twin; a twin needs another person in order to be itself. Historically, Arabs thought of twins as deficient, or weak, because they grew in the womb alongside someone else. Consider, for example, the verse by the pre-Islamic poet 'Antara b. Shaddād al- 'Absī:

What a hero! His clothes cling as though wrapped 'round a tree,
    his feet are encased in softest leather. No lowly twin is he!

My name, on the other hand, is Tamim. He who 'completes completely' from the verb *tamma* ('to complete, finish'). It's an exaggerated form of the active participle 'completer', as if to say Tamim is 'extra-complete'. Thus in reality my teacher was insisting that my name means the opposite of what it actually means. She was a good person, and well-intentioned, but imperialism, which forcefully installed itself as the teacher and guardian of all conquered peoples, deliberately changed our names. Imperialism transformed us from a whole people into a nation of twins, each in need of a sibling who's nowhere to be found. The Arabic language bears this out: we don't call the people living between the borders that the invaders drew for us *nations*, we call them *peoples*, a word that comes from an Arabic root meaning 'to branch out'. For us, these peoples are like branches split off from the whole. At the beginning of the last century, the generals overseeing the foreign occupation drew some lines on a map, which they called nations, and in turn they expected us to call them our countries. But the truth is that they're nothing more than oil companies with massive security apparatuses plus some flags, and anthems, and a border patrol. The armies, police forces, and rulers in these places are just middle-men who mediate between us and the world powers who drew these borders. We didn't choose these borders, or these names, or these institutions. And like any occupation, or tyranny, the system isn't complete unless it penetrates the imagination of the subject, and even though our nation was indeed occupied by others, they never succeeded in colonising our imaginations entirely. They may have divided up the ground beneath our feet, but they could never split up the language we share. Arabic poetry is still Arabic poetry. It's not Kuwaiti poetry or Jordanian or Libyan. This unity of language reflects a unified imagination, and that in itself – no matter what a given poem is about – makes it a political act, an act of resistance.

It's been said that poetry in standard Arabic is pan-Arab, whereas poetry in colloquial Arabic is national and confined to national borders, but this doesn't begin to explain how three of the most important Egyptian colloquial poets – Bayram al-Tunisi, Fouad Haddad, and Salah Jahin – all had non-Egyptian backgrounds. If you look at the way they express themselves, you'll see there's nothing Pharaonic to it. Their colloquial poetry is Arabic in the same way that the *Epic of Bani Hilal* is Arabic. What makes them Egyptian is what makes them Arab.

Arabic poetry, like other varieties of world poetry, is connected to the rise of an imagined community. The nomadic Arabs couldn't know every member of their own tribes personally so they had to devise a symbolic system in order to link all the members of their tribe together. And while city dwellers in the ancient world could feel at home in their cities, imagining the roads, temples, and state institutions that bound them together, Arab bedouin who were constantly moving camp couldn't exactly build temples and roads or foster a sense of identity centred around place. The classical Arabic poem, the *Qasidah*, tells the story of the tribe: their lineage, the achievements of their knights, where they found water, the dates on which they fought their battles, the moral principles by which they lived, etc. and being part of the tribe meant memorising these poems of praise and belonging. If a tribe were to leave a place, there would be no trace of its having been there except for what the poets recorded. And the sons of a tribe could never be true sons of the tribe unless they imagined themselves to be so. The *Qasidah* was one way of binding the individual to the community, and individuals to other individuals, and two people to a third, and three to a fourth. The poem, therefore, itself created a community in the political sense.

Moreover, Arabs were in the habit of turning eloquent lines of poetry into proverbs; folk wisdom with moral authority, which could be applied to situations other than the one which prompted it. The implicit belief operating here is that something that is well said must be true. The eloquence of an expression is an indication of its veracity and the moral authority implicit in it. The poet Abu Tammam went so far as to mock people for the extravagant powers they granted to eloquent poetry, while at the same time boasting about it, in a verse praising his own poetry:

They say it's wise, though it's really a joke.
They do its bidding, though it becomes their yoke.

A poem's eloquence didn't just give it credibility, and moral weight, it also helped poetry circulate and gain fame among the tribes, elevating both the poet's reputation and that of his tribe. In the pre-Islamic period, whenever a poet's line of verse was made into a proverb, he and his tribe got a boost in the societal hierarchy of the Arabian Peninsula, provoking the envy of the other tribes.

This habit of mind made its way into mediaeval Islamic philosophy. According to Muslim belief, the Quran's eloquence gives it its credibility, and it is this eloquence that makes it inimitable, unique. This inimitability, in turn, is proof that it is a divinely authored text. It is also, therefore, the foundation of its moral and political authority. The Quran is divinely authored because it's eloquent. And because it's a divinely authored text it should be respected and all governments should derive their political legitimacy from one interpretation of it or other. Just as the poem, the *Qasidah*, created the tribe, the Quran created a community of believers: a tribe of individuals who memorised a text in rhymed prose that told the story of a specific community, detailing their attributes, values, and culture, and thus their political life.

Ever since the pre-Islamic period, Arabic poetry has been linked to the way the community defines itself. When the community regarded itself as a tribe, poets were tribal poets. And then when the community became a caliphate, and after that a collection of kingdoms, poets were called court poets. In the modern period when the community began to call itself a nation and a people, poets became known as poets of the people, or national poets. After the collapse of the Pan-Arab movement in the late 1960s and up until the late 1990s, as communal cohesion gave way to self-interested individualism, poets sang only of the self. This was the period that saw the rise of literary theories claiming that poetry is the expression of personal freedom, totally divorced from communal authority; that comprehensible language is produced by the community and that a poet's dependence on it hobbles his creativity and by giving into the community he constrains his freedom; that a poet must invent his own language, which hardly anyone other than him or those like him can understand. Poems intended to be incomprehensible to almost everyone were all the rage, but the aloof and gloomy poets who wrote them were simply reflecting the attitude of society at large by running away; they belonged whether they knew it or not.

Then, from the 1990s on, and especially in the period of successive American wars on Iraq, whose victims during the sanctions regime from 1991 to 2003 totalled more than one million people – more than half of whom were children according to UNICEF estimates – as well as more than a million people who died as a result of the American invasion and the subsequent civil war that raged from 2003 to 2011 – from that period on, there has been, I believe, a growing trend among Arab writers toward isolation, grief, and depression. Although inventing a language that no-one else can understand is a luxury we cannot afford. Rather – in order to survive – we desperately need to muster strength from any and all sources, and our cultural heritage is one of them; it bears weight, it does not burden.

Imperialist control over the affairs of Arab countries is the greatest threat to the Arabic language today – to its use and the feeling of belonging it engenders – and poetry is under threat because it is the densest form of the language. The language was never divided up like the land, and that's why a poem written by Abu al-Qasim al-Shabbi could be turned into a chant in Tunisia and be echoed in Yemen; and a poem written by Badr Shakir al-Sayyab in Iraq could be repeated in Egypt; and *The Saga of Bani Hilal* as told in Upper Egypt could come to be told in southern Tunisia. What's more, most colloquial poetry, which one would have expected to participate in creating national identities, canonising these tiny states, which had been given borders and governments by the invaders, actually ridiculed these identities. The *Saga of Bani Hilal*, by far the greatest work of colloquial poetry in Egypt, links Egypt to a cultural sphere that stretches from the Caspian Sea to Tunisia. The epic recounts the history of the Bani Hilal tribe, some of whom live in Upper Egypt today: their origins in Najd (in the Arabian Peninsula), the marriage of their hero to Na 'isa daughter of Zayd al-'Ajjaj, king of Persia, and their journey westward to Tunisia to take revenge against the ruler there, himself of Yemeni origin, who had mistreated their uncles from the Hijaz (also in the Arabian Peninsula).

In the modern era, when the cultural flank of the Egyptian nationalist movement – led by the Wafd party, which is now no more than a shell of its former self – was championing Egypt's ancient Pharaonic heritage to the exclusion of everything else and the Museum of Egyptian Antiquities was being built along European lines – don't forget of course that Egypt's rulers had been hellbent on making the country into a slice of Europe ever since the mid-eighteenth century – it was Bayram al-Tunisi, one of the great Egyptian colloquial poets of the first half of the twentieth century, who ridiculed the government's entire project. Ahmad Shawqi's poems in standard Arabic and Bayram al-Tunisi's in the colloquial in praise of the Ottoman army during the First World War defied, and even threatened, the authority of the Sultan of Egypt, who had been appointed by the British after they'd made the country a protectorate in 1914.

Therefore, Arabic poetry, whether in standard Arabic or colloquial, is a threat to the current structure of power in Arab countries simply by virtue of its existence. It is the voice of the people, and the people are, by definition, the body politic.

Poetry also affects the imagination, however, and rulers exist only in the imagination of those whom they rule. If enough people decide that their ruler is actually a vegetable pedlar, he'll have no choice but to take his cart to the market the very next day. The only power a ruler actually has can be covered by a shirt and trousers; everything else comes from the obedience of others. They will only obey him if they imagine that it is their duty to obey, whether motivated by dread or delight. And of course these notions – dread and delight – are themselves products of the imagination. Words give the imagination form, and if poetry is words best expressed, then it is better able to shape the imagination than any other form of expression, and is therefore a ruler's greatest threat.

The modern governance of Arab states began with Napoleon's occupation of Cairo and ended with George Bush's occupation of Baghdad. These modern states – with borders, bureaucracies, police forces, militaries, and economic policies imposed on them by others – have failed. They have failed to achieve the most important mission for which states are founded: to protect their people. What we have now is the occupation of Iraq and Palestine, the presence of American military forces in the Gulf, and in all the other nominally independent Arab countries abject economic, political, and military subservience. There was a time during the Cold War when Arabs thought there was a chance they could succeed by following a non-colonialist European model of government – the model proposed by the socialist camp in its many guises – but the defeat of 1967 and the catastrophes that followed all the way up to the occupation of Iraq, drove people to give up the idea of taking control of the state. Rather they began to build an alternative state: one without borders or bureaucracy, without an externally dictated economic system, free from international law and military transparency. Since the end of the twentieth century and the beginning of the twenty-first, we in the Arab world have seen numerous examples of non-governmental organisation: groups that engage in defence and policing, that provide health services and education, that run media networks, and that even carry out foreign relations, with little regard for the government. They don't aim to seize control of state institutions; they simply carry on as if those institutions didn't exist.

The Lebanese resistance fought without the army and the first Intifada set up local councils in Palestinian townships without any institutional structure resembling a state. During the Tunisian Revolution, the people of Tunisia were able to organise themselves outside the governmental framework and protected their neighbourhoods when they were attacked by Ben Ali's thugs after the fall of his regime.

In Egypt, the ruling Supreme Council of the Armed Forces itself acknowledged that twenty million Egyptians took part in the demonstrations and sit-ins that gripped the country from January 25th to February 11th, 2011. The people who were gathered together in Egypt's squares practised medicine without any Ministry of Health, covered the news without any Ministry of Information, protected themselves without any Ministry of the Interior, defended themselves during the Battle of the Camel without any army, and negotiated with Mubarak's collapsing government without any ambassadors or Ministry of Foreign Affairs.

Egyptian society carried on for several months despite the complete absence of the police, and in fact the Ministry of the Interior's support of this complete and criminal withdrawal was an attack on that society. The police forces were the main driver of the crime wave and still the society managed to stick together. The people made do with an unwritten constitution and instinctive laws, and they triumphed.

Poetry is political in the same way that those people were politicians. They managed to pursue a politics more beautiful and more successful than anything they'd been offered by the modern state with its colonial pedigree. This was thanks to the way they spoke to one another and the way they imagined themselves to be a cohesive unit. The only leaders of the revolution were the people's demands, their thoughts, their imagination. The people followed their imagination; an image of themselves they'd dreamt up and decided they wanted to be.

A nation, *ummah* in Arabic, is nothing more than a group of people who follow a leader, an *imam*, and in Arabic an *imam* can be a person, a book, or an ideal. In fact, the tool that builders use to measure a building's centre of gravity, the plumb-line, is also called *imam* in Arabic. Furthermore, the nation, the *ummah*, is itself an *imam*; it is its own leader. The nation pursues its own idealised, imagined notion of itself. In Arabic, a nation (*ummah*) can consist of a single individual. If someone has an image of his or her self that they decide they want to live up to, then that individual becomes a nation and its own leader.

That's why the verb *amma*, the root of the word *ummah* ('nation'), is one of those linguistic contradictions in Arabic: it means to lead and to follow. If you say 'amamtu so-and-so', it either means you led someone in prayer or you went toward someone, as though they were a target. It's a verb of movement and it's no accident that the verb 'to head toward' should be the origin of the word 'nation' (*ummah*) just as another verb meaning 'to head toward' (*qasada*) gives us the origin of the word for poem, *qasidah*. A poem, a *qasidah*, is an ideal image of the world as imagined by society. If they head toward it, they will become it. By this logic, the people gathered in Tahrir Square wrote a poem and were themselves its verses. They brought into reality on the ground an imaginary, idealised image of themselves and turned the imaginary into politics, power, and authority. They were a nation who challenged the state, poured out from it and overwhelmed it. But of course this wasn't anything new. As I said before, the ruler only exists in the imagination of those who are ruled. When enough people had decided that Hosni Mubarak was no longer their ruler, and that the leader that should take his place was in fact this idealised, imaginary vision of society, and that every individual was responsible for making sure that they were behaving in such a way as to accord with this vision, Hosni Mubarak fell and the idealised vision took over. The dictator fell and the nation rose; the state fell and the poem ruled.

The party politics we see today is a step backward. People have given up on the ideal vision of politics in the hopes of getting their hands on those same state institutions, which the colonial regimes established. Today a given party or a given president is prepared to defy the will of the people – defy the sovereignty of the people as encapsulated in that ideal vision – in exchange for control of the legal authority of the modern state as established by Lord Cromer. This person would prefer for the people to obey him – not because he resembles the ideal in their imagination – but because the founding documents, which Lord Cromer drafted for them and were approved by all the puppet rulers who followed, say they should. Because the UN and the US and some judges and some army generals say he's the president.

Turning away from the ideal vision – or in other words, abandoning the leader (*imam*) – has broken the rhythm of the collective poem and this has dire consequences. A poet, or an experienced listener, notices a break in the rhythm straight away, and though it may take a poetry novice slightly longer to notice the interruption, the ruler will realise sooner or later that the true source of power is the people's imagination. Documents and laws and constitutions are nothing more than a means of persuasion; a pointless means of persuasion. And if he should abandon his leader, that is, the vision set down by the people, the ideal upon which they built their expectations, he will lose his power over them sooner or later.

A love poem by a Palestinian poet in standard Arabic may not seem like it's political, but it joins with thousands of other images, imaginings, reports, and visions, to create a sense of Palestine in Egypt, Morocco, Lebanon, Syria. It helps to shape – alongside other creations – Egyptians' conception of what power should be, of what is meant by war and peace and justice. This notion, if it grows and matures, and if it attains self-confidence and *esprit de corps*, soon becomes feet on the ground, tearing down thrones and putting up new ones.

CENSORSHIP TODAY

Engines of silence

by Hannah McGill

Politics and political engagement were a major theme of the Edinburgh World Writers' Conference, and a whole strand of the worldwide debate was devoted to the question of censorship – one of the areas where the politics of writing becomes active and visible. However a writer might choose to incorporate political thinking, states have their own interpretations of political intent – and machinery to silence that which they consider dangerous or objectionable. Even without state intervention, restrictions might be imposed by editors and publishers; by the demands of an established readership; by the writer's own sensibilities; or by the mores of his or her society and time. Clarion calls for freedom of speech are easy to make, but as **Boualem Sansal** put it in St Malo, 'The line between censors and libertarians is uncertain: censors live amongst us, even within us.'

    Patrick Ness's keynote in Edinburgh addressed this idea: how much are we governed not by obvious totalitarian bars on our self-expression, but by what is acceptable within the particular contexts in which we operate? He identified the danger that a belief in 'free speech' can mutate into a belief in 'free speech for those only likely to espouse similar opinions to those I hold myself' – and that whatever openness to difference they might believe they enshrine, groups that regard themselves as all similarly enlightened close ranks against those they consider to be wrong. This is a highly visible conundrum for more than just writers, in these days of unfettered online babble and an internet that harbours something to frighten individuals of every political stripe bar absolute libertinism. Contradictions abound in the *causes célèbres* and *bêtes noires* of internet debate. Loud demands for free speech for the Russian punk band Pussy Riot dwell on the same Facebook page as exhortations for bans on 'lad mags', internet pornography, marches and rallies by extreme political groups and offensive humour on social media pages. Support for 'slut walks' – protests that trumpet the right of women to wear whatever they want – jostle with aghast calls for female pop stars to cover up and dance less dirty.

What about being public with one's spiritual beliefs? Openness about one's faith can draw out vivid reactions, even from people who would purport to be advocates of free expression. Consider the openly Christian writer: how long could the matter of his or her faith be out in the open before triggering an angry response in a reader, fellow writer or critic who objects in principle to Christianity? When in 2005 the Disney film adaptation of CS Lewis's *The Lion, The Witch and the Wardrobe* was released, journalist Polly Toynbee spat in *The Guardian* that 'adults who wince at the worst elements of Christian belief may need a sickbag handy for the most religiose scenes.' But Lewis was a Christian; he put in his story what he believed to be worthy and true. When Marilynne's Robinson's *Gilead* came out in 2005, I was involved in a group discussion of it for publication in a newspaper. For one of my fellow critics, there was no way around it: Robinson's Christian faith rendered the book suspect, made it unambiguously a piece of dogma. Because *Gilead* issued from a Christian place, a Christian's sensibility and morality, he could not critique it objectively as art. It was tainted. Such reactions might not constitute a drive to ban or censor, but they do indicate an angry reaction against those who are 'not one of us, not really' – a sense that some modes of expression or sets of values are inappropriate or wrong.

Taken in a wider sense, censorship of voices, thoughts and ideas can be seen to include the long-term exclusion of writers and thinkers from particular social groups – and the prevention, via sustained exclusion, of a literary culture developing at all. The Conference repeatedly came back to the endemic dominance of the English language and the dearth of effective translation and distribution of books from non-English language cultures: inevitably, much talk of literary culture, however informed and knowledgeable the speakers, must be understood to refer only to 'literary culture as it is broadly known and understood', which means a culture dominated by western modes and by the English language. In specific territories, this has specific resonance. Speaking in Melbourne, **Larissa Behrendt** drew attention to the complexity of the issue of free speech around marginalised and minority social groups. The voices of indigenous Australians having been institutionally silenced, she explained, constitutes an ongoing mode of censorship, comprising not only the direct repression of stories and testimony from that group, but also the restriction of its education and the artificial interruption of its oral tradition. 'Among all of the insidious ways a people can be colonised,' Behrendt said, 'denying them the tools that allow them to communicate in the imposed and dominant culture is one of the most effective in disenfranchising, disempowering and continually marginalising them.' But the protection of that colonised group, and the redressing of the historical balance, also demands the restriction of what can be said to or about it by its oppressors, she argued. 'I believe free speech is important but, like any other right, needs to be balanced with others, including the right to be free from racial discrimination and vilification.' And perhaps liberals should not be afraid to accept the idea of selective censorship, for free speech bears caveats in any sensible culture: 'It is regulated, rightly, in relation to defamation and libel. It is regulated, rightly, in relation to trade practices, to ensure that consumers are not duped by unsubstantiated claims.'

Inevitably, however, the acceptance that certain forms of language can hurt or damage – and that certain writing, as **John Burnside** put it in Edinburgh, 'appeals to violence and endangers life' – requires the concurrent acceptance of gatekeepers deciding on behalf of the rest of their society where those lines ought to be drawn. The Young Adult authors participating in the Conference shared their concerns about the restrictions on certain forms of information being shared with the young, with **Melvin Burgess** describing the 'press hysteria' that attended publication of his work in the UK on the basis that it dealt with 'risqué' themes such as sex and drugs, and **Keith Gray** pointing up the pressure for age certification of books in the UK and describing the exclusion of his books from the libraries of Catholic schools due to objection to their sexual content. Should institutions instil such barriers, or should parents and carers or indeed children themselves be trusted to impose appropriate limits? Even those with a blanket approval of free speech for all would surely instinctively seek to protect children from material that might present them with information for which they are not intellectually or emotionally ready.

Regimes that censor widely are often accused of treating their citizens 'like children', within which analogy rests the assumption that censoring material for children's eyes is appropriate. But when speaking openly to an adolescent audience about sexuality or drugs strikes one onlooker as an educative responsibility, and another as an attack on innocence and an invitation into corruption, who makes the rules? Can such a responsibility be trusted to the state, without sacrificing the element of challenge and discovery in young people's writing that makes them into receptive and responsive adult readers? Can it, come to that, be trusted to parents who might simply be absorbing media hype or passing on their own prejudices? The children's author Judy Blume has been unequivocal on the subject: 'I believe that censorship grows out of fear, and because fear is contagious, some parents are easily swayed. Book banning satisfies their need to feel in control of their children's lives. This fear is often disguised as moral outrage. They want to believe that if their children don't read about it, their children won't know about it. And if they don't know about it, it won't happen .... Books that make kids laugh often come under suspicion; so do books that encourage kids to think, or question authority; books that don't hit the reader over the head with moral lessons are considered dangerous .... If every individual with an agenda had his/her way, the shelves in the school library would be close to empty.'

Yet honesty and openness can leave harm in their wake – for children who are presented with material they cannot process, or for individuals who might be left to live with the consequences of another's free speaking. An audience member in Cape Town spoke of having seen footage from the Holocaust as a child, and having 'nowhere to take' the resulting feelings. In the same debate, writer **Damon Galgut** raised the subject of a protest at the 2012 Jaipur writers' festival, from which Salman Rushdie was 'disinvited' due to a threat of violence; a number of his fellow writers read aloud from *The Satanic Verses*, before leaving the country to evade the legal consequences of reading from a banned book. 'If you believe that freedom of expression is absolute ... why would you flee the consequences of that act?' Galgut asked. 'If you know that people are going to die and that it's probably not going to be you, is there not a responsibility to limit what is said and done? ... Are there damaging forms of expression that should be restricted?' The free expression of, say, a documentary filmmaker working in a politically charged situation is challenged by the fact that he or she might endanger the lives of his or her subjects by capturing them on film. More intimate damage can result from a writer placing sensitive information about or unflattering depictions of real people in his or her work. In terms of both real-world political scenarios, and real people's rights to privacy, most writers self-censor by balancing honesty and openness with a degree of responsibility or sensitivity.

Some would argue, furthermore, that censorship and self-censorship have positive political functions: that artists should use their personal power by refusing to visit repressive regimes, and that readers should refuse to consume the cultural product of such regimes. To **Li Er**, speaking in Beijing, the overarching system has outgrown and overpowered censorship as a mode of social control: while 'censorship in publishing and the media has, by and large, no effect on the reception of information … the power of the system, the power of capital, the power of industrialisation and technology, has formed a new system-level force that can devour anything new, and is constantly draining the individual's subjectivity.' What he calls 'the self-regeneration of the novel' thus becomes a necessary form of resistance to a manipulation of the self that is infinitely larger and more effective than the mere redaction of certain combinations of words. Mass media, he argued, and the 'fragmentisation' it promotes in life, is a more significant force for writers to resist than straightforward forms of censorship. But of course, that very fragmentisation also provides access. Chinese novelist **Chan Koonchung**, who spoke in Toronto, saw his satirical political novel *Fat City* banned in his homeland but disseminated widely in pirated online editions. The constant effort of the Chinese government to control content on the internet via censorship is no less constantly challenged by a generation committed to getting around 'the Great Firewall'. 'Someone has to do it,' Chan said. 'If not us, then who? Someone must keep telling the truth, otherwise we will all live in lies.'

Voices of unreason

by Boualem Sansal
Keynote, St Malo, May 2013

I don't want to review the whole history of censorship. We would have to go back to the Roman censors, the magistrates whose absolute power meant their decisions couldn't be appealed against, and who were meant to maintain moral standards in the City. We are familiar with censorship, we know the myriad official and unofficial ways censors have used over the centuries to muffle speech, and we know how the state punished those who broke the law of silence. Each and every human institution – whether religious, civilian or military – has had a go. At some times, in some places, the system was so ignominious that it has left a lasting imprint on human consciousness. Such totalitarian behaviour has left us words we still cringe to hear: inquisition, deportation, banishment, self-criticism, purge, gulag .... Such words speak of death, of the arbitrariness and the suffering of our world. They make us truly uncomfortable.

Yet we also know how men and women, intellectuals, writers, journalists, film-makers, playwrights, have spoken up against censorship, putting their own lives at risk. That goes back a long way: to Socrates and to Galileo. The list is long, and is full of prestigious names: Voltaire, Zola, Solzhenitsyn, Heinrich Heine, and so many others. It speaks of the courage and resilience of humanity for the cause of freedom of speech, a freedom without which life is worthless.

But the world is not divided into two groups. The line between censors and libertarians is uncertain: censors live amongst us, even within us. We all know that freedom of expression and its cause can be easy excuses for those who actually want to impose their truth and their censorship onto society. That is what extremists do. They speak up against censorship and want to impose their own, as Islamic fundamentalists – the latest addition to the double-speak scene – do. Someone like Tariq Ramadan is the greatest advocate of democracy and freedom of expression in Paris, London and Geneva. We have to admit it even though we know his ulterior motives: to spread Islamic fundamentalism, democracy's sworn enemy. Conversely, ardent proponents of freedom of expression have, on occasion, approved of or even called for its restriction. For instance, the Gayssot Act [passed in France in 1990], establishing the offence of denial of crimes against humanity, does exactly that – but draws on positive inspiration. In its introduction, it states that it institutes a ban not to violate freedom of expression, but to oppose the virulent antisemitism of the *Front National* and of Holocaust deniers. Since then, Islamic fundamentalists have joined and even overtaken them. This goes to show that laws are only as effective as the resources made available to implement them. In this case, the resources are minimal. As we know, legislation, when not enforced, will support the trend; it becomes an incentive to do what it is meant to prevent and sanction.

For a radical anarchist such as Noam Chomsky, it is evil. He claims freedom of expression only makes sense if it is unfettered. He has therefore heavily criticised the Gayssot Act. It is easy to imagine what would happen if the law were repealed and if freedom of expression were unrestricted, as Noam Chomsky would want. There is a host of deniers and manipulators, they would soon get us to forget all the genocides committed, against the Indians in America, against the Armenians in Turkey, against the Jews in Europe. We would forget about large-scale colonial massacres. They would try to convince us that slavery and colonisation were collateral damages in the forward march of history and civilisation. In fact, they have already tried.

A law was passed in France in 2005. Article 4 asked historians to highlight the positive aspects of colonisation. And Article 13 extended the benefits enjoyed by those repatriated from Algeria to all OAS [Organisation de l'Armée Secrète] activists, including those convicted of terrorism and murder by French courts. This was going to lead to a comprehensive reworking of history and to a new form of censorship to gag all dissenters. Historians rebelled; the revisionist provisions were withdrawn; but those who put them forward are still sitting in parliament expressing the same beliefs – which, incidentally, are becoming more popular. It is democracy killing off democracy.

Significant voices, including Elisabeth Badinter, Marc Ferro and Alain Decaux, have called for the repeal of all restrictive or prohibiting historical/memory laws, such as the Gayssot Act on revisionism, the Taubira Act on slavery, the act of 2005 on the Nation, and others. Should we do so? It is a real issue, and the question is as old as censorship itself: is prohibition or restriction always an act of censorship? Orhan Pamuk – who probably shares Noam Chomsky's views – was sentenced not for denying a historical truth but for acknowledging it. In the Holocaust and the Armenian genocide, we have two crimes against humanity serving as the focus of two contradictory forms of censorship. In one case, whoever denies genocide is condemned; in the other, condemnation awaits anyone who acknowledges it. Orhan Pamuk was reviled at home but praised and honoured abroad. In many countries, those who deny the European Holocaust are welcomed, listened to and honoured. In Iran, for instance, learned symposia are often organised at which people claim that their voice is muffled in Europe at the instigation of the Jews and of Israel.

The questions of racism, xenophobia, homophobia, sexism, islamophobia and anti-westernism are similar. Do we need a Gayssot-type potion for every ill? Or do we need more freedom where there is already so much unreason, madness and ignorance and so little sound common sense?

I would like us to look at this from a slightly different point of view as we open the debate on censorship. I feel we know enough about the way censorship operates, who fights it and who supports it, but too often we overlook the basic issue of legitimacy. I mean the validity, or otherwise, of the reasons that – at a given moment, in a given country – lead the dominant classes (civilian, military, religious and financial, and other institutions whose purpose is to give meaning to society, such as universities, masonic organisations, learned society and the media) to state the truths and the way they should be observed, and to claim that straying from this would threaten public order. They have the power to direct, and possibly, force people. That should be enough, but no, they want everyone to share their philosophy and to support their domineering project. Wherever the spirit of censorship takes root it spreads, becomes all-pervasive and prescriptive.

It may also be interesting to see how writers de-legitimise censors' arguments and legitimise their own. In truth, they have forgotten how to do it. De-legitimising Islamic fundamentalists by saying that they want to introduce Sharia is stating the obvious: Sharia is part of Islam, it is perfectly normal that Muslims should want to be governed by the laws of their faith, just as democrats would want to be governed by the laws of the democracy they believe in. The same applies when it is said that Sharia is violent. Capital punishment in the USA, China, Japan or elsewhere is no less violent. That, to me, is the reason why censorship lasts. We don't always know how to de-legitimise its bias and its claims. Quite the contrary: our arguments too often support it. To criticise the means without unpicking the underlying ideas is to support these very ideas.

It isn't really a debate between advocates of opposed opinions but a vital struggle between two contradictory views of society. Secrecy is part of human history. Some want to keep it untouched and untouchable as it guarantees their power, and will do all they can to protect it. Others want to remove it as it obstructs and keeps men ignorant and destitute. Writers stand on the cusp, between these two worlds, the worlds of secrecy and transparency. They are not all looking in the same direction. Some denounce the censors. Many also denounce their victims and those who support them. In Paris, the global capital of human rights, Left-wing intellectuals came and accused [Soviet defector] Viktor Kravchenko for denouncing Soviet totalitarianism [a film about him was shown at the St Malo conference]. Are those who side with dictatorship sincere? Do they truly believe that good can come from evil? That some evils are worse than others?

Looking at censorship from this point of view means looking at truth. What is truth? Who holds it? Who can confirm that it is real and more useful to society than doubt, questioning or mistakes may be? These are so many basic yet relative questions. Definitions are entirely different from one country to the next.

Censorship is no longer an official institution in democratic countries. It is pervasive and enforced through legislation: anyone – public or private institution, voluntary organisation or individual – can turn to the courts to impose censorship on an article, a book, a film or a painting. They will mention defamation, infringement of privacy, breach of the peace, blasphemy, sexism, racism, anti-Semitism, homophobia, and so on. In a democratic environment, there is a double difficulty for writers active as defenders of freedom of expression. Firstly, it is difficult for them to speak against censorship as they are talking of court rulings, handed down on the basis of existing legislation, and against which it is always possible to appeal to a higher court. Secondly, confusion is such in society that speaking against censorship can be seen as supporting the action that gave rise to the initial complaint and the court case. When the magazine Charlie Hebdo printed the cartoons of Mohammed in support of the Danish *Jyllandsposten*, which was being threatened by Islamic fundamentalists, many accused it of Islamophobia, blasphemy, racism and the like. The fact is, defenders of freedom almost always end up in the dock, and the censors are justified in their ways. It is a vicious circle.

Everywhere you turn you hear people saying, with despair in their voices: we can't say anything about this or about that, about homosexuals, about Jews or Israel, about Muslims or Islam, about insecurity in the neighbourhoods. Censorship is so pervasive across democratic societies that speaking up will lead to criticism and reproach or even physical violence and litigation. Ironically, silence has become a form of freedom. Saying nothing is saying it all, but it is also depriving you of any action when the struggle for freedom requires, first and foremost, a practical commitment.

Speaking freely

'Censorship is a very Sixties word in a way,' mused the Scottish writer **John Burnside** in Melbourne. He was thinking about how much the political scene has changed since the original writers' conference – the world of letters too. The twists and turns of the global conversation suggested that things have moved on since 1962, when the court case that led to the lifting of the ban on DH Lawrence's *Lady Chatterley's Lover* was still fresh in the minds of the assembled novelists. And back then, political censorship in its crudest form was still a fact of life for writers in many parts of the world: the Soviet bloc, China and many other authoritarian countries. It was only five years since the sensational publication in Italy of Boris Pasternak's *Doctor Zhivago*. The book had been refused publication in the USSR due to its perceived anti-Soviet tone. Its appearance in the west led to furious attacks on Pasternak at home, and he was forced to refuse the Nobel Prize for Literature when it was awarded to him in 1958. 'We have moved away from that,' said Burnside, 'to talk about silencing and marginalisation.'

Certainly there was much discussion of the subtle and all but invisible ways that censorship (or something that delegates chose to term censorship) can affect fiction and other kinds of writing. It took the Burmese writer **Ma Thida** to remind the Conference that the old-fashioned, heavy-handed state suppression of the written word still exists, that novelists can still be gagged and bound by their national governments. She spoke with immense grace at the meeting in Kuala Lumpur.

'First of all, I'd love to express my pleasure and gratitude for being here,' she said at the start of a speech headlined 'Freedom and Literature'. 'For us, as citizens of Burma or Myanmar, the very title "Freedom and Literature" would have seemed surreal in the recent past.' To explain why, Ma Thida told her own story – and this too had an element of the surreal.

'In my country, we had a Press Scrutiny Board for nearly five decades. In the early 1980s, it took at least a year or two to get permission to publish a novel. Even with permission, there would be much editing. Sometimes writers decided not to publish because of the immense and nonsensical editing by the censorship board. Periodicals were censored not at the manuscript stage, but before distribution. The censorship board would ask us to remove paragraphs or whole short stories or articles from printed periodicals. So we would have to paint black or silver ink over certain paragraphs, or glue pages together, or rip pages out before the magazines went on sale .... I began writing short stories in the 1980s. But because of my political activities and written criticisms of the government, my pen name was on the "brown list", and most of my short stories were banned. In 1993 I was sentenced to twenty years' imprisonment for crimes including the printing and distribution of illegal materials. All of my writing was banned, and I was put on the black list. Though I was released after five and a half years, no publisher dared take my books. I really wanted to run a news or current affairs journal, but I knew it was impossible. And because of the censorship board's heavy pressure, no publisher would take me on as an editor. So even when not in prison, writers had very limited freedom to publish.'

For Ma Thida, the new freedoms to read and write in Burma are more than just a barometer of political tolerance. She sees the act of reading as something that is liberating in itself, as a pursuit that manufactures freedom out of thin air. 'Readers have a perfect freedom to imagine; the words and sentences encourage readers in their imaginative power. A simple sentence saying "the sun rises" can be imagined differently by different readers (while a movie scene of a sunrise can only be the same for every viewer). So I dare to say that, while it may be easy to prohibit writers, it is hard to suppress creativity. For writers, creativity helps to expand the boundaries of freedom that are permitted by censorship. Writers do not need permission from the censorship board to be creative. And as for readers, their imagination helps them to read between the lines, to look behind the words or even peep inside the vocabulary. Literature is an art that contains and preserves freedom. Writers engender it through their creativity, readers by their imaginative power. So we can say: literature requires freedom, yes, but it also brings freedom. Censorship prohibits the publishing of the literature, but cannot restrict its freedom. The free nature of literature and of the appreciation of literature – these things endure, even in censored works.'

Ali Smith, in her keynote on style, remarked in passing that nothing is harmful to literature *except censorship* – but perhaps even censorship can work as a creative constraint, like the unalterable fourteen lines of a sonnet, or the dimensions of an artist's canvas. **Benjamin Markovits** suggested that this might be the case, and that censorship was one of the backhanded compliments that politics pays to art. 'One of the amazing things about censorship of novels is that it shows such faith in the power of literature. In England if you really want a book to make no difference you just publish it.' Then he added: 'Theatre works best when there is a certain element of censorship, and you have to modulate your political thought into something that is more concealed or aestheticised. In Eastern Europe before the collapse of communism, theatre was immensely popular, because people could go and see something that was supposedly a production of Shakespeare, say, but was in fact a coded critique of the autocratic system under which they functioned. After the fall of those regimes, the audiences for theatre vanished overnight. So, as soon as there was a much freer environment where political statements didn't need to be channelled through the arts, through something symbolic or representative, there was no market for that art.'

The Malaysian playwright **Huzir Sulaiman** ruefully agreed, and joked darkly about the failure of the democratic countries to understand the aims and the status of writers in authoritarian regimes such as his own, or in thoroughly oppressive ones such as Ma Thida had endured. 'The western media, and even the westernised Asian media, are much more comfortable seeing an author from a developing country as an expression of political dissidence.' he said. 'You are evaluated according to how much you fight your third-world regime, and in return, how much you are repressed by it. There's a pecking order that goes: censored, banned, intimidated, arrested, tortured, imprisoned for life, murdered. If you are murdered, you win.'

Jonathan Bastable (ed.)

The censors within

by Patrick Ness
Keynote, Edinburgh, August 2012

I had intended to open this polemic with some version of this true story: earlier this summer, I was having dinner with friends and our conversation turned to the role of the veil in Islam, starting with how to explain a burkha to a son raised to believe that men and women are equal, before leading into the veil's potential as a form of oppression against women. The friends I was having dinner with were two women: one a Palestinian, raised in Jordan; the other English, raised as a Muslim. And as our conversation progressed, it turned into how – for a number of reasons, some of them perhaps very good – it is far easier for them to discuss the issue of the veil publicly than me, a white western male, no matter how nuanced or well-intentioned my views.

Now, this is exactly what I wanted to address: the things we disallow ourselves to discuss. But a funny thing happened. I found myself drafting and re-drafting the way I opened with that anecdote again and again and again, working so hard to make sure my role in that conversation was clearly understood – and therefore impossible to misunderstand – that I found myself pounding the sentences into such painfully careful neutrality that they would end up meaning almost nothing. But why? Why did I obviously think such care necessary, even while being painfully aware of the irony of this being a polemic about censorship?

Part of my hesitation is of course my own genuine impulse not to be in any way racist, a truly held wish to accommodate cultures and views not my own. There is also my desire not to have this polemic be just another tediously calculated controversy, like the ones Martin Amis seems to pull out every time he's got a new paperback on the way. But if I'm honest, isn't part of it also fear? Fear of having whatever I'd say about the Islamic veil – no matter how thoughtfully I'd said it – misappropriated, misquoted or badly paraphrased in the inevitable tweeting that's going on right this very second? Fear of having my words turned into something they aren't, and having to suffer the consequences. Because the price of being misunderstood is very high. In the online world, nothing can be unsaid and nothing is off the record. And once you're forced, fairly or not, to start saying something like 'I'm not a racist', haven't you lost the legitimacy of your voice forever? Is that something a writer can risk?

What I've done, though, by being so careful, by even perhaps keeping silent on this or any issue, is disallowed myself a real voice in the conversation. I who consider myself a brave writer, one unafraid to push boundaries, to speak truth to power, I who believe these things about myself as much as any of you, I have in this instance self-censored. In a polemic about self-censorship. And my argument is that, paradoxically, in this age where everything is connected and every voice is heard, this form of self-censorship is on the increase. What we disallow ourselves to discuss – sometimes for good reason, yes, but sometimes for bad – can curtail our voices as effectively as any government or corporation ever could.

Now, the larger issue of censorship, by those very governments and corporations, is still obviously a huge one. But what I've faced with this polemic is what Mary McCarthy grappled with in 1962 when she delivered it. She said, 'I imagine it has occurred to the audience … that there is not going to be much problem with today's topic as there can't be too much disagreement.' Fifty years later, she's still right. I could easily have given an impassioned fifteen-minute talk about China's censorship of the internet, for example. Or how book-banning in schools remains a persistent problem in the US, even in 2012. I could have spoken of the hate tweets to Tom Daley or Louise Mensch or Fabrice Muamba. Or the disgrace of the Pussy Riot trial in Moscow. Or Great Britain's own problems with censorship: its outdated libel laws, its alarming flair for super-injunctions, its plans for secret courts, and on and on. Censorship has not left the world. It only finds new avenues.

But as in 1962, these are all easy things to rise in opposition to, without much risk, without possibly even disagreement. Would we agree here today that Salman Rushdie has the right to produce *The Satanic Verses*?

Would we agree that his experience during the [2012] Jaipur Literary Festival is a depressing blow against free speech? There might be a few dissenters, but I suspect on the whole, we'd rally around Rushdie, and loudly – and proudly – claim our right and willingness to speak on any issue at any time.

But would we be correct? Ask yourself, truthfully, would you sit down tomorrow morning and start writing a novel with Mohammed as your central character? A Mohammed treated as a fallible man rather than a prophet? A Mohammed perhaps even criticised? This is a different question than: 'should you be able to write this book?' Because I suspect, again, that we would probably agree here in this room – if perhaps less so in the world at large – that of course you should, if the need to tell that story was great enough. But who actually would?

Or consider something more benign, at least on the surface. However ashamed you might be to admit it, has the threat of a Bad Sex Award ever made you pause while writing a sex scene? It's entered my mind, and frankly, it pissed me off. I wrote the scene anyway, of course, but even the thought that I'd momentarily hesitated made me angry. For the record, I loathe the Bad Sex Award. I think it started as a funny idea, but in order to gain headlines and get writers like Haruki Murakami on the list, the otherwise intelligent people who – I hesitate to say 'judge' it – have to temporarily pretend they understand neither context nor tone. So rather than what the Bad Sex Award could be – a discussion on how sex can be written honestly – it is instead an occasion for tittering and humiliation of the most public-school kind.

However, having said that, have I now guaranteed that every bit of sex I might ever write will automatically be scrutinised by the Bad Sex Award? Does that enter my mind before both writing a sex scene or criticising the award itself? Do I have to make the conscious decision not to self-censor rather than write freely, as an artist should? What about if you're here today, among what is probably – correct me if I'm wrong – a fairly politically liberal gathering. What if you're here in this group, and you believe deeply in the freedoms I argue for: freedom of speech, the battle against censorship. But what if you're also, say, against abortion? For you, it's a moral position you can't budge, no matter how socially liberal you otherwise consider yourself to be. In your heart, you believe abortion to be the taking of a life. Would you venture to speak that opinion here? Would you write a work of art that espoused that opinion?

Now, this is interesting, because I suspect you might not. But what if you did? What if you expressed that opinion here in a thoughtful but clear way? That opinion would have consequences, wouldn't it? We'd like to pretend it wouldn't. I imagine we here think of ourselves as open-minded and accommodating to points of view other than our own, but how would an anti-abortion writer be received in a group like this? Politely, respectfully, I'd imagine. But within that politeness, would that writer's opinions on other topics be ignored because some of us would secretly think he or she is 'not one of us, not really'?

Because this is the other self-censoring problem growing with the interconnectedness of the world. Instead of bringing us all together in an omnipresent, multi-faceted discussion, the internet instead has made sectarianism an almost default position. The nature of mass debate has become solely binary: you're on one side or the other. Factor that in with whatever combination of debates you've been forced to take sides on, and the number of people willing to listen to you – because they agree with you – shrinks daily. Try stating a strong opinion on gun control, for example, on Twitter and see how many followers you lose.

That's not the only example. This polemic is going on *The Guardian* website, and though no-one really wants to say so out loud, most of us seem to accept these days that the comments on articles like this, while occasionally containing interesting replies, are far more often the domain of outraged point-missers, incandescently furious pedants, and trolls who don't bother reading past the sub-headline. And again, did I pause about whether to include that paragraph, knowing this article will have comments beneath it? I did. More importantly, have I, by all that frankly liberating name-calling, just committed the same crime myself by dismissing any discussion I find unpalatable?

Because this is the kind of risk you run by saying something like that opinion about abortion. We here would almost certainly argue for your right to hold it, but in this sectarian, connected world, we'd then maybe stop listening to you. In a way, you'd be suddenly free of censorship because you'd be able to say whatever you like, you'd just be saying it to fewer and fewer people. And importantly, you'd be left out of conversations you'd like to be having.

Can an artist do this? Should an artist? Certainly, there are artists who are happy to talk to their own small sect in exchange for complete freedom to say whatever they will. But isn't the pushing of an artist into a small sect also a kind of censorship? And if chosen by the artist, isn't it a kind of self-exile? Of giving up on engaging? Of possibly even changing things because you're no longer part of a discussion that might? For example, if you're a writer who wants to affect the world and engage with a large audience, would you risk being marginalised in the US by talking about your atheism? Would you risk the same marginalisation in England by talking about your devout Christianity? Would you loudly proclaim a pro-Israeli position in Europe? Or a pro-Palestinian one in the US? Or go anywhere in the world and suggest Israel and Palestine may both have dirty hands?

Now, of course there's a natural elision between what we say in private versus what we say in public, but in a time where everything that you say is said to the entire world, are there areas where you've allowed that elision to justify not speaking what you see as the truth to save yourself from the consequences that could result? How does an artist speak freely in this environment? I don't have a simple credo that answers this. I press on, I try hard, I work to say what I want to say in a way that keeps my voice both heard but also truthful, also standing up for what I believe in the most effective way I can. But I don't always get it right, I don't always make myself proud, and most importantly, I find that the struggle grows daily in the way the world now connects.

And so I ask you today, what do you not say? What do you censor when you write? Because I'm afraid I can't believe that you don't. You may be willing to do some of the things I've mentioned today, but all? I like to think of myself as a fearless writer, and I'm sure that you all do, too. But are we really challenging ourselves enough to keep that true? I don't think the question behind censorship today is any longer should you be able to say these things. Nor is it any longer a question of if you *can*. The question has become, if you *do*.

Everything is permitted

The discussion initiated by **Patrick Ness** in Edinburgh led to much soul-searching on the subject of self-censorship. For the most part it was taken as read that it is a bad thing for a writer to self-censor. Most of the delegates began from the assumption that there is something cowardly or dishonest about letting one's writing be shaped by exterior forces – such as a publisher's commercial interests, a government's menace, or even a desire to please one's readers and be liked. Because all these things (it went without saying) were likely to distort or degrade the truth of the writing.

'The worst thing a writer can do is to sit down with an idea of what you can and can't write about,' said **Larissa Behrendt** in Melbourne. 'The writing should always come from the desire, the absolute passion for telling a story. The act of *uncensoring* as a writer is important – you should just write. I've sometimes had compliments about my writing such as "Wow that was brave", and I always think: Gee, what have I revealed about myself.' **Ali Alizadeh**, chairing in Melbourne, lent historical authority to this view, adding that it was a particular problem in the west, where the marketplace is king. 'Self-censorship is probably one of the prevalent forms of censorship in our free, liberal democracies,' he said. 'It goes back to Thomas Hobbes: yes, we are all free to do what we want, but we regulate it by fear – by fear of the offence that we might cause, by fear that we might get punished by the sovereign – even if the sovereign is not a totalitarian, despotic dictator.'

Back in Edinburgh, **Keith Gray** suggested that dealing with Hobbes' sovereign, whatever form he might take, may be more a matter of tact and diplomacy than a question of intransigence and courage. 'I wonder if self-censorship could be seen as a skill that good writers develop. Maybe the best writers can navigate, and still tell their story without losing any of the power or the potency of the integrity, and without patronising the audience.' **Jackie**

Kay pointed out that not all characters in books are fictional, and that this too might make a writer think twice, for good or ill, about what goes onto the page. 'There is no form in which you are more likely to censor yourself than in the memoir,' she said. 'In memoir, how do you deal with people who are still alive and might object to what you are saying? Do you have the right to write about such people? The memoirs that are really wonderful are the ones where self-censorship hasn't gone on.'

China Miéville, taking part in the same debate, was far less timid. 'Is there nothing we shouldn't say?' he asked. 'There are millions and millions of things we shouldn't say. We all self-censor all the time, and a bloody good thing too. Our minds are washing-machines full of the crap that we pick up over the years on this earth, an earth that is full of prejudices and nonsenses. So one of the fundamental problems of this argument is the elision between having the legal right to say something and having the moral right not to be told off for saying something objectionable. When some free-speech warrior thinks they should get to say whatever they want, and then complains if someone complains, that's not censorship. Censorship is when the police come round and tell you: don't say that! One person saying to another "That is thoroughly objectionable" is not censorship; it is just part of civilisation.'

Miéville turned the debate on its head by suggesting that our liberal distrust of censorship sometimes serves as a Trojan horse that gives abhorrent ideas access to the society-wide discourse on difficult and delicate issues. 'There is a massive libidinal investment among reactionary people in presenting themselves as incredibly brave. So you will never just hear someone say "I hate Muslims", they will always say "I know I'm not supposed to say this, I know the politically correct brigade are going to knock down my door and throw me in a dungeon, but actually I'm just going to come out and say it : I think Islam is a problem ..." – as if that is not the default conversation in every pub in Britain, the quotidian prejudices of boors becoming a sign of amazing freedom! Two streets from here [in Edinburgh], right now, there is a shop in the window of which is a golliwog. Now, I don't want the police to go down there and close that shop. I want the people who run that shop to realise that this is spitting in the face of many of the people who walk past it, and have the decency to stop what they are doing.'

Miéville produced a connected, book-related example to demonstrate that the censor's blue pencil – a rewrite imposed for reasons originating outside the book – is not always a force for evil. Moreover the censor can sometimes quite properly be the writer herself, or in this instance, someone who has a close interest in the writer's reputation and legacy. 'Here is a quote from Enid Blyton's daughter: "My sister and I came to the conclusion in the 1980s that, because of the multicultural society we now had, the gollies should disappear from the books. We felt that it was not right in this day and age to use them if they were considered to be a parody of part of our population." How incredibly polite and sensitive and decent! None of this stuff disappears from history. Archivists are always going to be able to find it; this is not "the commissar vanishes", or some Stalinist piece of airbrushing. It is just saying that context matters, and that we should self-censor all the time.'

The German novelist **Matthias Politycki** reacted strongly to Miéville's invocation of political correctness. He too thought it was part of the problem – but he had a different take. 'Political correctness is the word for censorship in the western world,' he said. 'As a writer I would like to come back to what happens to our languages when we self-censor in our politically correct world. I have a lot of problems in presenting my theses to the public without causing shitstorms in the press or on Facebook. One example: gypsies. That was the term used until the late-1970s, when political correctness informed me that the correct term in Germany is "Sinti and Roma". In Switzerland there is a different tribe and they have another name. Nevertheless, we have to call them Sinti and Roma – which sounds a bit clumsy if you write it in a novel. But I went to Budapest and there I had a taxi driver who insisted that he was a gypsy. Every gypsy I met there said "Use that word, please, because we are neither Roma nor Sinti." He had a point. Now that 'African-American' is the accepted term, how are Americans to call people of ancestral African origin who are not American? How do we handle the awkward fact that not all Eskimo people are Inuit, that – to the Inuit themselves – the terms are not synonyms?'

Many of the delegates were uncomfortable with Politycki's remarks – though presumably they would all have defended to the death his right to say it. The thoughtful Argentinian writer **Carlos Gamerro** provided a neat and considered let-out. 'At the 1962 conference,' he said, 'William Burroughs said: "Nothing is true, everything is permitted." That is a wonderful summary of what fiction can do. The characters are your alibi: you can always say "I am portraying a racist or a homophobe; it's not me saying this."

But in poetry or an essay or a piece of journalism the author is speaking in his own voice, and there the problem of self-censorship is maybe more acute.'

In one of the serendipitous coincidences that were a mark of the Conference worldwide, **Sorj Chalandon** in St Malo had enlarged on this very point – using a rather fine and thought-provoking image from his own experience as a writer. 'I am a journalist,' he said, 'and journalists are not supposed to be the subject of what they write, they are not supposed to show their emotions. So our problem is to censor what we are as men and women, so as to convey objective information. Self-censorship for me means not writing about my own fears and sorrows. I have seen wars and written about them, but never allowed myself to bring in my own emotions. I write in pads – on the right-hand page I put the material that is going to go into the article, and on the left I write about myself, my feelings, the stuff that is not going to go into the article. I found a way around this self-censorship by killing the journalist in me and becoming a novelist. Whenever I write a novel, I wonder if they are really all about everything that is written on the left-hand page.'

Jonathan Bastable (ed.)

The gatekeepers

by Keith Gray
Keynote, Cape Town, September 2012

When I was fourteen I was an outstandingly mediocre student but a voracious reader and a determined wannabe writer. I read many 'How To' creative writing guides and even crowbarred some money out of my father to be able to attend a local creative writing night-class. And the advice I kept hearing, what seemed to be the golden rule was 'write about what you know.' Although I may have broken that rule many times over the years, for the following few minutes I believe I'll stick to it pretty closely. I write for children and teenagers – this is my perspective on censorship from within the world of kids' books.

I'd like to start by reading a letter I received a couple of years ago:

> Dear Sir,
> I found the language in your book *Warehouse* most objectionable. At a time when schools are struggling with literacy standards, do you really have to use language of that sort? I note from the cover that it is 'unsuitable for younger readers'. I am 76, how old do I need to be?
> Yours sincerely,
> Mr AD Cartwright

Now, I'd love to dismiss Mr Cartwright as narrow-minded or, at his age, out of touch. It would be so very easy to simply ignore him. But I can't. Because Mr Cartwright is possibly a grandfather. And as a grandfather, he's definitely a Gatekeeper.

Despite what you think you may know about the world of children's and teenage books, we are not all frightened by the big bad wolf or the troll under the bridge (and if you ask me, Lord Voldemort was just given bad press). What keeps us awake at night, what makes us rewrite and redraft and redraft and rewrite, what we're terrified of finding lurking beneath our beds when the lights go out, are the gatekeepers.

It's all about access. Young people accessing books – writers accessing their readers.

Unlike many adult readers, the majority of young readers don't buy books. They are given books as gifts, they have books forced on them in the classroom, or they borrow books from a library. I may write a novel with an ideal reader in mind, perhaps thirteen or fourteen years old, but before my book reaches my reader it will be confronted, challenged and vetted at several stages – approved or not by the gatekeepers.

There are obviously the publishers and editors – and it goes without saying that all writers need to keep them onside, but they have been known to be a disappointingly timid bunch when it comes to the more provocative children's books. There are also the librarians, the majority of whom I've found to be brilliant, knowledgeable and passionate about children's books. But then there are those who bring a personal agenda to their shelves …. Next are teachers, who often unfortunately have much less knowledge or passion for current children's books and who can decide against using a particular title in their classroom. And of course there are the parents and grandparents, who on the whole have the least amount of knowledge about children's books – except for the books they read when they were young. 'You know, the *nice* ones?'

If any one of these people takes the slightest offence, if the book cannot successfully navigate these gatekeepers, then somewhere along the way a gate closes shut. That book shall not pass! And my ideal reader may never discover that the book I wrote with them in mind even exists. It's also possible I may never discover a gate has been closed either. So often these gates ease shut with a whisper, rarely ever with a clang.

So what is it that the gatekeepers are keeping their beady eyes out for? Which blips on their radar are indecent Exocets primed ready to explode the sweet nature of the nearest unsuspecting youngster? Well, there's the 'F-bomb' for one. Language is often the biggest complaint – as Mr Cartwright points out in his letter. And I do, yes, freely admit to using the F-word twice in my 68,000-word novel. But I also feel Mr Cartwright is showing his age here. I don't think he's taken into account that all language, even profanity, evolves. Sexual swear words have lost much of their power with the younger generation. The vast majority of young people don't give a fuck about the F-word. They don't use it to offend each other; they use it to offend their elders. So if I cut that word, for whose sake is it that I'm doing censoring? My readers', or the gatekeepers'?

This immediately brings into focus one of the great dilemmas of the teen fiction writer: Do I mirror the lives of my teenage readers no matter how distasteful, or do I attempt to teach them some kind of 'better way'? Many gatekeepers believe books for young people should be worthy, character building, educational. It's a flawed argument I'll come back to.

But from sexual swear words to ... sex. Here's a topic that can get the gatekeepers not only closing the gate but also melting down the key, as I've personally discovered with a book called *Losing It*. It is an anthology that I put together for Andersen Press in the UK, published in 2010. It contains eight different authors, eight original stories, all tackling the same tricky subject of first sexual experience. I was invited into a school in Scotland to give a book talk to a group of 15 year-old students, and the session had been arranged three months in advance, but the week before I was due to visit the school I received an email asking me not to talk about *Losing It*. I promised I wouldn't read from the book, I promised I wouldn't perform it, but I said I'd like to mention it because, you know, it was my most recent book and maybe .... But, no.

I called the school up and spoke to the head teacher, tried to explain that the book wasn't a 'How To' guide or even a biology lesson. The contributing authors included Carnegie Medal winners, a UK Children's Laureate – established writers who handled the subject matter with great care and sensitivity. But, no. The head, who did seem genuinely concerned, read aloud the blurb on the back cover. He didn't need to; I knew what it said, because I'd written it. He said going by the blurb he didn't feel the book was suitable for his school. 'You've not read any of the stories?' I asked. 'Maybe if you read the stories you'd ...' But, no.

He told me his biggest worry was the parental reaction to having this kind of book on the school library's shelves. I asked him: what kind of book did he mean? He read me the blurb a second time. But it hadn't changed from his first reading. So I gave up and said I felt it best to cancel my visit.

He told me he was sorry I felt that way, but after our discussion admitted he agreed. He finished by explaining that they were a Catholic school and as such – and this is where I will quote him directly – 'we will only teach lessons about love and sex from the moral perspective of the Catholic faith'. That hurt. Was he calling me immoral? After I'd put the phone down I suddenly wished I'd said: 'The book isn't meant to teach lessons. That's not why it was written.' I tried to phone him back to say so. But he was too busy to take my call.

I also wished I'd thought to ask about his anxiety over the parental reaction. He hadn't once said he was concerned how the book may affect his students. His main concern was pissed-off parents. I wish I'd asked: for whose sake was my book banned?

Here's the rub: If I wrote novels for adults and someone took umbrage at what I'd written they'd call me 'distasteful', maybe 'offensive'. But as a writer for children and teenagers, I get accused of 'corrupting' the readers. It's a strong and worrying distinction.

Since that phone conversation I've learned of a second school that has banned *Losing It* from their library – and there are rumours that more may follow suit. This second school, in my home of Edinburgh, is unfortunately another Catholic school. I say unfortunately because these bannings don't seem to be due to offensive language or the subject of sex itself, but because the book doesn't conform to a particular worldview or philosophy. Do these schools only want their students to read approved, sanctioned, authorised books? Unfortunately it seems they do. But approved by whom? Authorised by whom?

There does seem to be a stealthy and silent censorship when it comes to children's books. I've always believed reading is about opening your mind, about learning empathy, about looking at the world from stranger's point of view. All notions I believe should be front and centre when writing for young people. So am I really claiming certain books get banned or censored because they make young people think *too much*? Are we scared they'll not think the way we want them to if they read the wrong book? Do we not trust young people who can think for themselves? I mean, it's one hell of a conspiracy theory ….

I recommend you browse the American Library Association's list of challenged books, you'll find it on their website. Every year the ALA publishes the top 100 most challenged books and the reasoning behind the challenges. *Bridge to Terabithia* written by Katherine Paterson, challenged because 'death is central to the plot' and it 'encourages disrespect of adults'. *James and the Giant Peach* by Roald Dahl, challenged because of 'profanity' and because it 'encourages disrespect of adults'. *Harriet the Spy* by Louise Fitzhugh, challenged because it 'teaches children to lie, spy, talk back to adults and curse.' *How To Eat Fried Worms* by Thomas Rockwell, challenged because it 'encourages children to engage in antisocial behaviour' (at a guess, frying worms, and then eating them). *A Light in the Attic* by Shel Silverstein, challenged because it 'promotes disrespect' and more specifically one of the illustrations 'might encourage children to smash plates so they don't have to dry the dishes'.

The list goes on and on. And I'll ask this one last time: for whose sake would these books be banned? Somewhere a gatekeeper has become concerned that a book could undermine their implied authority or set a child off along a path of which they do not approve. Meaning, a gate has been closed and there are children who may never know these books even exist. Access denied.

In many of the book protests I've encountered the implication seems to be that the supposedly wrong type of book could corrupt, not only the minds of children, but society as a whole. And yet if this were true, wouldn't someone have spotted the correlation between reading 'challenged' books and criminal behaviour? Surely our prisons must be brimming over with the grown-up readers of banned books?

It appears the opposite is true. I'm yet to hear of a convicted criminal who acknowledges with a heavy heart that his unlawful behaviour was influenced by *James and the Giant Peach*. A survey conducted by the UK's National Literacy Trust in 2008 discovered that 70% of pupils who have been permanently excluded from school have difficulties in basic literacy skills, while 25% of young offenders have reading skills below those of the average seven-year-old. These troubled youngsters would unfortunately struggle to read any children's book, never mind a challenging one.

Young people need good books. Actually, they need *great* books – the *best* books. Here's the thing that's so wonderful for me as a teen-fiction author: the readers. Teenagers are such a wonderfully open-minded audience. Ask yourself: when was the last time you read a book you didn't want to read? Not only read it but studied it, dissected it, took it apart sentence by sentence and wrote essays about it? It's so rare for us as adults to read anything we don't care to. We read novels that bolster our political views and confirm our beliefs and make us feel secure in what we already know we know. It's not often we genuinely challenge ourselves with our reading. Yet every day at school teenagers may find themselves in the situation where, not only are they forced to read a novel that challenges their views and beliefs, but they also then have to study it with enough discipline to be able to pass an exam.

And here I am, an adult kicking off this debate, but let's be honest, I don't expect any of you to change my mind on any part of this subject. As a forty-year-old, I'll argue to change *your* mind because me, I'm already pretty satisfied with what I think and what I believe, thank you very much. But if I was a fourteen-year-old, I'd still be figuring out exactly what it is I think I know. I'd be arguing not to change your mind, but to discover my own. Reading at that age is an exploration and hopefully a discovery of who you are, where you fit in and what you aspire to be. What an exhilarating, inspiring, challenging audience to write for!

Perhaps this is the reason some worry that the 'adult' literary novel is stagnating. I can't help but get the impression that in the adult world it's often a case of writers writing for themselves, and for people just like them. Where's the challenge in that? We teen fiction writers don't write for ourselves. Because we're not kids anymore. We have an audience and we have to be much more inventive with our fiction for them. Please, go read David Almond, MT Anderson, Aidan Chambers, Jack Gantos, John Green, Margo Lanagan, Patrick Ness, Meg Rosoff – a few examples among many. The adult novel may well be in trouble, but the teenage novel is flourishing.

Something I would say about writers for young people is that, always conscious of the gatekeepers, we do a heck of a lot of self-censoring. And perhaps the best kids' writers are the ones who see it as a skill, as part of the craft. They are able to successfully navigate the gatekeepers without losing any of the power, potency or intention of their writing. And most importantly, without patronising the readers. I've seen teen-fiction novels fail to reach their audience because the gatekeepers have barred the way, and I've seen others fail because young readers have found the book to be weak or patronising. I'm beginning to believe self-censorship is a valuable skill or talent a writer for young people needs to attain.

Before I finish I feel I must mention age-banding which has yet again raised its ugly head in the UK – the idea of putting an age certification on the cover of books, similar to movies and computer games. It's a notion Mr Cartwright might buy into, at least he'd know exactly how old he needed to be before a librarian or teacher or parent would allow him to read my book. But age-banding is a notion the majority of the UK-based children's authors have fought against these past few years because that number on the book's cover would just become another gatekeeper by proxy.

I believe young people should be allowed access to books tackling subjects which even we adults find unpalatable. If a child or teenager lives in a world where bullying, racism, suicide, faith, love, sex, terrorism are all everyday concerns, should we really be banning them from gaining knowledge of these issues? If a young reader is granted some access to that world from the relative safety of a novel, it could help them towards getting their heads around the issue long before they are forced to encounter such a thing in real life. These issues never get age-banded in the real world after all. Are we committing a disservice to the next generation under the guise of protection?

Back when I was a fourteen-year-old wannabe writer I witnessed abuse, I encountered drugs, I lived in a nation rocked and rocked again by IRA terrorism, I was an inventive swearer, I fell in love and I lost my virginity. All the while I was repeatedly told, the golden rule if I wanted to be a real writer, was to write about what I knew. But I didn't want to distress my parents or displease my teachers by admitting my true knowledge, so I wrote ghost stories instead. I remember thinking there seemed to be little point in writing books that none of my friends would be allowed to read.

On taking offence

'Censorship is unavoidable,' remarked the Chinese writer **Xi Chuan** in Edinburgh, 'because wherever you have taboos – historical, religious, social, political – there is censorship. It is everywhere, it is in the air.' In other words, the banning of books, or the subtle restriction of access to them, is a cultural phenomenon as well as a governmental one. It is often a matter of what one's fellow citizens view as acceptable, what they are prepared to stomach in the name of free speech. And of course a protest against the written word does not require a majority of one's fellow citizens. It can be a noisily outraged minority.'

    John Kampfner, speaking in Jaipur, raised a concern about 'how we deal with cultural sensitivities. I see a worrying phenomenon, which is the public's desire to raise the right to take offence to the level almost of a human right.' **Shoma Chaudhury**, speaking on the same panel, expounded on that phenomenon in relation to her home country – and drew a distinction between voluntary and involuntary cultural exposure. 'I am extremely worried about the status of freedom of expression in India. As a society we must assert the right to hurt people's sentiments. As Tim Garton Ash has said, we should respect the believer but not the beliefs. We must have the right to mock each other's beliefs, to question each other's beliefs. I am a freedom absolutist. There can be no substitute for the freedom of speech. When we talk about freedom of speech we are talking about two things. One is cultural production: cinema, art, music, theatre; in that realm there should be absolutely no restrictions, because if you don't want to engage with it that freedom lies with you. The much more complicated arena is about public discourse: if someone is giving a speech to a large public gathering, or if there is an advertisement or a hoarding that I cannot ignore on my way to work, that is intrusive into my presence, then that is different because I can't exercise choice.'

If Chaudhury worried about accidental or unwilling exposure to potential offence, **Keith Gray**, in his keynote speech, had described an almost opposite situation: the danger that a silent string of nixers and naysayers can keep young people from exposure to good and useful books. These opposites overlap, because the strident, willfully offended fundamentalists (of whatever stripe – Islamist, Christian-evangelical, sexually mono-dimensional ...) are almost certainly not representative of the views of society as a whole, and neither are Gray's gatekeepers. The kind of outrage that leads to cultural censorship is never a reflection of a broad consensus, of democratically agreed norms regarding what may be written and what can be read.

Nicola Morgan, speaking in Kuala Lumpur, linked the question of children's books to the earlier discussion of self-censorship. 'At first I thought, I'm not censored, am I?' she said. 'Then I remembered that as a children's writer I am censored all the time in my writing. Aren't we all censored all the time right from when our parent's say "Don't say that", or "You mustn't ask an adult their age" (these things are different in every society). There are constraints on us as humans in society that we have to live with. And as a writer for children I have to do that very much. I am entirely comfortable with that – perhaps because as a UK writer, I don't feel that there is anything I can't talk about in my teenage fiction. Everything we write is self-censored in the sense that we are selecting and deselecting, choosing to write certain things, and not to write all the other words that we could have done.'

Morgan added that 'this is completely different from the situation where you are afraid of being arrested,' – but one might wonder whether the process she was describing was censorship in any sense. Choosing what to write and what not to, what to keep and what to cut, is surely part of the writer's craft, an essential element of the storyteller's technique. When a sculptor chisels away at a block of marble, is he in a meaningful sense 'censoring' the scraps of stone that fall to the floor? Of course not: by being chipped away and discarded they are contributing to the finished work of art. Editing is not censorship – not when it is done by the writer, nor when it is done by a writer's publishing house. Yet some of the writers taking part in the global Conference saw their own publishers as potential censors, because they tend to ask successful writers always to deliver more of the same. Several people made the point that in a capitalist economy, the money-making imperative tends to stifle experimentation and creativity, because these things always represent a commercial risk. Publishers see books primarily as 'product', and are unwilling to invest time and effort in unquantifiable or unpredictable wares.

Alan Bissett had said in passing that a writer's relationship with the publisher was more in the nature of a negotiation – meaning that a clever writer writes the book that he wants in a manner that he knows will appeal to his publisher. Patrick Ness agreed, and said that he didn't mind this compromise at all. Some delegates, while perfectly happy with their publishers, made a censor of the more ephemeral and shifty concept of 'the market'. Because when badly written but easily digested fiction goes supernova, it has a doubly deleterious effect: it pushes serious books to the periphery, starving them of publicity and their authors of a living wage; and at the same time it coarsens and debases the tastes of the readership. The result is a vicious circle in which, eventually, only a tiny proportion of readers are interested in literature or equipped to read it. Lourd de Veyra, speaking in Kuala Lumpur, said that this state of affairs had already arrived in his home country, the Philippines. 'When it comes to fiction, novels, poetry, the audience is super-insubstantial,' he said. 'Writers are read by other writers, and the literary scene has become incestuous.' This is surely the censor's dream: a situation in which it is no longer necessary to police literature and writers, because no-one want to read books any more.

Jonathan Bastable (ed.)

A death penalty for thought

by Emmanuel Dongala
Keynote, Brazzaville, February 2013

'In traditional Africa, when you visit a village, does anyone ever take you to the hut of the opposition after having taken you to the chief? No! In our African tradition, there is only one chief!' That is how Zaire's Marshal Mobutu justified the censorship of writers and journalists as well as the rejection of any form of opposition. But before coming back to the censorship of writers in Africa, which is the main theme of this article, I will start with a general overview of censorship.

The Robert dictionary of the French language defines censorship as 'the act, demanded by the authority, of examining literary works, shows and publications before authorising their release'. Even if the definition is correct, I am not happy with it. I much prefer Victor Hugo's definition; after all, he fell victim to implacable censorship for his great work *Les Misérables*. To him, 'censorship is the death penalty of thoughts'. By quoting Victor Hugo, I wanted to show from the start that censorship has been practised one way or another all over the world, even in those countries that pride themselves on being models of democracy. Censorship has a long history. As early as 387 BC, Plato banned poets from his Republic, and then suggested that Homer shouldn't be read by immature readers.

If some books hadn't been written, our modern civilisation wouldn't be what it is today, and it is hard to believe these books we now consider essential once fell victim to censorship. I'll let you work out your own list of favourites.

Today, states are careful about their image and censors no longer act like ignoramuses, they no longer organise *Fahrenheit 451* book burnings (although when it comes to Salman Rushdie's *Satanic Verses* …).The approach is more subtle. Often, it isn't the state authority that bans books, but local pressure groups. This is particularly true of the United States, where the federal government hasn't officially banned books since 1960, after the Federal Appeal Court overturned the ban on the publication and distribution of Lawrence's *Lady Chatterley's Lover*. However, at local level, community or religious groups, the so-called guardians of public morals, often bring pressure to bear to ensure that books are taken off public libraries' shelves. In order to raise awareness of these practices, the American Library Association sponsors the 'Banned Books Week' each year in September. During that week, books or lists of books that were banned or challenged at some point in the past are displayed in libraries. The mind boggles when you see on those lists books that shaped America, like *The Adventures of Huckleberry Finn* by Mark Twain, *Beloved* by Toni Morrison, *The Catcher in the Rye* by JD Salinger, *Of Mice and Men* by John Steinbeck, *Moby Dick* by Herman Melville, to name but a few. The main reasons given by these groups for banning books are: explicit sex scenes, offensive language and texts unsuited to age group.

In France, books and writers are no longer officially subjected to censorship either. However, certain recent events give us food for thought. Remember Robert Millet, who wrote *A Literary Eulogy for Anders Breivik*, an abominable cold-blooded criminal who killed 77 people in Norway in 2011. The book wasn't banned, but, whether rightly or wrongly, because of press and peer pressure, the writer had to resign from his post in the Gallimard publishing house's reading committee. Another example is provided by Frédéric Mitterrand, French minister of culture, who decided to remove French author Céline from a list of personalities to be remembered at an annual national ceremony in 2011 because of his antisemitic past.

What about censorship of writers in Africa? I don't know the detailed situation of every country, but globally the fate of writers at the start of the second decade of the twenty-first century is much better than it was in the late 1990s. Unlike journalists, who are still arrested, imprisoned or persecuted, very few writers are currently in prison for their work. This hasn't always been the case. The worst period for writers started in 1970, a dozen years after the move to independence, and ended in the late 1990s, a few years before the advent of national conferences, 'African springs' of sorts. I would like to illustrate my point by taking a few of the many authors who were persecuted during that time.

Remember Ngugi Wa Thiong'o who was arrested and detained in 1971 because his play written in Kikuyu was such a success in rural areas that it caused panic among Kenyan authorities. Remember Cameroon's Mongo Beti, who had the honour if I may say so of seeing his book *Main Basse sur le Cameroun* (*The Rape of Cameroon*) banned in Cameroon and France. Think of Malawi's poet Jack Mapanje, who was imprisoned in 1977 for four years by the administration of President Hastings Banda for his collection *Of Chameleons and Gods*. His case became a *cause célèbre*. Organisations that fight for freedom of expression, such as Amnesty International, took up his cause. And famous writers such as Wole Soyinka protested for his release. Harold Pinter gave a public reading of the forbidden poems outside the Malawian High Commission in London. Both Pinter and Soyinka would become recipients of the Nobel Prize for literature. A more dramatic example is writer and playwright Ken Saro Wiwa, who was hanged in 1995 by General Abacha's regime. In fact, in his eulogy to that writer, Harold Pinter cried out that 'murder is the most brutal form of censorship'. Finally, remember the fate of the most famous Mauritanian writer, Téne Youssouf Guéye, who was left to die in a Mauritanian prison in 1988. It is during that sad period that many writers, including very famous ones, decided to go into exile.

Journalists were subjected to censorship after the move to independence. Leaders wanted to enjoy their newfound authority without any opposition after the withdrawal of colonial powers. They saw daily news commentators as a threat because the stories they told were different from the authorities' propaganda. As for writers, they were long ignored, sometimes even despised, not out of leniency but because of a misunderstanding. Leaders took for granted the commonplace statements that books didn't have any impact in Africa because most of the population was illiterate, that books were written in a foreign language and were expensive, and that when given the choice between culture and food, Africans generally chose their belly. But that was only partly true and they forgot about the way communities work. If one person bought a book, that book changed hands, and ten or twenty people read it. I bear witness to that. Those who read it commented on it, and those who hadn't built on those comments and added their own. In other words, oral tradition, an important feature of African communities, took over the written word by giving it a threatening dimension in the eyes of the authorities. This is how books were banned by censorship commissions without being read and writers were arrested and detained not because of what they had written but because of what was being said about those works.

When debating the issue of censorship, it is important not to overlook the complicity of some intellectuals. The role of European and American intellectuals who defended the worst crimes of Stalin or of fascism is well documented (names such as Céline and Ezra Pound come to mind), but the role of African intellectuals who suppressed their colleagues' work is little known. The quote I gave by Marshal Mobutu at the start of this article doesn't come from nowhere, but from the teachings of a philosophy called 'Authenticity'. This philosophy advocated a return to an 'authentic African tradition' which never existed in the first place. It was put together by academics and intellectuals, including writers and journalists.

In Congo-Brazzaville, which is where I am from, censorship was created by true-blood Marxist intellectuals, again including journalists and writers. They imposed a single party and a dogma according to which 'the party rules the state'. Every writer, every artist had to agree with the standards imposed by that single party, otherwise works were banned and writers sent to prison if needed.

Take Sony Labou Tansi's great novel *Life and a Half*: I am not alone in saying that its impact on francophone African literature was similar to James Joyce's *Ulysses* on twentieth-century literature. That book featured in the list of banned books, as well as Tansi's *The Shameful Work*. And who, even among experts of African literature, has even heard of *Chômeur à Brazzaville* (*Unemployed in Brazzaville*) published by NEA Editions in 1977? This wonderful novel is one of the first to mention the harsh reality of daily city life and the population's disillusion after independence. Because it was banned, not only is the novel utterly unknown today, but even the name of its writer is forgotten (for your information, his name is Pierre Biniakounou and I know nothing whatsoever about him).

Allow me to digress and talk about me. My collection of short stories *Jazz and Palm Wine, and Other Stories* ended up on that famous black list. For reasons still unknown to me, I wasn't arrested or detained, but friends and family were summoned by State Security and questioned, so my scheming plots could be found out. Copies of the book were taken off library shelves, even at the local French Cultural Centre. Even stranger, the head of a bookshop called the Evangelic Bookshop of the Congo was arrested because he was selling copies of my book, even though he hadn't ordered or read it, it just happened to be among a list of newly published books he received automatically.

However, during that period when writers, journalists and artists were arrested as a matter of routine, it was comforting to see how quickly readers understood the undertones of writings that censors thought harmless. And readers even taught writers how to manipulate official propaganda and turn it into ridicule.

One day Sony Labou Tansi told me how he managed to get rid of security agents tasked with watching the rehearsal of one of his plays with his company Le Rocado Zulu Théâtre. As soon as the agents arrived, he'd ask the actor on stage to repeat the same movements and the same sentences ten, twenty times around. After an hour, sometimes less, the agents who were bored to death started yawning and ended up leaving the place well before the end of the rehearsal. Essentially they wondered how something so boring could be subversive. After a few weeks, their visits became rarer and they ended up not coming back at all.

As for me, I'm a chemist. In chemistry, some molecules, like our two hands, are not superimposable on their mirror image. Where one molecule rotates a polarised light beam to the left, the other rotates it to the right. You then refer to left-handed or right-handed molecules. This notion is fundamental for life molecules. To ridicule censors, I programmed a much advertised academic conference mysteriously entitled 'Of the notion of left and right'. They fell into the trap. Just imagine, the author of the banned collection of *Jazz and Palm Wine and Other Stories* was going to say who belonged to a Right- or Left-wing ideology in the country, when this was the sole prerogative of the party's Political Bureau! Given the number of agents who came to my conference, I have to admit I was proud of having turned several members of the political police force of the country into organic chemistry enthusiasts. As you can see, even during the darkest years of censorship, we still managed to have some fun.

One of the great philosophers when it comes to freedom of thought, Voltaire, wrote that 'it is characteristic of vicious censorship to give credence to the very opinions it seeks to annihilate'. How very true! Once, in

Brazzaville, I was stopped by a policeman for driving through a red light that clearly wasn't working. I knew the drill and didn't want to waste my time so I immediately took out my driver's licence together with a 2000F note, and handed them out to him. He discreetly hid away the note, pretended to look at my driver's licence, and all of a sudden his face lit up when he saw my name. A big smile appeared on his face. 'Are you the one who wrote *Jazz and Palm Wine*? Do you know it's banned? I secretly read it. It was great! Keep on writing great stuff like that for us'. He took the note out of his pocket and gave it back to me together with the driver's licence. 'Good luck' he said, and he turned away to get back to his lookout. I couldn't believe my own eyes. Coming from a cop in the street, what a tribute for a banned writer!

Today, in Africa, writers are no longer routinely arrested, but that isn't due to a sudden kindness on the part of leaders. It is because writers have never stopped fighting, either openly, or by subterfuge, and when they had to go into exile, they didn't keep quiet. In the end, they managed to get the idea across that their word isn't any less legitimate than the authorities'. Today, when you re-read novels such as *Bound to Violence*, *The Suns of Independence*, *Life and a Half*, *A Man of the People*, *The Laughing Cry*, *Unemployed in Brazzaville* – and the list isn't exhaustive – it is incredible to think that writers were able to anticipate the future of their communities thanks to their imagination and their creativity. The very imagination and creativity they refused to curb in the face of so much censorship and so much repression.

Sousveillers and fifty-centers

With a respectful nod to the Burmese dissident Ma Thida, who was sitting by his side, the Filipino writer **Lourd de Veyra** made this strange confession at the Conference in Kuala Lumpur. 'Many of us fantasise about the notion of jail or a charge of sedition, about the authorities clamping down on us in an Orwellian manner,' he said. 'But no government is quaking at the knees because of a novel. No poem will bring down a government.'

It is undoubtedly true that governments worldwide are now less afraid of the printed word than they are of the glimmering screens of the laptop, the tablet and the smartphone. These days, the internet represents the real threat to power, and activists and authorities alike know it. The Arab Spring could not have happened without the viral spread of news and information over the web; popular protests movements such as those that have filled vast urban squares in Kiev and Moscow would be impossible without the swift, subversive organisational capability of social media.

In Toronto, the Chinese novelist **Chan Koonchung** followed de Veyra in invoking Orwell – but unlike de Veyra he was in deadly earnest. He was discussing the Chinese Firewall, the immense effort of the Beijing government to control and delimit what Chinese citizens can access on the internet. 'In the novel *Nineteen Eighty Four* there is huge scarcity – the protagonist cannot even find a razor blade.' he said. 'That is not the case in China, where there is abundance. On the Chinese version of Amazon there are thousands of titles to be bought – so how would you even know what had been censored out? Less than 5% of netizens even try to climb over the Chinese Firewall. And yet on the Chinese equivalents to Twitter and Facebook, something you were reading five minutes ago can suddenly be deleted. In this way the young people who use the internet see that there is a Big Brother watching. The authorities meanwhile get the internet providers to police the content. They employ nannies to trawl the net and delete things. There are estimates that between 50,000 and 100,000 people do this work. They are called 'the fifty-centers', because they are paid piece-work style, per deletion. Often they over-delete, erasing all reference to a subject or person. That too gives the younger generation a little awareness. I am not sure that they know what to do with it, but they know that they are not totally free.'

John Kampfner, speaking in Jaipur, made the point that it is not only authoritarian countries that are worried. 'In so-called developed countries, and in the emerging powers too, there is an almost desperate attempt to control the internet. [We are witnessing] the state's backlash, the state's attempt to introduce legislation around the world. In the UK we saw off (albeit, I think temporarily) an appalling piece of legislation dubbed 'the snooper's charter', which would have given the state unbridled powers to require internet service providers to store all internet traffic or email traffic or text messaging for a year and to hand over whatever is wanted not just by the security services, but by local authorities, the fire service, pretty much any authority. There is no ideal jurisdiction, no paradigm for free expression, but some countries are resisting this urge more than others.'

Marina Mahathir, in Kuala Lumpur, said that cowardice on the part of editors is making the situation worse, that fear of the backlash can prevent valid discussion from finding its way into print or onto a news-led website. 'The two things that editors worry about are politics and religion. And now there is the relatively new idea of 'insulting' a religion – on the internet, on a blog, or on Facebook. It's very vague, strange – and scary.' **Nicola Morgan**, speaking in the same discussion, said that ancient English acts of parliament were being deployed against free speech on the internet – like maces and battle-axes wielded to smash blinking web-servers and chop through fibre-optic cables. 'It is inconceivable in the UK that a novel or a poem would be banned for its content, but what we have in the UK are very strict libel laws, so when you are writing non-fiction – a blog, say – you have to be incredibly aware of what you can and can't say. And I think it's right to say that the libel laws in Britain are more stringent than in pretty much any country – to the extent that if you are accused of murder the prosecution has to prove that you are guilty, whereas if you are accused of libel then you, the defendant, have to prove that you are innocent. Our libel laws really can threaten freedom of speech.'

For **Orlando Figes**, historian of the Russian revolution, 'the founding principles of freedom of speech' were the key issue. He felt that in Russia the framework of free speech was largely absent – and, as in England, the problem boiled down to old habits. 'Firstly, there should be a marketplace of ideas; and secondly freedom of speech must underpin democracy. I am concerned with a post-totalitarian and (now) authoritarian state in which the underpinning of free speech is very questionable. Before you can have free speech, you must have people who are able to think independently. A poll done in 2010 showed that most Russians were quite happy with the ownership of media by state or quasi-state organisations. They were perfectly aware that there was, say, an imbalance in the presentation of the main candidates in presidential elections, but they thought that was OK, because to them the nature of television is to represent order and security. So that's a problem that comes before we get to the free exchange of ideas.'

But for **Lourd de Veyra**, the real problem of internet censorship remained the Orwellian one that he identified at the start: the fact that anyone can now speak to anyone else also means that everyone can watch everyone else, and of course denounce them in the blink of an eye. 'We are no longer talking about surveillance from above, but "sousveillance" – which comes from below. There are little eyes, anonymous eyes, becoming Big Brother. Big Brother is us.'

Jonathan Bastable (ed.)

The whale on the rock

by Larissa Behrendt
Keynote, Melbourne, August 2013

At the end of Kate Grenville's novel *The Secret River* there is a powerful image of a colonial mansion, the new home of ex-convict turned wealthy land-owner William Thornhill and his family, being built on rock that has a sacred Aboriginal carving of a whale on it. The house represents the wealth of the new settlers, those who have conquered the Australian landscape, made their fortune and built their future here. The foundations of the house are the Aboriginal people and their culture.

The power of Grenville's metaphor is that she preserves the Aboriginal presence and connection to land. It is not destroyed in the face of the oncoming colonisation; it is buried. Although it lies hidden, one day, when the civilisation eventually crumbles, the rock with its carved etching, will once more be revealed, the ancient connection to land continuing.

It is easy, when thinking of censorship, to think first of legal definitions. But Grenville's image evokes a broader, more complex reflection on the concepts of silencing, one that goes beyond the arbitrary and shifting concepts within the dominant legal system. What lies hidden beneath and unseen – like the foundations under a stone house – is also silenced.

Winners vanquish losers; we all know they write history. But each instance of conquest has its own historical peculiarities, its own legacies. And within those historical distinct events and repercussions are a multitude of experiences, the plethora of stories. Some of those stories triumph and become canonical. Others are suppressed, still handed down from parent to child and transmitted amongst subgroups and subcultures, but outside of the dominant national narrative.

The capacity of Indigenous people to tell their own stories was impeded in several complicating ways as part of the process of the colonisation of Australia. As an oral culture, Aboriginal and Torres Strait Islander cultures relied upon transmission from generation to generation through stories, ceremony, dance, music and art. The high mortality rate from introduced diseases, the processes of dispossession, dislocation and relocation, and the policy of removing Aboriginal children from their families, are all factors that made the continuing transmission of these oral traditions difficult, especially in the areas where colonisation was most aggressive. And secondly, while the removal of Aboriginal children was supposed to give them the advantages of dominant culture, education levels were appalling and Aboriginal young people, no matter what their talents, were earmarked for manual labour. Boys were to work on cattle stations; girls were to work as domestic servants. Among all of the insidious ways a people can be colonised, denying them the tools that allow them to communicate in the imposed and dominant culture is one of the most effective in disenfranchising, disempowering and continually marginalising them.

Literacy rates in Australia have improved gradually but even today there is a large gap between the literacy rates of Indigenous and non-Indigenous students. The gap between Indigenous and non-Indigenous students emerges early. Non-Indigenous students out-perform Indigenous students in benchmark tests for reading, writing and numeracy in Year 3 and Year 5. By Year 7, the gap has widened, even more so for numeracy and competency in science. As Indigenous children get older, the gap continues to widen. Indigenous students are 2.2% of the population in the age groups that can engage in higher education yet Indigenous students make up only 1.3% of student numbers. While 82% of all Australian students enter tertiary education through their previous educational attainments, only 46% of Indigenous students enter university this way. The gaps in their earlier education mean that Indigenous students often have to do additional studies to be able to enter university. It is not a matter of the students not being clever enough for tertiary studies but they were denied the shortest pathway and come to university studies later in life and through a more circuitous route.

The resilience of living cultures must frustrate those hell-bent on assimilation or achieving a cultural hegemony. Attempts to assimilate – no matter how extreme or how subtle – often have the opposite effect. They further bind an identified and persecuted group through a shared suffering and its associated experiences and trauma. Discrimination only succeeds in reinforcing difference, in testing attachment to culture and reinforces a sense of identity.

Attempts to reintroduce marginalised voices into the dominant narrative are not always welcome. My grandmother was removed under the policy of removing Aboriginal children from their parents. Her experiences as a ward of the state – and my father's childhood in an orphanage – inspired my first novel, *Home*. Growing up, I was surrounded by other children, well-meaning but innocently ignorant of these historical practices of separating Aboriginal children from their families as part of a policy of assimilation. Their views were sometimes crudely racist and often lacking in empathy. I had always thought that if Australian children were taught this history, it would increase the understanding of the issues facing Indigenous people. Even if it would not win people over to the Indigenous point of view, at least it would explain why Indigenous people face the issues we face and why we have the political agenda we have.

But the response to the publication of the *Bringing them Home* report – the detailed national investigation into the extent and impact of the children removal policy – was instructive and sobering. The official response was to dismiss the report by saying that 'only one in ten' Indigenous people were removed, that the term 'cultural genocide' was too emotive and that, whatever the report concluded, the motivation for the removal of children was often done with the best of intentions and for the best interests of the children involved.

Aboriginal poet, novelist and historian Tony Birch wrote of this response to the *Bringing them Home* report:

> Indigenous communities across Australia have become the memory bank of white Australia's violence by proxy. It is time for white Australia to take over that responsibility. Perhaps it is time to make an ethical withdrawal of responsibility. Such a need has become more acute in recent years, with the outcome of the Human Rights and Equal Opportunities *Bringing Them Home* report providing an opportunity for white Australia to take ownership of its colonial past in a more than selective manner. Unfortunately the backlash against *Bringing Them Home* has

been more substantive than any acceptance of, and responsibility for, the colonial violence that it has provided testament to. It was the delivery of the report that motivated the most ferocious elements of the History War; an orchestrated campaign conducted by the right in Australia against the legitimacy of Indigenous memory.

Birch's observations resonate with me and are a reminder that the 'history wars' or 'culture wars' that waged amongst academics and writers of opinion pieces may have argued the semantics and the numbers in the halls of universities and on the pages of broadsheets but, like the stone hidden under William Thornhill's house, the lived experience of Aboriginal and Torres Strait Islander people affected by those polices remained unchanged by those debates. The ideological battle was not really about Aboriginal history; it was about the competing narratives that non-Indigenous Australians want to tell about themselves. And this reaction, which included the official government response, showed me that I was wrong to believe that hearing the stories of people who had suffered under the removal policy would be the pathway to better understanding of Indigenous history and culture.

The response was much more complex than that. What it did show was that evidence in its most human form can be so powerful that it is simply too confronting and the easiest way to deal with it for some people is to attempt to silence it, dismiss it by falling back on to contested statistics or distract from it with semantic debates. This reaction does, however, give testament to the power of stories. The *Bringing them Home* report was littered with extracts from testimony – not just from those taken away, but from the parents, grandparents and siblings left behind. So many government reports are written after investigations, contemplation of the research and a list of sensible recommendations to address the problem to sit on shelves, gather dust and fade into the mists of bureaucratic memory. What challenged people more than any legal or historical argument made in the report, what made it so dangerous to those who felt so challenged was the power of human testimony, the power of their stories. George R. R. Martin, author of the now culturally iconic *Game of Thrones* wrote in another novel, *A Clash of Kings*, that 'when you tear out a man's tongue, you are not proving him a liar, you're only telling the world that you fear what he might say.'

The impact of the removal policy has been a strong theme through much Indigenous writing – not surprising since it formed such a large part of the contemporary Indigenous experience. Sally Morgan's *My Place* and Doris Pilkington's *Follow the Rabbit Proof Fence* are quintessential examples of this – and the response to the Philip Noyce film adapting Pilkington's book to the screen was met with a similar response to the *Bringing them Home* report from, predictably, the same quarters.

Telling stories is not just an essential part of Indigenous culture; love of stories is instinctive and primal to all human beings. So it is no surprise that there is a vibrant creative drive within the Aboriginal and Torres Strait Islander communities in Australia to continue to tell stories. The renaissance of Indigenous writing, which has been driven by writers such as Tony Birch, Alexis Wright, Ali Cobby Eckermann, Kim Scott and a pantheon of others. It has been accompanied by other Indigenous storytellers using other mediums: Stephen Page and his work through the Bangarra Dance Theatre; Wesley Enoch and his work on the stage; the rise to eminence of Indigenous art whose aesthetics point to ancient connections to country; the new wave of Indigenous film makers, including Ivan Sen and Warwick Thornton; and the establishment of National Indigenous Television Ltd. All these new technologies have been adopted for the telling of our most ancient stories.

So coming from this perspective, it might seem natural that I would blindly embrace the concept of the 'right to free speech'. But it is more complicated than that. An essential part of any rights culture and of any human rights framework is the complex balancing of rights. I believe free speech is important but, like any other right, it needs to be balanced with others, including the right to be free from racial discrimination and vilification. Where that line is drawn should be the debate of a healthy and inclusive participatory democracy. Observing the psychological and emotional scars of racism enacted as policy or disseminated through popular culture and political narrative, I am wary of blanket claims of absolute rights, suspicious of extremes demanded by a dominant culture that has only championed its own interests, not those of the groups it has marginalised.

The heightened precedence given to the right of free speech against other rights is a particularly American value but also symptomatic of the way that our civil and political rights are often given precedence over economic, social and cultural rights. For marginalised and culturally distinct groups, exclusion from economic and social participation and freedom of cultural expression are perhaps valued more and seen as being of equal importance to the civil and political rights that more easily engage members of dominant cultures and political elites. Besides, the notion that any society supports the concept of free speech in an unfettered way is absurd. It is regulated, rightly, in relation to defamation and libel. It is regulated, rightly, in relation to trade practices, to ensure that consumers are not duped by unsubstantiated claims.

I find it difficult to support blanket statements about the concept of censorship. For me, the arguments about where to draw the lines in theory are slippery and contradictory. Of more interest, and of more importance, is the question of what is seeking to be censored and why. When the censorship is one where the weight of the dominant culture is used to silence dissenting views and to silence the marginalised, I think it raises a complex set of moral and ethical questions. I don't pretend to know where that line is but I believe that the balancing of the right to free speech against other rights is one of the ongoing conversations in a healthy participatory democracy. This might sound utopian but I say this as someone who is inherently suspicious of the way the dominant culture's laws sometimes draw lines. The fact that the dominant culture often gets to decide that line is often problematic. Its adjudicators are never without their own cultural bias even though they often assume that they can be objective on such matters. But I do think the discussion about where those lines are drawn needs to be an open, honest and fluid one and needs to include voices that are often marginalised within the dominant culture.

It strikes me that one of the deepest cultural differences between Indigenous culture and dominant Australian culture is around the concept of knowledge. Within the spiritual life of Indigenous societies there was a clear delineation about knowledge-holding. There were issues that were 'men's business' and 'women's business' and the concept of 'secret and sacred' knowledge, which only the custodian or the initiated were entitled to know. The concept that there is information that you are not permitted to know is one that sits uncomfortably with European intellectual tradition. It remains the case today across Australia that there is still knowledge, images, practices and artefacts that remain sacred to Aboriginal and Torres Strait Islander people and cannot be shared.

Respecting that, I do not, however, subscribe to the view that a non-Indigenous person can never write from the perspective of an Indigenous person. Writers with talent can write from any perspective. The trick is to get the authenticity – the truth – of the situation, the characters and the essence of the interaction. The challenge in crossing any divide – gender, religious, cultural – is that unless the writer can stand in the shoes of the character, can adeptly interpret the perspective, the writing will ring hollow, will ring untrue.

In this way, Indigenous writers are advantaged. They better understand, by virtue of their interaction with the dominant culture, the views from the other side of the cultural divide. It has always challenged Australian writers – even writers of great skill – to be able to interpret well the world of Indigenous people. That is not because it is impossible but just because the level of understanding needed to write authentically is so deep, that the general ignorance of Indigenous culture often makes the translation a challenge for those seeking to interpret it from the outside.

Patrick White, one of our greatest writers, meditated on the perspectives on Indigenous people within Australian culture in several of his books. He did so reflectively in *Riders of the Chariot* and *Voss*. But he was much less successful in his novel inspired by the shipwreck of Eliza Fraser in the 1860s, *A Fringe of Leaves*. During the heroine's time amongst Aborigines, she becomes closer to her more natural state and, as part of this psychological reconnection, engages in a ceremony that includes an act of cannibalism. Instead of understanding that there was no practice of cannibalism within Indigenous communities in Australia, White buys into this myth – and thus perpetuates it – but seeks to excuse it by using the act of consumption of flesh as a metaphor for our most primitive desires, the instincts our society represses. White paints the Aboriginal people in this novel in the classic noble savage role. I've argued elsewhere that the depiction of Aboriginal people in this romanticised role is as unhelpful and dangerous as the portrayal of Aboriginal people as savages.

Grenville avoids this trap in *The Secret River*. She tells the story of William Thornhill's conquest of his land and the Aboriginal people who lived there before him without romanticism. Her novel also tells the story of Aboriginal people, and she chose not to do this by creating an Indigenous character to guide us through this perspective but by telling us the same story from the unsympathetic viewpoint of a white Australian who sees Aboriginal people fearfully – fearful they will retaliate, they will fight, they will challenge. And through the eyes of such characters, she says so much with deep truth about the underlying unease which not only pervades the contemporary relationship between Aboriginal people and the dominant Australian culture, she also explains why so much unease and conflict remain amongst that dominant culture about the way in which they tell the story of their own history.

This is a deft skill, but I want to conclude by celebrating what uncensored, unselfconscious writing can achieve even when it misses the mark. Another great Australian novelist is Thomas Keneally. Within his enviable body of work sits a book, *The Chant of Jimmie Blacksmith*, written in the 1970s when Australia was confronting a new political era in its relationship with Indigenous people. Influenced by the civil rights movement in the United States, a black power movement and a land rights movement had emerged, along with a new kind of Aboriginal activist. Keneally's novel is inspired by the outlaw Jimmy Governor and explores the inevitable consequences of trapping a young man between the ambitions available to white people and the discrimination against his own black skin. What blind ambition to try to write a book about this subject matter. And in the most part, Keneally succeeds. But the portrayal of Aboriginal women seemed so one-dimensional, especially contrasted to the insights Keneally showed for Jimmie's own plight as an Aboriginal man.

That aspect of the book annoyed me in contrast but I have a great affection for both the book and the author, and for his audacity. Keneally has since written that he would write the book differently if he wrote it now. I am glad he wrote it when he did. It gave me more to think about, more to contend with, a greater slate against which to try to articulate my own views about my feminism and the intersection between my gender and my race and what that meant in contemporary Australia against this historical backdrop. Along with *A Fringe of Leaves*, Keneally gave me a book that provoked me to articulate my own views, providing me with a conversation of depth and intelligence I could find nowhere else within Australian society. That is the gift a brave, thoughtful, imaginative and uncensored writer can give.

So I don't think the territory is off-limits, but I think that the challenge for writers who want to explore that terrain is that the extent to which one must be familiar with it if coming from the position of the privileged, from a position where many of the voices will be hidden, is very difficult. And such is the skill of great writers. They translate. They interpret. They hold a mirror up. And that's why they are, when talented, so threatening.

A NATIONAL LITERATURE

Marking your territory

by Hannah McGill

Not without exception, but pretty overwhelmingly, the Conference speakers and delegates responded with suspicion to the subject heading 'A National Literature'. Rather than regarding shared geography, culture and heritage as formative creative influences that might express themselves positively, or even radically, most read the conscious assertion of national identity as at best severely limiting – and at worst sinister. Perhaps too many of these writers grew up in sight, or at least in news-media earshot, of bloody national uprisings, ethnic strife and rising fascist movements for issues of nationality to exist for them without negative trappings. Perhaps too many of them undertook tertiary education at a historical moment when post-colonial studies were fashionable to look on questions of national identity with anything but weariness. 'The literature of a nation is a mirage because the concept of nation is a mirage,' said **Kapka Kassabova** in her keynote in Brussels. 'The real task in all our lives is to find a true spiritual home.' **Miriam Toews**, speaking in Toronto, said that 'a writer is not a soldier or Olympic athlete, flying a national flag.' And **Anjali Joseph**, speaking in Cape Town, said that writers' self-selected peer group was a greater influence than 'the vertical lineage of nationality'.

If, as these writers suggest, an individual's subjective interiority, or the shared experience among a group of writers of just being writers, represent more useful and significant formative factors than any aspects of selfhood drawn from geographical or cultural experience, one might wonder: why make a conference international? Why get on planes and visit so many lands, if writers truly believe their specific cultural experience to be irrelevant to their practice? The Edinburgh World Writers' Conference could surely have featured writers from one territory only and lost no richness or diversity.

To other delegates, issues with foregrounding nationhood were more political than existential in nature. The fear of a controlling state claiming artists as its minions overshadowed any sense of national identity as a positive creative motivator or unifying – and potentially anti-authoritarian – social force. 'Nationalism and patriotism are designs of the state,' argued **Sema Kaygusuz** in İzmir, Turkey. 'The writer who is reduced to being a local representative cannot progress past being a parrot.' Anjali Joseph cautioned that definitive views of nationhood and literature could move us 'away from lived experience and into the generic'; a book ought to have a freer reach, the imagined geographical potential of 'the magical flying carpet in the Hans Christian Andersen fairy tale.' This was in fact an airborne collision of national myths: Andersen wrote of a flying trunk, while the carpet is an image drawn from his early influence, *The Arabian Nights* – but in any case, writing literature was to Joseph an attempt to communicate the incomprehensible, a project which to her 'has very little to do with national boundaries.'

Other writers saw actual dangers, as well as mere restrictions. 'The line between national and nationalist literature is very fine,' warned **Velibor Čolić** in St Malo. As Yugoslavia splintered, he explained, literature became central to the construction of a national myth – and the myths came to be read not as myth at all, but as historiography. 'This confusion between genres, between history and literature, was a tragedy,' noted Čolić. Myth took on a fatal power; storytelling became justification for bloodshed. New, consciously created national literatures, he argued, can present new dangers – and the potential for new tragedies – because they overwhelm reason.'

Irvine Welsh noted that cultural identity can define itself most clearly not in separation and self-definition, but in resistance to absorption by a colonial power. 'I see a thriving national literature in Scotland, perhaps ironically because of the country's non- (or quasi-) nation status,' he said. So is the need to self-define a symptom of cultural insecurity? As **Margie Orford** put it in Cape Town, countries have seemed to need national literatures until they achieve their independence, whereupon the idea disperses. Dominant cultures don't seem to ask themselves the question of whether they have a national literature. (Although we might query in this context the perennial search for the 'Great American Novel' – a term that has proved interestingly tenacious since being coined by John W. De Forest in 1968, and that surely represents a dominant culture endlessly seeking definition through art.)

By originating and kicking off in Scotland, a country poised at that historical moment for a referendum on independence from the United Kingdom, the Conference was well-placed to reference a culture in the throes of debating, and possibly remaking, its own identity. For some Scottish delegates, this was exactly the moment to be starry-eyed about national identity, and the deployment of literature in its construction – a situation that put them at odds with the general resistance to the foregrounding of nationhood. **Alan Bissett** backed the idea of a specific Scottish cultural identity as a positive force, arguing that 'you can't have internationalism without nationalism'. **Jenni Fagan** noted from the crowd the importance to her as a reader of having seen her own cultural experience represented through Irvine Welsh's writing – an experience that English readers growing up in Britain could take for granted a good deal more. This point was echoed by Scottish children's writer **Theresa Breslin** in Krasnoyarsk. Though she revelled in the work of Robert Louis Stevenson and JM Barrie as a child, said Breslin, 'when it came to stories set in modern times I found nothing that related to me and the circumstances in which I lived …. When I was raising my own children the situation was essentially the same. I found it difficult to find books that reflected their lives'. A spur for her own first efforts at writing, she explained, was the desire for 'stories for my children where the characters spoke as they did, and had similar life experiences'.

The desire to be understood and recognised is universal, but the yearning to surround oneself with the familiar and the similar, rather than the different, is double-edged. Does indulging it, whether in childhood or thereafter, aid in the formation of a positive national identity, or encourage cloisteredness and jingoism? **China Miéville**, in the discussion that followed Welsh's keynote in Edinburgh, made a stirring point when he questioned why either localism or universalism were desirable approaches in literature. 'Why is the aim to see our lives reflected?' he asked. 'Surely literature can also be fantastic by completely shocking and astonishing us?'

Risking, perhaps, the very 'confusion of genres' that worried Čolić, writers – Bissett among them – were vocal in the Scottish independence debate, particularly as part of the campaign for a Yes vote. The National

Collective, an organisation of pro-independence artists, made prominent efforts to attach positive associations to the idea of a separate Scottish spirit and identity and to associate the idea of an independent Scotland specifically with creative and artistic freedom and innovation. First Minister Alex Salmond actively courted the assistance of writers in creating a stirring independence narrative – which didn't stop them from occasionally straying some distance off-message. Alasdair Gray, who in his seminal 1981 novel *Lanark* queried whether Glasgow and by extension Scotland had yet secured the identity that comes with being 'imagined' by artists, raised hackles by criticising the prevalence of English 'colonists' within the Scottish arts extablishment.

Shena Mackay took things farther than is comfortable for most pro-independence activsts when she told *The Guardian* in 2011, 'I want Scotland to be Scottish through and through – I hate to hear English accents in the shops there'. (It was a mantra for the Yes campaign that being pro-independence had nothing to do with anti-Englishness or ethinic purity, but change 'Pakistani' or 'Polish' for Mackay's 'English', and just see how that looks.) James Kelman declined to participate in the Edinburgh World Writers' Conference once he noticed that it was co-organised by the British Council, a 'patronising umbrella organisation', he wrote in explanation, 'that just happens to be utterly opposed to our existence as an independent country'. Alan Bissett, in a recent polemic/poem entitled 'Vote Britain', scathingly cited Rupert Brooke's 'corner of a foreign field' (from *The Soldier*) as emblematic of the literary glorification of England to the exclusion of Scotland. In Bissett's imagined scenario, a bereaved military mother in Kirkcudbright experiences through her recollection of Brooke's specifically English poem the denial, the deliberate effacing of her specifically Scottish grief.

Kelman's objection to the British Council is founded in mistrust of and opposition to the British state –not just the desire for Scotland to be amicably separate from England that was the preferred mode of the Yes campaign. 'Why enter the lion's den to express my right not to be eaten by the lion?' he wrote of the Conference, in a piece that depicted the event as nothing less sinister than a stealth rally for English language dominance and British – that is, English – imperialism and colonisation. Bissett, however (who did attend the conference) raises by his invocation of Brooke's war poetry the point that Scottish pride in Scotland must logically co-exist with English pride in England. For if there's a grieving mother in Kirkcudbright deserving of our empathy, is there not one in Stevenage no less so? Kelman's argument might be that both of them are victims of exploitation by the upper-class English military machine. But is the English mother thereby denied a pride in her son's sacrifice, or in her nation and its culture generally, that might be willingly extended, at least by Bissett, to her Scottish counterpart? Is the cost of being a citizen of a historically dominant, colonising culture the renunciation of one's right to patriotism, or pride in one's cultural identity?

Certainly English pride is a loaded concept for most British people. Just as **Rachida Lamrabet** speaking in Brussels associated Flemish pride with prejudice, discrimination and ethnic division, so the concept of taking pride in Englishness for many has direct associations with Far-Right parties, football hooliganism and racist thuggery. The Union Jack flag remains an ambiguous symbol for many (in spite of a degree of modish reclamation during the 'Britpop' years), thanks to its forceful identification with the British National Party. The English St George flag is even more fraught, linked as it is to the Far-Right English Defence League.

It was apparent at the Conference that a sense of English patriotism sits uneasily with people who might be less inclined to question patriotic pride in Scottishness, Welshness or Irishness. And if few writers much want to claim their Englishness, whence and whither an English national literature? 'In the last forty, fifty, sixty years, the Celtic nations have thought an awful lot about our national literature,' said **Owen Sheers** – of Welsh origin, writing and living in England – at the Edinburgh conversation. 'Post-devolution, there's a conversation to be had: what is *English* writing? It seems as though the Celtic nations have a slightly more nuanced idea of what the United Kingdom is. We need an England that's asking that question too, not just through its politicians but through its writers and readers.' But to Irvine Welsh, the invisibility of an English identity spoke of dominance, not insecurity: 'Upper-class Englishness is the cultural yardstick against which all literature must be measured'. Alan Bissett was happy to declare himself as 'writing for Scotland'. Hoping to get someone to speak positively about Englishness after the Edinburgh Conference, I asked another delegate born in England to comment on his national identity, and got an uncomfortable response: 'I'm not sure I fully understand what you're driving at …. I feel no responsibility for having been born in England'.

If Scots can be 'proud' of 'writing for Scotland', must English writers consider themselves to be writing against or in spite of England, to evade the taint of fascism or imperial arrogance? What can that mean for a literary culture? The problem of claiming and celebrating a contemporary Englishness has been addressed in various forms and from various political perspectives by commentators, philosophers, pop culture figures and poets – among them Roger Scruton, Jeremy Paxman, Morrissey, Billy Bragg and Simon Armitage – but remains sticky for fiction writers. JK Rowling, whose Harry Potter series cushioned its magical elements with comfortable clichés of boarding-school life familiar from earlier eras of English children's fiction, resides in Scotland. Martin Amis, famed debater and debaser of English values, morals and habits, chose to raise his second set of children in New York, and has a prickly relationship with the British literary establishment. 'Englishness' and 'Britishness' will tend to be used interchangeably about the work of Julian Barnes, Jonathan Coe and Ian McEwan; and new generations of their compatriot writers are even less likely to assert themselves as specifically 'English', let alone proud to be so. Carol Ann Duffy, the Scottish-born, Irish-rooted poet laureate, has said 'When I go to Scotland I feel Scottish and when I go to Ireland I feel Irish .... I suppose the one thing I don't feel is English.' Writers who have reinvented national identity from a multicultural perspective, taking in the experience of immigrants and children of immigrants – Hanif Kureishi, Zadie Smith, Hari Kunzru – are safer emblems of Englishness for a politically nervous intelligentsia, because their portrayal of Englishness incorporates ambivalence and critique, and cannot be confused with that of the EDL.

Perhaps, after all, it's a question of entitlement. If you live with the benefits of being part of the dominant race in a dominant nation, you give up the consolations of aggressive national pride. Arguably, after all, you don't need it. Your battle's won. Patriotism needs an oppressor to distinguish it from dangerous triumphalism.

'Overall,' says Irvine Welsh, 'I think writers must value their independence and be very wary of being co-opted into anything governmental, whatever colour of flag is wrapped around it.' (James Kelman, an acknowledged influence on Welsh, would doubtless pull him up here on having contradicted this stance by his very participation in the Conference.) As to writing for England, there are those – Duffy as poet laureate, Andrew Motion as her recent predecessor, Frank Cottrell Boyce as scribe of the Olympics opening ceremony a third – who might be said to have embraced roles specifically sponsored by or supportive of the British state, which might – certainly for those of Kelman's political stripe – be conflated with the English state. Writers accepting the Queen's honours (or complaining, as a plaintive Martin Amis did to the Observer in 2012, about never having been on her list!) accept an explicit alignment with the establishment. It was this interpretation of the concept of national literature that seemed to dominate the collective thinking of the Conference: nationality as an imposed structure; art conscious of its nationhood as inherently co-opted, compromised, suspect. One sensed that a writer bearing one of the Queen's titles might have taken some stick for it. But **Marlon James,** keynote speaker in Trinidad and Tobago – itself a former British colony – had a suggestion. 'Maybe we need to rethink the term,' he said, 'and it's not just the literature that needs to evolve, but also the national.'

So – the key to a positive way forward? Flexibility; an acceptance of ambiguity, fluidity and even conflict, rather than a search for fixed definitions; an awareness of differences forged by origins combined with a willingness to push and alter them. **Kamila Shamsie**, summing up the debate in Edinburgh, made a pertinent point relating to the torrential downpour that had commenced outside the tent during the event. In a British novel, she noted, rain tended to indicate sadness, disappointment, negativity. In her native Pakistan, rain spelled blessed relief from the heat, and thus symbolised breakthrough and renewal.

It's perhaps once one recognises that such symbols are unstable that an unmoored attitude to belonging, identifying and connecting becomes possible for writers, and a sort of airborne overview of nationality can be developed. In Hans Christian Andersen's *The Flying Trunk*, a playboy fritters all of his money, leaving himself with nothing but a trunk, a pair of slippers and a dressing gown. He packs himself into the trunk, which proves to be magic; it flies him to Turkey, where he fits right in on account of the fact that 'the Turks always go about dressed in dressing gowns and slippers'. Thus attired in ersatz national dress, the flying playboy is accepted as a 'Turkish angel' by royalty and peasantry alike. He takes to entertaining them with fairytales, and ends the story as a beloved, globetrotting storyteller, never needing to go home.

Negotiations against difference

by Irvine Welsh
Keynote, Edinburgh, August 2012

I've always considered myself belonging to the school of writers who should be read but not heard, so I don't know what set of circumstances leads me to be standing here today. I suppose the subject matter, a national literature, is a compelling one for me, given the current political situation in these islands, what with the independence referendum, and the fact that I'm now in genuine exile in the US, rather than a half-arsed one in London or Dublin.

It only really hits you living outside the UK, how much the casual remark 'I'm Scottish' or 'I'm British' is, bizarrely, such a political statement. I speak as someone who has been described over the years in British Council, and other, literature as both. My friend Phillip Kerr and I find it amusing how I can be described as 'Scottish' while he's referred to as 'British' in the same festival brochure, as we grew up about three miles from each other in Edinburgh, and both left that city in our teens, to go to London. This, like so many things, is down to perceived social class differences. I don't want to get sidetracked by dwelling on class; at this stage let's just acknowledge the fundamental veracity of its relevance to this debate, and leave it at that.

As this discussion originated in Edinburgh half a century ago, I'm going to focus mainly on the Scottish situation, as it's a pretty unique one. For we live in a country that isn't a nation, but has been lurching, almost apologetically at times, towards that status, picking up some of the trappings of such an entity en route. But, lest we forget, this is still a region of the UK.

The political and cultural landscape was unrecognisable fifty years ago, when Hugh MacDiarmid delivered his lecture on a national literature, provoking his famous spat with Alexander Trocchi. We'd come through the horrors of war and Holocaust, and people who regarded themselves as progressive politically saw internationalism as unambiguously good and desirable. It was forward-looking and inclusive, respecting the culture and aspirations of all, and based on fraternal, even socialistic notions. Nationalism, even dressed up in 'national liberation' clothes, was seen as morally dubious and inherently divisive.

Now the dominant model of 'internationalism' is capitalist- and media-led globalisation, levelling national and regional differences into a monolith of confused, debt-fuelled consumerism and bland, disposable culture. Today it's difficult to imagine, even without underestimating the formidable power of Scottish contrariness, that kind of discord existing between such freethinking mavericks as Trocchi and MacDiarmid. I'm quite sure that both, whether their vantage was the Scottish borders or New York City, would look at the UK in a globalised world and acknowledge that there were bigger fish to fry.

As both a nation and a national culture, it's important to remember that the UK ascended on the back of the first imperialist epoch of globalisation, when world markets were dominated by militaristic nation-states. Paradoxically, the current era of globalisation has, in some ways, strained the relationship between a national-cultural identity and a nation-state, which, certainly in Britain, is starting to disappear. Rearguard actions by the establishment to promote a monocultural British nationalism are usually unable to move beyond the traditional bedrock of that nationalism; what Stuart Hall calls 'the idea of an assumed Englishness', which has always negotiated against difference. This negotiation against difference is mirrored by the current mass production and dissemination of culture, whereby overt regional and national differences in this context, are in the first instance, perceived as troublesome barriers to mass sales.

We can spend all day debating what is national and regional literature to the point where it becomes meaningless. In an American context, look at Wikipedia, and you'll find writers as diverse as Stephen King, John Steinbeck, Mark Twain, William Faulkner and Raymond Chandler all described as 'regional'. The criterion for being a 'national' writer often seems to be as trite as living close enough to Manhattan to be able to attend the occasional *New Yorker* cocktail party.

Global mass culture is now largely governed by an increasingly image-dominant, rather than linguistic-dominant, means of cultural production. Therefore, it's more difficult for it to be limited by national boundaries. In such an environment, the main question for storytellers who see themselves as working outside the global cultural highway of London, New York and LA is, what kind of room for manoeuvre do we have, in a global literary marketplace, to express national or regional culture? Moreover, can writing still be undertaken – and indeed, writers be formed – within a 'national' culture?

The Scottish experience says a resounding yes to this. Prominent novels that have come out this year, from Alan Warner, James Kelman, Jenni Fagan and, less obviously but still emphatically, Ewan Morrison, John Niven and Dougie Johnstone, clearly could not have been written by non-Scots. Even genre fiction writers, often derided as writing into marketing holes, must convey a sense of place, and perhaps even of national character or archetypes.

Yet, Scottish fiction has an uneasy relationship in the 'British' literary paradigm, dominated by this imperialistic idea of an assumed Englishness, which, as Hall reminds us, exists to negotiate against difference. Only one Scottish novel has won the highly imperialist-orientated Man Booker Prize, routinely chosen by a largely upper middle-class English panel, and alternating around 50-50 between largely upper-middle-class English writers and citizens of the former colonies, presumably to stamp legitimacy on this 'global accolade'. Kevin Williamson of Rebel Ink, and Scottish Writer of the Year Alan Bissett, both recently attacked the anti-Scottish discriminatory nature of the prize, producing hard, sobering statistics in support of their arguments. That they haven't been deemed worthy of a reply can only be due to either the arrogance of hierarchical power, this negotiation against difference, or in this case, more likely, that the Booker apologists simply have no arguments to refute these observations. Hegemony not only breeds arrogance; it also promotes intellectual enfeeblement. The Booker prize's contention to be an inclusive, non-discriminatory award could be demolished by anybody with even a rudimentary grasp of sixth-form sociology. The academics who are custodians of the prize however, can only offer bland and complacent corporate PR speak in defence of an award based on the conceit that upper-class Englishness is the cultural yardstick against which all literature must be measured.

The key point is that competing groups, ranging from national politicians to non-governmental organisations to indigenous activists, have come to see culture as a valuable resource to be invested in, contested, and used for varied socio-political and economic ends. This idea has largely been expressed on the Left – both traditional and modern – in terms of the Gramscian notion of cultural struggle for hegemony. Now, everything from the Jubilee to the Olympics, to all of us sitting here, illustrates that cultural agency, at every level, is negotiated within globalised contexts; dominated by the active management and administration not only of culture, but the circumstances within which it develops. In most cases, this is seen as a legitimate, even essential mode of urban development. So these rituals and everyday aesthetic practices are mobilised to promote tourism and the heritage business, in countries where mass culture-reliant industries often comprise significant portions of the GNP.

Writers such as George Yúdice assert that a new international division of cultural labour has emerged, combining local difference with transnational administration and investment. Yúdice contends this doesn't mean that today's increasingly transnational culture – exemplified by the entertainment industries and the so-called global civil society of non-governmental organisations – is necessarily homogenised. In other words, no matter how strong economic and cultural hegemony is, there is always room for maverick opposition. The biggest shock about the 2012 London Olympic opening ceremony was that after thirty-odd years of neo-liberal governments, such a genuinely anti-imperialist, multi-and-popular cultural event could actually take place in contemporary Britain.

So national and regional differences still function, and shape the meaning of cultural and political phenomena, from pop songs to anti-racist activism. Yúdice considers a range of sites where identity politics and cultural agency are negotiated in the face of powerful transnational forces. For example he analyses appropriations of American funk music, and a citizen action initiative in Rio de Janeiro, to show how global notions such as cultural difference are deployed within specific social fields. He provides a political and cultural economy of a vast and increasingly influential art event — the inSite triennial festival, which extends from San Diego to Tijuana. He posits on the uses of culture in an unstable world where censorship and terrorist acts can interrupt the usual channels of capitalist and artistic flows.

With that point in mind, I'm only digressing slightly when I focus on a piece of work, *Tales From The Mall,* by Glasgow-based writer Ewan Morrison, which was published this year by Scotland's innovative Cargo Press. In the simplistic nature of market classification, this book is hard to tritely define (and therefore stock). Not only does it not fit the genre-dominated fiction boxes into which everything must increasingly be shoehorned, (again, retail-, not publishing- or artist-led), but it's not a fictional novel, short-story collection, multimedia experience, or a treatise on modern architecture, consumer capitalism, authority structures and the negation of democracy, yet it's all of these things.

Tales From The Mall, therefore, has gained little exposure, other than a fantastic word-of-mouth through the cognoscenti. This publication posits an exciting future for storytelling, from the so-called margins. It's an innovative book that is set largely in Scotland, but which has a global reach, as this small country interfaces with a globalised consumerist culture to produce truly zeitgeist writing.

But the supposed crisis of national culture and writing in our globalised world is, like most of our current ills, fundamentally a crisis of democracy. Faced by the seemingly impregnable forces of multinational capital, imperialist structures and their slavish spokespersons, overloaded by impotent debate, people must have forums and space for dissent and positive resistance. I emphasise the 'positive' only because we must never forget that local ethnicities/nationalities can become as dangerous as 'nation-state' ones when they simply fear modernism to the extent that they retreat into national and defensive identities.

As I know through my own experience, the market will always convert art and culture into mass entertainment. When my first novel sold 10,000 copies, I was a local hero. When it sold 100,000, people grew more dubious. At a million copies I was a sell-out, whoring out my culture for the entertainment of outsiders. Now ... I can't even think about it. The point is, that many people locally felt an ownership of the book, and a pride in it. What was an affirmation, an attestation to a place, a way of life, a language, a class, a culture and an attitude, became seen as something else. Obviously, the book was the same; I hadn't changed a word of it. Let me make it clear that I'm not complaining about making money – any writer that does is either a liar or crazy – just stressing that the marketplace can force the writer into a set of relationships and perspectives they might not have recalled signing up for.

So from an aspiring author's point of view, if you're from the so-called margins, do you play the current publishing game – e.g. shoehorn yourself into writing genre fiction, and 'work within the system', as the successful Scandinavian writers have done in crime fiction, effectively globally rebranding (at least in the eyes of outsiders) an entire genre – or do you exercise the freedom of the author and simply do what the fuck you feel like? I think I know what both Trocchi and MacDiarmid would do, but I'm suggesting that there is legitimacy, and not necessarily a dichotomy, in doing both. But wherever a writer, or their writing, is placed on the spectrum, what interests me, personally, is work which in some way, speaks the truth to power. To my mind this is still is the greatest freedom a writer can have. The celebrated, marvellous, Indian writer and political activist Arundhati Roy was reported to have said: 'It's all right speaking the truth to power, but just don't expect it to listen.' While I understand what she means, I don't think we speak the truth to power for power's ear, but for the ear and the imagination of future generations, who would seek to live in a world free from the malign and self-serving influence of those who wield it.

So the call to arms is a twofold one: firstly, let's have a look around, it's a big world, and if bits of it move you, don't be afraid to write about it. Second, be bold, and proud of who are and where you come from. Express your culture, your concerns and those of your community and the voices within it, however movable a feast that is. Because if you don't, the chances are that it might not be around in the future. So do what Trocchi and MacDiarmid would do: don't get obsessed with histories and legacies or markets and 'rules', just hit those keys and see what happens.

Brit lit

As Hannah McGill noted in her introduction to this chapter, the Conference slightly tied itself in knots over what might be termed 'British literature'. That exact term was rarely used, and it sounds unnatural for all sorts of reasons. But much was said about English and Scottish literature, and remarks were passed on Welsh and Irish literature, as if there existed some kind of loose notional United Kingdom of writing: four traditions that happen to co-exist on the same set of islands, but are separated by navigable seas of idiom and permeable borders of intent.

And it so happened that the discussion of literature in Britain, initiated at the opening chapter in Edinburgh, raised many of the broader questions that recurred throughout the Conference – not just in the connection with the UK. Here are some of them:

Is national literature defined by language, by the ethnicity or citizenship of the writer, or by some more elusive and complex formula?

From the point of view of literature, what in fact is the nation?

Can literature promote a national cause such as independence, and should it try?

If so, is it part of the function of literature to paint a picture, flattering or otherwise, of a region or a nation?

By what process or principle are works of literature co-opted into the national canon?

And is there, once you pick it apart, any such thing as national literature?

Ian Rankin chaired the discussion that followed **Irvine Welsh**'s keynote. Several of the above issues were zipped up in the first question he put to Welsh, and in the answer he received. 'Do you think of *Trainspotting* as a regional or a national novel?' asked Rankin. 'And if it's national, is it saying things about Scotland or about the United Kingdom?'

'When I was writing it I wasn't aware that it was coming from any particular place,' replied Welsh. 'That comes after the event. I was thinking about character and story, not the political or socio-cultural context.

'Is it critics and reviewers who do that, then?'

'Yes, and so they should. But it comes a shock to the writer, because you go into yourself and live in your own world while you're writing. It's only when it is done that the rest of the world has its say.'

So Welsh did not set out to write a novel that would become part of the wider world's view of his homeland. But as was often said at the Conference, writers have no control over how their work is received or interpreted once it is published – and they cannot legislate for all the uses to which is put. 'It's not Irvine Welsh's fault – of course it isn't,' said **China Miéville**. 'But it's a fact that *Trainspotting* is used to promote the Bonny Scotland brand.' Welsh agreed, adding cheerfully that his seedy tales of drug addiction in Leith have been used in advertising on trains bound for Edinburgh. **Alan Bissett** coined a metaphor that, perhaps unintentionally, tapped into that image of a piece of selling-copy in a moving railway carriage. 'National literature is a negotiation, not a fixed destination,' he said. And in enlarging upon the theme he came closer than any delegate to suggesting that writers have a patriotic duty to fulfil. 'There is not a permanent canon of works that say: this is what Scotland looks like. There is a constant discussion about what it means to be Scottish. And if we leave that up to other forces, such as politicians or the market, they will define this country in ways that most of us are uncomfortable with. I am writing for Scotland – I make no apology for that. If Scots don't write about Scotland, and take pride in their own culture, then who will?'

The trouble is: not everyone sees the core national texts the same way. Even books that tell the national story in glowing and attractive terms can have an ambivalent effect on the most enthusiastic reader, as **Theresa Breslin** recounted in Krasnoyarsk. 'As I child I never found "me" in a book,' she said. 'When I was young I read everything I could lay my hands on, but the Scots in my storybooks spent their time fighting glorious battles, rowing across lochs, or escaping over moors of purple heather. Even those Scots were hard to find. For at school, we recited poetry according to the set texts. I can remember my father's reaction when I came home chanting *Drake's Drum* – a stirring homage to the great English Elizabethan adventurer and explorer:

> Drake he's in his hammock an' a thousand miles away
> Capten art tha sleepin' there below?

'My father's antidote was to point me in the direction of Sir Walter Scott's border ballads and the poetry of Robert Burns. When I had to learn Wordsworth's *The Daffodils*, which begins:

> I wandered lonely as a cloud
> That floats on high o'er vales and hills,
> When all at once I saw a crowd,
> A host, of golden daffodils;

my father retaliated with Sir Walter Scott's *Young Lochinvar*:

> Young Lochinvar is come out of the West,
> Through all the wide Border his steed was the best;
> And save his good broadsword he weapons had none,
> He rode all unarmed and he rode all alone.

'A favourite in our house – because each of us six children could have a part to act – was *Lord Ullin's Daughter* by Thomas Campbell. It is about a Highland chieftain's attempt to elope with his true love. Fleeing from the wrath of the girl's father, who has threatened to kill him, the chieftain fears his blood will stain the heather. Now, no disrespect to Mr Wordsworth, but when you are nine or ten years old there is no contest between a bunch of daffodils – golden or otherwise – and blood on the heather.'

English readers might object to the implication that all literature south of the Tweed is rather effete compared to the Celtic north – as **Stella Duffy** did in Brussels, where she was on a panel alongside delegates from Scotland, Wales, Northern Ireland and the Irish Republic. 'I find it frustrating that generally to be English is perceived to be like something out of Downton Abbey, or at least middle-class, and to be the coloniser. I am not any of those things – and nor are the hundreds of thousands of immigrant English. Nationality is something that others stamp upon us.' And some Scots might not be happy always to equate Scotland with its highlands. Burns was not a highlander – nor was Hugh MacDiarmid, defender of Scottish literature at the 1962 Conference; nor, for that matter, is Irvine Welsh. In their writing they are all masters of Lowland Scots dialects.

The essence of Scottish literature was proving as hard to grasp as a holographic saltire. But the qualifying attributes of English literature were even more elusive. The Welsh poet **Owen Sheers** thought the time was ripe for English delegates to pay some attention to their own situation. 'I am a writer who works in London,' he said. 'But I have been informed by Welsh writing and the Welsh landscape, but I prefer not to call myself a Welsh writer – for two reasons. First, because the national tradition of writing in Wales is split between the two languages; second, because I don't want to be bound by the borders of my country – I want to be expanded by my country. In a post-devolution UK, one of the fascinating things is the nature of English literature. In the past forty, fifty, sixty years, all of the Celtic nations have thought a lot about their national literature, but there is still a question about what English writing is. I would like England to question itself – importantly, through its writers.

Melvin Burgess tiptoed carefully through the minefield of Englishness. 'When nationalism in these islands is discussed, there is always the question of what it is to be English. Orwell, one of my favourite writers, was asking seventy years ago: how do you go about being English now? How do you do that without embracing the empire? Even in our day, it looks lovely if a fairly recent immigrant to this country wraps himself in the Union Jack at the Olympic Games – but it would look like a very different thing if I did it, I would look like I was in the BNP.' **Alan Gibbons,** by contrast, charged straight past the danger sign – or perhaps he was pelting off in the opposite direction, back towards the safer ground of literary universalism.

'When I write,' he said, 'I want to refract through particular experience universal themes that people will understand in the Basque country, in South Africa, in Asia. I am not writing for bloody Englishness. I am writing for love and peace and power and rebellion and being bloody human.'

In Kuala Lumpur, **Suzanne Joinson** spoke about what it meant to her to be writing in English and to be a writer in England. Later she turned her comments into a short essay which is a kind of meditation on perimeter fences – on being within them, passing through them, looking back on them from somewhere outside. 'I write in English, within an English tradition,' she said, 'but I'm unsettled within those confines, and any sense of contributing to a literature that sits within the framework of national borders is as paradoxical and complex as my feeling towards home. The most emotive places for me are actually the points of exit: Victoria Station and Gatwick airport. It is as if I don't fully belong, and am only happy in England if I can leave.

'The mongrel English are islanders, much as they conveniently forget this. The sea is everywhere, and the houses are small. It is a claustrophobic country, and people cling to a regionalism to fend off the conflict or tension that comes with a national sensibility. Writers from Scotland, Ireland, Wales, London and the north of England are often fiercely territorial. They stake their ground with pride and dignity. They reference themselves within a context, emit a sense of community. What is left of Englishness and the literature that sits within its contours these days? Following what we might call a melancholic withdrawal of empire and faith, there isn't much bar a profound state of identity crisis. And the literatures arising from this are by necessity shifting, questioning and fragmented forms. Nationhood is about identity, but the more one hunts down one's own stories, the more fractured any sense of identity becomes. In my writing, the islandness of England becomes highlighted: the sea around it, a compulsion to leave it, the isolation, all of that examined. Yet I couldn't possibly write with a consciousness of my national identity, because what kind of writing would that produce? A writer can only tell the stories that haunt her, but hauntings are chaotic, slippery and contradictory.

'I don't really believe in nationality, or in a literature that conforms to the edges of a rigid definition. Stories are more often than not born in the no-man's-land of not-quite-belonging, in transitory existences or in-between places, in those zones and states of mind. And landscapes tend not to have borders ...'.

Jonathan Bastable (ed.)

Allochthoon, autochtoon

by Rachida Lamrabet
Keynote, Brussels, March 2013

A few months ago I was invited to give a lecture for the occasion of the 200th anniversary of the great nineteenth-century Dutch writer Hendrik Conscience, the man who taught his people, the Flemish, to read.

This writer played a historical role in defining the identity of Flanders, the Dutch-speaking part of Belgium. Conscience wrote *The Lion of Flanders*, an epic novel about the brave Flemish resistance in the Battle of the Golden Spurs of 1302 against French dominance. He wrote in Dutch, which was quite revolutionary. Flemish writers of his time and those who came far behind him, were only taken seriously if they wrote in French. The Flemish writer Maurice Maeterlinck, our only Nobel prize winner for literature, said for instance that the Dutch language was 'un coassement de grenouilles, mis en grammaire'. Or in plain English; 'the croaking of frogs put into grammar'. Maeterlinck wrote in French.

Conscience defended the importance of the Dutch language through his literature and played a major role in promoting the idea of a Flemish people. He adhered to the idea 'that language is the whole of the people'. And those who read him began imagining a nation for that Dutch-speaking people. Unfortunately, it is that very idea that divides today our country. Conscience's legacy became an important symbol of the Flemish movement, a movement which at its worst was not afraid to go in alliance with Nazism and racism. So you can understand that I was unenthusiastic towards the kind of national literature that Conscience represented because it was too often used to define a rigid notion of people and of citizens; it was used to justify a politics of exclusion, and it caused an obsession with identity. Referring to a national literature was, in my eyes, referring to something archaic and closed, a monolith that would not change even if the world was changing. I felt more comfortable with Ben Okri who said 'I was born in the world and I'm at home in the world's myths'.

So when I was asked to say something about the meaning of Conscience for me as a writer who came in the 1970s with my parents from the north of Morocco to this brave new country, it was that idea of an almost hostile national literature that dominated my thoughts: a national literature that I could not touch or add to. It left no room for other stories, because these other stories were simply not considered to be part of the national patrimony, part of the collective narrative. Sure, these other stories could be very interesting and informative, but they remained stories from the periphery, stories of others who could never affect or alter what was considered as the centre and the norm. As Marc Cloostermans, a book reviewer of one of the two important Flemish newspapers, plainly puts it: 'We like to read allochtonous writers, but only if they meet our criteria and if they make bold statements that we secretly enjoy.'

Here you have it: there is even a word to describe writers like me. I'm considered to be a special kind of writer; I am called an *allochtoon* writer. Let me explain to you what that word means, because there is no equivalent for it in English. It sounds unfriendly. I can assure you, it is unfriendly. The word allochtoon is of Greek origin and means 'someone who came from elsewhere', as opposed to an autochtoon, which is the word used to indicate the Flemish people and means 'from this land'. The reality in this society is that there is a semantic division on the grounds of ethnic origin. You either are an allochtoon, from another land, or an autochtoon, from this land.

The only chance to get rid of the allochtoon label in this part of the world is to be a brilliant soccer player who leads the national team to victory and fame. Guess it's too late for me to make a career in soccer and so for writers like me, it is not obvious to just be part of that great guild of writers. Regardless of the fact that I write in Dutch, my writing is not considered to meet the norm that has been set out by the centre. I write about identity, about migration and a changing super-diverse world. That is the kind of world we live in today here in this country, and yet, some readers and critics are convinced that my literature has nothing to do with them; it is the literature of the others, as opposed to national literature. I write about

Antwerp and readers would talk to me about my work as if I had described a world far away from them. My characters are strange exotic individuals for the mere fact that their names are Younes, Mariam and Marwan and not Isabel, Jan or Peter.

I'm not so very young anymore, but I'm still very naïve and I thank God for that. It's why I decided to challenge myself for my lecture about Conscience. I wanted to emphasise the things we had in common, to take Conscience's writing in his time and in his troubled society, when his language was not recognised, and make a connection to my writing today in my society. In Antwerp, Brussels and Ghent alone you have over 170 different nationalities living together. These people brought their languages, their stories and their convictions to this country. For me the main question was how the dominant society reacts to claims of recognition of one's own cultural identity. I think that the way that society responds to those claims can tell us a lot about how that society defines itself, about how self-confident it is in a changing world.

I had the brilliant idea, so I thought, to make a comparison between Conscience's striving for recognition and the aspirations for cultural emancipation of the new minorities in Belgium. I wanted to show how literature could be of help when you are trying to form an identity and trying to define your place in the world. I tried to connect the search for identity of young citizens with non-European roots and Conscience's cultural and linguistic struggle. I was convinced that in his time Conscience asked himself the same questions as do the young men and women who live today in the big cities of this country. Questions such as: Who am I? Where do I belong to? What is home, and what does language mean to me?

And then, of course, I went too far. I crossed the line, I came too close, and asked my audience what Conscience would think of Dyab Abou Jahjah, the former leader of the demonised organisation the AEL, the Arab European League, which advocated the emancipation of the Arabs in Europe and Belgium. Jahjah launched the provocative idea of making Arabic one of the national languages of this country. My mainly white and middle-class audience was not amused, I can assure you. That idea encountered resistance in the audience because there was the fear that their constructed national identity, a Flemish identity that has been won through hard battle, would be transformed by our multicultural, non-Flemish compatriots into something else. I could see the horror in the eyes of my audience. That same fear that makes it difficult to really open up to other stories, to let those stories really change ideas, opinions, and the way we look at things. As long as they don't get too close and risk changing the norm, then these stories are okay. But for how long can a society shut out its own reality?

Not for very long, because it bangs at the door. In fact, this evening, I declined an invitation to a funeral – the funeral of a word. The city of Ghent decided, at the instigation of a few organisations and artists, not to use the word allochtoon anymore. And at this very moment, on the international day against racism, its funeral ceremony is taking place in Ghent's town hall. After the word is buried there will be an enormous feast. Perhaps, after this meeting, we could all take the train and join the people of Ghent for this celebration of the semantic birth of citizens. History is made by people who have a great deal of imagination.

Words of war

by Velibor Čolić

One of the problems with the concept of a national literature, as **Rachida Lamrabet** intimated in her Brussels keynote, is that it can become a kind of exclusive club that – like many a club – exists for the sole purpose of deciding who is worthy to join and and who is not. But the national idea can be a good deal more poisonous that that. At its extreme, literary exclusionism becomes an effective and sinister weapon. Books can be as deadly in their way as bullets, part of the ordnance of wartime propaganda. In St Malo, the Bosnian writer **Velibor Čolić** made an impassioned speech about the role that writing played in paving the way for the Yugoslav conflicts of the 1990s, and in justifying their cruel excesses. Here is an edited version of that address.

'The line between national and nationalist literature is very fine,' said Čolić. 'Back in the former Yugoslavia, I was the witness to the rise of an elitist literature which very suddenly became a national literature. Writers, through their books and their "national language", came to define the spiritual space of the people; and on their heels came the military – to ink in the borders. This led to the triple crime – genocide, memoricide, urbicide – that took place in my country soon after.

'That war was the by-product of a national literature. The writer Dobrica Ćosić is known as "the Tolstoy of the Balkans" and also as "the father of the Serbian nation". In his 1954 novel *Koreni* (*Roots*) he concocted a national-literary manifesto that is infused with Balkan flavours. According to one spellbound critic, his great rustic family-centred *roman fleuve* addresses 'Serbian cults of freedom, their ancestral and national mythology, their patriarchal despotism'. The same critic says that the book *magnificently* denounces 'individualism, the Europeanisation of Serbian intellectuals, the destruction of the agrarian world'. In 1954, the nation had the same enemies as today: Europe, cultural diversity, the west, cities, individualism. The Tolstoy of the Balkans was in favour of home-made, serious national literature, a perhaps boring but tragic one, in which (he says) "Serbs always lose in times of peace what they gain in times of war". The result: the uprooting of the people and even the complete disappearance of the nation. In 1992, Ćosić became the future ex-president of the rump Yugoslavia (Serbia and Montenegro). The triple crime – genocide, memoricide, urbicide – was committed by Ćosić's own disciples – among them Radovan Karadzic, the leader of Bosnia's Serbs, who was a nationalist poet.

·

'The written word is never the direct cause of a war, but it seems to me that the root of this evil can lie in a national literature which acknowledges the soil, and spiritual borders as defined by language and religion, which more or less openly accuses neighbours of being the true enemies: communists, the Albanians, the 'Turkish' Muslims in Ćosić's works. Or which points the finger at hidden enemies –someting much more insidious because that category includes everyone, anyone .... The Serbian and then Croatian or Bosnian nightmare began precisely at the moment when the masterpieces of Ćosić and his ilk became a *political project*, and when their novels started being read as history books – and *vice versa*. The confusion between genres, between history and literature, was a tragedy for everyone. Intelligence and common sense should allow us to distinguish between myth and reality, to distance ourselves and to exercise reason. But new national literatures work on an emotional and a collective level to erode understanding. And when almost no space remains between national literature and the nationalistic kind, writers stand aside and make way for the military.

'Ideas of a *national* culture, of a *national* way of life all originate in the same place, from shortcuts, pre-fabricated phrases, historical re-draftings, Holocaust denial, populism. Nationalist literature is chameleon-like. Back in the former Yugoslavia, we sometimes called it patriotic literature or traditional literature, and very often we called it popular literature. Generally, novels of that genre are written in an old-fashioned idiom, but using common vocabulary. There are epic poems that intentionally blur the lines between ancestral tales and the current, usually straitened circumstances of the nation. The Serbian ethnologist Ivan Čolović gives an example: during the most recent war in Bosnia, Serbian soldiers shouted out the names of heroes from popular literature as they went into battle, as though citing the historical evidence for their cause.

'National literature cleanses our nation of all its sins, and turns it into a metaphor. Our homeland is no longer a geographical location; it is instead a pretty young woman who has been raped and defiled, or the resting-place of our grandfathers, or a white dove. Recent national works by Serbians, Croatians and Bosnians depict the homeland as a sort of maternal monster that wants our blood. The lyric of a popular Croatian song goes:

Do not be sad, oh mother Croatia
Call us, just call us, and like falcons
We will give our lives for you.

'Nationalist literature always speaks in the name of the people with this same kind of heroic rhetoric. It finds scapegoats, it makes our enemies visible, and it either accuses or forgives in the name of the people. National literature is like a church in that everything contained within is sacred. Our soil is sacred, our language is sacred, and most of all our freedom is sacred. This kind of literature is also necrophiliac: its writers are either already dead, about to die, or ready to be sacrificed on the altar of the nation.

'This cheap and shoddy literature sees humanity in very uncomplicated terms: good and bad, us and them. It is a world where the allegiances are as straightforward as on the terraces of a football match. National writers prefer to see us as victims – of the spread of Islam, of globalisation, of various world conspiracies. We become a mere handful of brave, clear-sighted people standing up to a cunning and ruthless enemy. (A Serbian satirist once said: "Before the war, we had nothing; then the Germans came and destroyed everything.") The enemy, meanwhile, are barbarians whose names and faces may change, but whose nature remains the same: wild, destructive and decadent. Usually this type of literature languishes on the margins, where it belongs. But in my country it heralded a fratricidal war in which a 100,000 people died and 2,000,000 were made refugees.

·

'So should we believe in literature? I hope that, when the perverted political games are done with and the era of crazed and bloodthirsty national bards is over, we will see a new age of literature. It will be a nomadic and human literature, a mobile and multicultural literature, it will be dishevelled and undisciplined, it will bear no passport and carry no visas.

'In 1992, during the war, I wrote a text in my soldier's logbook. Perhaps it was foolish, certainly it was naïve, but I was frightened. I wrote it as a kaddish of sorts for my country.

> In times of war, believing in literature means not accepting ready-made words, not accepting necrophilia or death as biblical necessities symbolised by the four horsemen of the Apocalypse. It also means working on the magic which makes words come together, recognising evil and condemning it. That is how, in Bosnia, we can go beyond a purely aesthetic literature. It means remembering, time and again, the bright and sacred nature of the sacrifice of victims, in order to believe there is meaning again, in order to breathe new life into literature, without thinking about the fact that this story has already been told numerous times. It means believing in the primeval cry of life, as wise and old as the hills; in the cry of the child who, pushed by survival instincts, rends his mother's womb to announce the clear and definitive triumph of creativity over absurdity, violence and destruction.

> Yes, that is what believing in literature means. A literature that cannot be altered. Because it holds the secrets of life's eternal nature.

'Just a few months later, the soldier that I was went into exile. And this text, which I'd written on my knees in the trenches, became a book. There is a gypsy proverb that says: they can kill all the swallows, but they can't keep spring from coming.'

Serve the story

by Miriam Toews
Keynote, Toronto, October 2012

Last month I was at a literary festival in Mantova, Italy. Most guest writers were Italian, but there was a handful of writers from other countries, and as it turned out I was the only Canadian in the programme. I figured that during appearances and interviews I would be asked a few questions about the literary scene in Canada, perhaps about Canadian politics, but I quickly realised that for the Italians, my Mennonite identity was of far more interest than my Canadian identity. For them, I was a Mennonite writer. I had no problem going along with this, I've been in this position before, but it reminded me again how so much of our self-identity is determined by others, how the person we're imagining ourselves to be, the self we expect to impose on the world, is always in negotiation with the identity given to us by other people.

Granted, I was there to talk about my latest novel, *Irma Voth*, which is about a nineteen-year-old Mennonite girl named Irma who lives in a religiously conservative community in Northern Mexico. *Irma Voth* is my sixth book but it's only the third time I've featured Mennonite settings and characters. I'm happy to answer questions about Mennonites, and in Italy I talked about their history, their practices, their beliefs – all the while thinking: what an odd position to be in! I'm not a historian or sociologist or theologian. I'm only a fiction writer. And though I *am* a Mennonite – born and raised in a religious Mennonite town in Manitoba – I am not a *good* Mennonite, at least for a great number of people in the Mennonite community who continue to regard me as an irritant, a shit disturber, and most certainly the last person who should be telling their epic tale of persecution, exile, and hard-won religious independence.

I can't count the number of times people have made a point of telling me – in writing or to my face – that I've besmirched the reputation of Mennonites, made a mockery of the very community that raised me up to be who I am. In fact, during a recent interview with a publication in Manitoba, I was asked how I feel about the fact that my novels reinforce negative stereotypes of Mennonites and fail to represent the educated, cultured, tolerant, urban Mennonites who are very much open to the secular world.

It was one of those questions that is also an accusation, and it told me I should feel guilty, ashamed, and repentant. But the truth is I have never set out to expose flaws in the Mennonite community. Fiction writing, for me, comes from a much more childlike impulse. There are stories to tell and I dive right in.

But it would be bad faith to say I simply can't understand why certain Mennonites would object to my books. We don't want people to think we're unsophisticated inbreds, mad for cruel practices like shunning and condemning gays and lesbians to hell. It's a natural, defensive gesture to say 'Wait, we're not all like that!' It has to do with arrogance and embarrassment. And self-image. But protests like that conveniently remove the onus of confronting difficult truths and lobbying for change. We know that some Mennonites were involved with the Nazi Party. Should we erase this from the history books? Should we say, 'Yeah but forget about that, most Mennonites are pacifists and apolitical!' (Is this even true any more?) And is it somehow my responsibility to write a novel about an agnostic cocaine-addicted Mennonite working at a New York fashion magazine who abandons her sophisticated, polyglot Wall Street boyfriend in order to fulfill her childhood dream of joining NASA and becoming an astronaut – simply to redress stereotypes of religiously retrograde Mennonite farmers?

No. I've come to realise what it is these Mennonites want from me – both the conservative Mennonites who have condemned me to hell as well as the secular Mennonites who regret the way I've depicted their other half: they want my *piety*. Not just loyalty to the community, but allegiance to whatever transcendent authority unifies the community. In other words, there are services to be rendered. They're fine with stories about Mennonites, they welcome stories about Mennonites, but only as long as the stories reinforce certain pre-determined narratives. The insinuation is always that because I fail to show piety towards my own community – especially this historically beleaguered community – I am a spoiled, mischievous, rebellious child, someone not to be taken seriously, a prankster, or worse, a morally directionless castaway who is best kept at a distance else I infect the community any further.

The parent-child analogy is inevitable when talking about identity. Identity is so much about inheritance. The Mennonite community often compares itself to a family, as do other minority communities. Even nation-states are sometimes described as families. In my life I've heard talk of the Canadian family, especially in times of crisis – during sovereignty referendums in Quebec for example: suddenly Canada is a marriage on the verge of divorce, or a family of several children, the eldest threatening to run away. You can be sure that whenever a politician chooses to describe the nation-state as a family, or extension of family, or even of a human personality developing into greater maturity, he or she is asking for your obedience, your allegiance to the status quo.

Like the conservative, religious men of my community, conservative nationalists want each one of us to conform to the identity they've imagined for us; they want our stories to become part of a larger authorised story. Which brings me to the dubious idea of National Literature. I say dubious not because I don't believe in the existence of a 'national literature' but because for me, a writer, it implies obligations and confinements, much in the same way that the 'Mennonite literature' label can sometimes feel like a confinement for me. Makes me think I'm about to be sent on a mission. I would never need or want to deny my Mennonite background and culture; even if identity is multiple and evolving, forever subject to the judgments of others, I'll always feel like and be identified as a Mennonite, and therefore possess that little extra authority on all matters Mennonite. I also see myself as a Canadian writer, very much implicated personally in all matters Canadian. Like every Canadian, I have been taught that one of the most important functions of art is to supply and elaborate the myths and narratives of nationhood. Northrop Frye said so: fictional stories are a secular bible for our imagined community. I get this: I wouldn't tell an Irishman that the great books written by Irish authors have nothing to do with who he is. So for me, to be granted a place under the banners of Mennonite literature and Canadian literature is an honour.

The problem is, the more defined these national narratives become, the less they have to do with the individual artist creating her art. The greater the number of stories that fall neatly into the category of 'national literature,' they more they threaten a writer's imaginative freedom. Fiction is perhaps the most emancipated artistic form; it's messy, shape-shifting, rebellious. Fiction is emissary to no embassy and child to no parent; a writer is not a soldier or Olympic athlete, flying a national flag. The only legitimate role of a writer, regardless of her community or nation is to tell the stories that are truly hers. I'll quote the American writer Dorothy Gallagher: 'The writer's business is to find the shape in unruly life and to serve her story. Not, you may note, to serve her family, or to serve the truth, but to serve her story.'

Serve your story and you are doing your proper business. You are also doing your part in the national project: helping to create an environment in which the diverse populations of the nation can develop freely and spontaneously towards a future that does not resemble the past. Ideas of national identity always belong to the past. By the time we've recognised a unifying national theme, we're somewhere else. And whether or not your stories are contributing to national literature is for other people to decide. Writers are off the hook, which should be a special relief to Canadian writers. As MG Vassanji says: 'To define [Canada] or its literature seems like putting a finger on Zeno's arrow: no sooner do you think you have done it than it has moved on.'

Literature is always moving on, quickly, daringly. If a story happens to serve someone's national agenda, then so be it. But it's most likely to do the opposite. Good fiction does not reinforce our complacent self-image; it makes us aware of identities outside our own. It brings to life complex characters who resemble real people, provides new points of reference, reclaims old territories and invents new ones, magnifies familiar moments into epiphanies. If anything, a good story will threaten the sanctity of the establishment and question the voice of privilege and tradition, and in doing so, evolve what it means to be a member of the community or the nation.

To many, serve-your-story-over-family-or-truth is the justification of a selfish and insensitive person. What if your writing hurts people close to you? Why would you want to expose the foibles of a vulnerable minority group that is so important to you? Mennonites need understanding, not critique.

These are important questions. I wouldn't have written *A Complicated Kindness* if my father had been alive. Not because I would be afraid of how I'd characterised him in the book, the character of Ray, my favourite and who is in the end the hero, but because of how sad it would make him to know just how critical I was of the community that meant the world to him ... so in a way, although I would prefer that he was alive, his death freed me up to write the book I needed and wanted to write.

I worried that Carlos Reygadas, the Mexican film director who was the inspiration for the eccentric filmmaker in *Irma Voth*, would take badly to the way he was portrayed – a man contriving chaos on the set and given to wild flights of somewhat pompous poetry. Some time after the novel was published, I went to see him. We spent hours talking before I finally had the courage to ask him: Um, what did you think of the book? He wasn't upset at all. He said he preferred the first half of the book, before the two sisters flee. I was relieved when he told me he liked it very much, and that he saw my blood on the page. Except, he just wished I had bled onto the page even more.

Many Mennonites have thanked me for my books, for telling my story, *their* story. This has been wonderful for me and deeply reassuring. On the other hand, there are the Mennonites who would be offended by any representation whatsoever. We all know that individuals who define themselves exclusively by the cultural group they belong to are less willing to acknowledge its inherent problems. I want to ask: to whom exactly am I *exposing* Mennonite foibles? I realise that a minority position is less secure than a mainstream one, but I fail to see why this insecurity makes its members less capable of rigorous self-critique. I think it's simplistic to assume that a mainstream Anglo reader (or reader from any other social tribe) confronts human foibles more courageously than other people.

Canada has, at times, represented itself as a country in a valiant struggle against powerful and menacing agents that are indifferent to its special practices and sensibilities – most especially American culture. It's the old, outdated garrison mentality. But even Canada, this highly regionalised, pluralistic, and accommodating country has a palpable sense of national community; it's manifest in our laws, institutions, and customs, in the unique conflicts of our history, in our differences from other nations, and yes, in our literature. So we've got no revolutionary war, no centuries-old Declaration Of Independence, no Walden in the woods, no American dream. Let's get over it. Let's embrace our insecurity, and continue to fall short of certainty. The concept of 'national literature' promises certainties and definitions and boundaries, all the things that literature withholds. The imagination is inherently subversive and cannot be mandated. A writer can only serve her nation by serving her story.

Writers as nation-builders

Many nations have a national poet. And in most instances that writer is specifically a *poet* – rather than a novelist or dramatist – since poetry, being harder to translate than prose, often gets 'stuck at home' (**Tibor Fischer's** words). Great novelists generally belong to the world; great poets are an unexportable treasure, and in their homelands they are all the more revered for that. Scotland has Robert Burns with his Lallans dialect; Italy, Dante; Ireland, Yeats ....

... And Slovenia has Prešeren, about whom the Welsh writer **Christopher Meredith**, speaking in Brussels, had a little story. 'A few weeks ago I was in Slovenia, a country that didn't exist as a state until the 1990s, but existed as a nation well before that. I went to Prešeren Square in Ljubljana, where a political event was taking place. There is a statue of France Prešeren in his square – though no-one knows what he looked like because the only portrait of him was done after he died. Various politicians were standing up to speak at his feet.' This seems to have struck Meredith as absurd – faceless power droning away beneath the blind bronze gaze of a generic poet-figure – but the symbolism of it somehow dramatised the strange function that national literature fulfils in nascent countries. Newborn nation-states need the validation of their dead writers as surely as they need a paper currency and a national anthem.

'Dominant countries tend not to ask whether they have a national literature or not,' said **Margie Orford**, speaking in Cape Town. 'But if you look at the history of national literatures in Africa, you find that there is a fantasy of the nation before it is achieved. Then independence happens, and that idea is dispersed. So the nation is something imaginary that you write towards, but that disappears afterwards.' **Denise Mina** said something similar in Edinburgh: 'The nation-state is a fictional character. Because it moves in the world, we tend to think of it as an actual character. But it's not, it's just a notion.'

If the nation is fantasy, a figment of the imagination, or a fictional character, then writers ought to be singularly well-suited to the task of helping to shape nationhood. And several delegates to the Conference maintained that a national literature – far from being a kind of anthology assembled *ex post facto* by politicians and cultural arbiters – is often something which precedes the nation-state. It may even be a necessary pre-condition for national identity. **Reza Aslan**, speaking in Jaipur about the Middle East, said: 'The idea of the nation was formulated not by politicians, but by writers and poets. They were the ones who gave birth to Arab identity as we know it. It was Turkish writers who defined what the modern state of Turkey means – as against Ottoman hegemony and western colonialism.' **Kirill Kobrin**, speaking in Krasnoyarsk about the European tradition, expressed the opinion that the nation-building project described by Aslan still goes on. 'In the nineteenth century the concept of nation defined what the national literature should be. First came the concept of the 'national', and 'national literature' followed on from that. Now we see that literature defines the national. That is, a nation is understood as a kind of cultural totality of such practices as literature, art, media and so forth. I think that is a great step forward, because it allows us freedom, because whatever you write, that writing is by definition part of the national literature.'

But all the same, is it a writer's job to be a flag-bearer in the national parade, or even to cheer from the kerbside? Some delegates thought not. 'Kapka [Kassabova, in her keynote] used the phrase "public kitsch" to describe the flags and bunting of nationhood,' said Christopher Meredith. 'As writers we must try not to be recruited as manufacturers of public kitsch.' **Imraan Coovadia,** in Cape Town, drew an analogy with architecture – then rejected it in favour of something more jazzy. 'I don't know how – in architecture, say – you distinguish between a national or indigenous style and the international style,' he said. 'I'm not sure there is any such thing as a national style of writing. What you can have is periods of unique cultural intensity and excitement: Russia between 1860 and 1910; Romantic England – from the 1790s to the 1870s. That is what I want from national literature: not a single style or a set of commandments, but a whole series of arguments and experiments. I want national literature to look like a kind of circus tent where every performer is keeping an eye on all the others in the ring.' **Anjali Joseph**, in the same discussion, pointed to Rabindranath Tagore, 'India's only Nobel laureate. He wrote endless Modernist short stories about poverty and caste injustice and all sorts of things that don't put the country in a good light. I dislike the idea of writers being encouraged to represent things in an attractive way.'

Nation-building is of course a political project. And in the Conference's parallel discussion of literature and politics it was often said that a novel that was *only* political, or that set out primarily to sell a political viewpoint, was bound to fail because it would be no more than a veiled tract or manifesto. The same logic applies to national literature: a novel in which the national idea is entirely central is merely a Baedeker populated with pretend locals. At worst, such a book could turn out to be a xenophobe's charter, or a hate-myth of the kind described by Velibor Čolić in his St Malo keynote (see p.238).

Marina Warner chairing in Trinidad wondered if there might be 'some middle way between the Soviet model and the market model', that is, between (on the one hand) national literature that is a department of the state's propaganda machinery and (on the other) national literature that is a kind of holiday brochure in narrative form. **Sema Kaygusuz**, who gave her keynote speech in İzmir, thought there might well be such a path, and that it was signposted language and memory.

'No language can be defined by nationality' she said. 'This is because language does not belong only to those of the same race, but to communities. What is more, just as a language can contain repertories of borrowed words from other languages, so can it play host to other languages that have melded into each other. In Turkish there are reams of words borrowed from Arabic, Persian, Greek, Kurdish, French and English. A person shares their language. And while language identifies a person as local, it also makes them a citizen of the world.

'I disagree with the idea of a nation being incubated upon a literature, as this is a form of social engineering. In Turkey, with the 1908 constitutional movement of the late Ottoman period, a full-blown national literature movement was born. Its intention was to take literature back to its early Turkic origin. This departure heralded the simplification of the language, and the replacement of the *aruz* meter with the syllabic meter. There was an attempt to depict local life in a nationalistic perspective. The literary efforts of this nationalistic movement were, paradoxically, influenced by French, Russian and English literature. Later, in the 1960s, Turkism twisted historical events and produced material that was brimming with native valour and that was disparaging to other countries. But despite its shallowness and transience, the movement left visible scars. The writers of this period fomented hatred and xenophobia, they contributed to the exclusion of those belonging to minority religions or different ethnicities in our country.

'Literature can only stay alive when it is authentic and unfettered. The respectable state of Turkish literature today is due to writers who have not been afraid to make their mark, who have contended with massacres, made a stand against fascism, attacked the official version of history, overthrown personal politics and put their guard up against all types of sexist, homophobic and heterosexist attitudes. If today we are able to write literary works with confidence and without apology, it is only thanks to the efforts of our libertarian predecessors: writers who made writing into an existential act.'

Jonathan Bastable (ed.)

Writing across boundaries

by Anjali Joseph
Keynote, Cape Town, September 2012

When I saw the subject of this talk, 'a national literature', I felt mildly depressed. It was an involuntary reaction, like the way one feels when made to fill in a form and categorise oneself: nationality, country of residence, address, that sort of thing. I immediately felt alienated at the idea of a national literature, and I don't think this was only because I'm an expatriate Indian who lives in England. The idea of a national literature sounded massive, like the kind of entity that would have a minister or an advisory committee, and a big white building somewhere with a security guard. I felt, 'Oh no, national literature has nothing to do with me.' Or maybe it could be something I would have read in a classroom somewhere. But it didn't speak to my experience.

Straight after that feeling of rebellion, I had another thought, which was remembering an image from a novel first published in 1928, in Bengali. This is from *Pather Panchali* by Bibhutibhushan Bandopadhyay. The title of the novel translates as something like 'Song of the Road'; it was made into a famous film by Satyajit Ray. It's about the life of Apu, a young boy, and his elder sister in a village in rural Bengal at the turn of the twentieth century. They come from a poor family and they play in the forest around the village, or near the river. I'm going to read a short passage in translation from the novel. Just before this passage, Apu's father has subscribed to a magazine called *Bangabashi* for them, and this is exciting because there are serialised stories in the magazine. The passage begins when Apu and his friend have gone out on the river in a small boat, and they realise an enormous storm is about to break.

He could think of nothing but the storm. His body was tense, his eyes staring straight ahead, now at the sky, now at the waves that rushed down upon them. The water danced wildly. The paddy birds were flying. The cloud mountains writhed in convulsions; and on the bank he could see the heaps of shells that the boatmen from the south had piled up. A floating island of water hyacinth swept by, so wide that it hid the water from sight. Suddenly he was voyaging to England like that man in the Bangabashi. His ship had sailed from Calcutta. Sagar Island in the mouth of the estuary was behind them, and they were threading their way through a host of little islands in the middle of the sea. The dark green line of coconut palms on the shore of Ceylon was already in sight, and on the far horizon he could make out blue mountains in a strange land, which reddened as he watched them in the light of the setting sun. Everything was different! New lands! New sights! And still he journeyed on, further and further, into the unknown.

Apu has an incredibly responsive imagination, and whenever he reads, the things he reads become a part of the place where he lives, even though they are set somewhere quite different. The river on which he and his friend are boating is a tributary of other larger rivers that finally lead to the Ganga, and then to the sea, and there is a way in which Apu's reading, also, opens him out to a much wider world than he would otherwise know. And his story, the story of a village boy reading serial novels and daydreaming of the world, is told in a serial novel which was made into a famous film that's known all over the world. There is a two-way movement here.

I didn't grow up in a village in turn-of-the-century Bengal, and yet this extract feels very close to me. I think it is because there is something universal in it: that is, the experience of what it is like to read, and find what you read weaving itself into the texture of your own life. There is a way in which perhaps each of us has at any time his or her own internal cry or thing that must be expressed, even if it isn't ever articulated in words. In Gerard Manley Hopkins' sonnet, 'As kingfishers catch fire, dragonflies draw flame' the poet says of 'each mortal thing': 'myself it speaks and spells, / Crying What I do is me: for that I came.' So, when we read we are looking for an answering echo of this cry in the world; we read to receive messages from the world. Sometimes we read to go on a journey, and be someone else, while still remaining ourselves. A book can be like the magical flying carpet in the Hans Christian Andersen fairytale.

The idea of reading feels close, but the idea of literature feels abstract, in fact like the idea of a nation. These notions seem more static and fixed, even congealed. When we talk of a nation, and literature, and national literature, we are talking about classes of things. 'This type of man.' 'An Indian.' 'A South African.' We move away from lived experience and into the generic. In fact, we become like some of the famous bores in fiction: like Polonius in *Hamlet*, or Monsieur Homais the chemist in *Madame Bovary*, who deal only with generalisations. Writers don't read only their own national literatures: they form affiliations, links of choice with the writers they have read and who matter to them. Maybe that means a French novelist such as Claude Simon reading William Faulkner, or a South African novelist such as JM Coetzee reading Samuel Beckett, or an Indian writer reading Yasunari Kawabata. And these links matter far more than the vertical lineage of nationality.

Perhaps the label literature has a defensive aspect. Possibly it is intended to validate or protect work that may not have an immediate appeal to everyone. Suppose I like reading and someone hands me a book and I open it and read this:

> To one on his back in the dark a voice tells of a past. With occasional allusion to a present and more rarely to a future as for example, You will end as you now are. And in another dark or in the same another devising it all for company. Quick leave him.

And suppose that after reading this I feel frankly a little upset, as though I want to cry, because I can't see the story, or the characters, or actually anything that I'm expecting, and I say to my friend who gave me the book, 'I don't get it, I thought you said this was a really good book.' And she says, 'Well, it's by Samuel Beckett and it's literature.' Maybe then I will carry on reading the book, and maybe in its very strangeness I will find something that makes me see my own experience in a way that is quite true but which I wouldn't otherwise have perceived; something in fact that brings me home to myself.

Because I think it is a myth that, inside, we experience ourselves in a linear way, like a nineteenth-century novel or a Hollywood film, a straightforward sequence of cause and effect where a virtuous action later results in a piece of good fortune. Maybe it sometimes feels like that, but often it doesn't. And this is the great adventure of the modernist novel: to create an image of the soup of memory and thought and desire and urges and advertising and the internet and newspaper and television and sex in which our brains exist, and to give us back this image, so that we can recognise it, and laugh, and for a moment, be liberated from it.

There is nothing stranger than a human being. Sometimes there is nothing stranger than oneself. And sometimes these different varieties of strangeness seem quite hermetically contained, quite sealed, each inside its casing, walking around, or issuing messages through the ether, through the internet, or in print. It is a small miracle that these messages transmit and are received. And writing, and reading, are two of the most discreet, tactful, and beautiful ways in which it's possible for a human being in a landscape to think to himself: 'I'm here.' And then feel lonely, and listen, and ask: 'Is anyone else there? Can you hear me?' And find a book, and open it, and realise, in a satisfying and internal way, 'Ah yes, there is someone there.' And it's a way for a writer to sit in a room and write something, and wonder, 'Am I mad? Does this exist?' and for the words that represent her thoughts to be printed and later found in a book by someone else, in another country, and for the message to arrive home. And the operation of that basic magic is why literature and reading matter to us, and why we respond to them, but I think that has very little to do with national boundaries.

News from elsewhere

'I have always been most enthralled by books set in places that are unfamiliar to me,' said **MJ Hyland** in Melbourne, 'the place that is strange, that is foreign, that is other.' And many times at the Conference, amid the talk of what a writer's attitude should be to his or her own country, delegates remarked that as readers they had a xenophiliac attraction to unknown or distant settings. What is more, this was usually not because those books were exotic (although they might be on the surface) but much the reverse: because despite having come from afar, they contained something recognisable and true. The Australian writer **Tony Birch** made the case beautifully when he described his own teenage encounter with Barry Hines' *A Kestrel for a Knave.*

'It is set in the depressed working-class north of England, geographically a long way from inner Melbourne,' he said. 'A bullying older brother, schoolyard thugs and psychopathic teacher repeatedly whack Billy Casper, the slightly built boy at the centre of the novel. His respite from violence is discovered in his love for a bird, a headstrong but graceful kestrel, and in the wonder of a nearby wood, itself a relief from the grime of coal mines, slag heaps and narrow overcrowded terraces of the town. No book left the impression on me that *Kes* did. I was convinced it had travelled the globe to find me. From the first pages, when Billy wakes in the early morning in his damp, crowded room and is teased and abused by his brother, I felt more than empathy for him. I was sure I was Billy.' Birch remembers exactly where he was when he started reading the book: it was on the platform of Melbourne's North Richmond railway station. 'I had a half hour to wait and I retrieved the novel from my bag. When my train finally arrived I continued reading, and after I got off the train and headed home, open book, I found myself walking into light-poles. Buried deep in the novel I went to my bedroom and finished it. Closing the final page, I rushed from the house, ran through the narrow streets of my life. I didn't stop until I reached the banks of the Yarra River, which, at the time was a maligned stretch of water, home to car wrecks, the homeless and neglected, and water rats. I lay in the long grass on the riverbank and thought more about the book until I became so excited I ran back home and read it again. We don't require a national literature to draw attention to issues of the human condition – or the heart. As my experience of *Kes* indicates, good writing migrates and finds a home. I want to read stories that travel – like a bird I adore, the Arctic tern, which bravely navigates the globe each year to nest on the beaches of southern Australia.'

So, as **Theresa Breslin** said in Krasnoyarsk, 'a story may be set in the landscape and couched in the language of a specific country, but express, in the particular, larger truths. It may draw upon what might be termed a national culture yet illuminate what it means to be human.' But nations needn't come into it. **Denise Mina** touched on this in Edinburgh when she said: 'I think we are conflating 'situatedness' with a national literature. Situatedness is essential to good storytelling.' The specific situatedness of *Trainspotting*, for example, could be said to be Leith, Scotland, Britain, Europe. Its in-written culture could be said to be that of Edinburgh, or of disaffected youth, or of drug addiction. In the end, these are all merely keywords, empty search terms that tell you nothing about what the book means. In Edinburgh **Ian Rankin** had said to **Irvine Welsh**: 'I imagine you were pleased when it turned out that the story that you had told was understood not just by local people, or people in Edinburgh or even in Scotland. 'Yes, ' replied Welsh. 'I went to Russia and people said; we've got a Begbie. Or I'd be in South Africa and someone might say: I know a Spud. Suddenly those characters were global archetypes that people identified with.'

Welsh now writes from Chicago – and it was noted in Edinburgh that many of the writers with strong opinions on the national theme were based in countries other than the one to which they owed national or cultural allegiance. And even when that was not so, some delegates seemed to feel that they were in some key sense foreigners in their own land, that in order to write they needed the sense of distance that a self-perception of otherness provided. 'A writer is always in exile, even when he lives at home' said the French-Moroccan writer **Tahar Ben Jelloun**. 'If I say I am a French author, the Arabs will call me a traitor; if I say I am an Arab author, the French will say: how ungrateful. I prefer to say my homeland is my language. And you are allowed to have several homelands.' In Brussels, the Irish poet **Gearóid Mac Lochlainn** read an anguished poem of his own which contained the line 'I wanted to go home, but I was home ...', an unwitting echo of Basho haiku that **Kapka Kassabova** quoted to different ends in her keynote speech ('Even when I am in Kyoto ... I miss Kyoto.' – see p.281). Kassabova herself was impatient with the whole writers-in-exile conceit. 'Exile is when they shoot you if you go back,' she said. 'All the rest is travel.'

The Turkish writer **Sema Kaygusuz** swerved past the slightly self-regarding exile concept by unilaterally renouncing national allegiance for herself and all other writers – while still, in a cake-and-eat-it way, laying claim to her own cultural inheritance. 'If I were to have to talk of what drives my own writing, I would have to step outside the framework of national literature,' she said. 'In fact, all the world's writers are stateless. Like many of them, I have an inescapable feeling of separation. I feel discord, disquiet, fragmentation. On the other hand, when I try to create for myself an intellectual framework, I experience a narcissistic comfort that comes from having roots which spread from the Mediterranean basin to Mesopotamia, and from the Middle East to Anatolia. In other words, there is some atavistic factor that allows me to confront the feeling of statelessness. My intellectual geography is made up of all the celestial religions, the Greek gods and the myths of Sumeria, the Persian poets and Arab philosophers, Jewish cabalists and Armenian legends, Hellenic architecture, the first winegrowers of Rum and the shamans of the Turkmen, Gypsy songs and Kurdish bards ...'.

That is a lot for one imagination, one sensibility, to deal with. But no writer filters everything that they know, all they have experienced or want to say, into the one book. A novelist's cultural background is a storehouse, or maybe something more like a junkyard or a flea market. It is a place that they return to when they need to, to pick over the bric-a-brac and take away what they can use. Some writers, meanwhile, never go near that place, and garner all the material they need from, say, their own private memories of childhood. It doesn't matter, and (as another mantra of the Conference had it) there are no rules in literature. Writing can have a national dimension, of course, but it needn't. Theresa Breslin said it right at the very end of her keynote address in Krasnoyarsk. 'My hope is for a literature that raises the language above the ordinary, that makes words both functional and emotional, that resonates at the frequency of the human spirit – the skill and insight of the writer lifting the parochial novel above the level of regional concern. Making it personal, national, and universal.'

Jonathan Bastable (ed.)

On the African novel

by Helon Habila
Keynote, Brazzaville, February 2013

We can begin by attempting to define the African novel. This shouldn't be hard to do; we can simply look at definitions already proffered by eminent critics, and by practitioners of the African novel itself, and we must remember that in some cases these were the same persons, because the earlier African writers had to also act as their own critics in order to bring any sanity and nuance to a field dominated by foreign critics who tended to look at African literature as nothing but a sub-branch of western literature. And so African writers had to write their novels with one hand and to critique it with the other hand, as it were. Their critical writing has defined the African novel in terms of both form and content, but it must be pointed out that in most cases they don't simply say what the African novel is, but what they think it can, or should be. This last point is very important because, compared to other art forms, the African novel is a recent thing – before the colonial contact there was nothing like the novel in Africa. This is a fact. But although there was no novel, it didn't mean that there was no storytelling.

Before the novel came, all the rhetorical devices of the extended narrative were there, waiting to be adopted into the formal requirements of this alien art form. And it is this combination of oral elements grafted onto the substructure of the European novel, and written mostly in European languages, that has come to define the modern African novel.

One of the best examples of the African novel would be Chinua Achebe's *Things Fall Apart*, and having said that, I must also add that no, *Things Fall Apart* was not the first African novel, there were others before it – *Things Fall Apart* was published in 1958, and before that date there were novels like Sol Platje's *Mhundi*, Amos Tutuola's *The Palm-wine Drinkard*, and novels by Francophone writers like Mongo Beti and Camara Laye – and many others.

But it is Achebe's unusual grasp of the tenor and mood of the immediate post-colonial period, and his ability to express it clearly, unapologetically pitching his tent with the colonised, and his exemplary ability to incorporate oral narrative devices into the novel, that made his book stand out, making it something of a model for other African writers. One of the problems with *Things Fall Apart*, if one were inclined to find fault with it, is that it succeeded too much in what it set out to do, thereby over-determining in many instances the idea of what the African novel should be. To most critics *Things Fall Apart* is simply the African novel against which every other African novel must be measured. And I promise you that even as we speak right now, somewhere there is a paper being delivered on *Things Fall Apart* by one of those critics.

Chinua Achebe's view of the writer is a very traditional one: he believes the writer should be a teacher, a guide for the masses whose voices are often drowned out in the din of everyday life, and in this he is simply affirming the tradition of the ancient African griot [storyteller]. The griot is a rather Homeric figure, wise, almost godlike, something of a seer and a prophet. Something, I am sure you will agree with me, most contemporary writers don't see themselves as.

A writer whose view is directly opposed to that of Achebe is the colourful Zimbabwean writer, Dambudzo Marechera – in fact I can safely describe Marechera as the anti-Achebe. Born in Zimbabwe in 1952, this writer lived over nine years in the UK, before returning to Zimbabwe in 1982. He died in 1987. He is best known for his first novel, *The House of Hunger*. I mention him here to give you an idea of how complex and diverse African literature is, and to show that Achebe's is not the only model we have of the African novel. Marechera, and others like him, see themselves as belonging more to the tradition of Kafka and James Joyce than that of the ancient griots, and might even object to being called 'African' writers. Marechera had, on some occasion, had his book turned down by Heinemann African Writers Series for being 'insufficiently African', and by this they meant it was too unlike *Things Fall Apart*. Marechera insisted, in defence of his own writing, that, 'Far from imitating the practices of past generations of European writers, African novelists have extended the possibilities and uses of fiction'.

And so, while there are some who believe that African literature should continue to be very traditional, some of them, like the Kenyan author, Ngugi wa Thiong'o, going so far as to suggest that African writing should be done only in African languages, there are others who think that African writers should be open to external as well as internal influences, whether it is in language or in craft.

And these two positions, broadly speaking, have been the two opposing positions the African novel and indeed modern African literature has found itself occupying since its inception. Aesthetic nativism, or traditionalism, championed by people like Ngugi and Leopold Senghor and all brands of nationalist critics on the one hand, and those, like Marechera, who are opposed to them, who see nothing pernicious in influence, who are grateful, in fact, for influence – for isn't the novel supposed to be ever-new, and ever-changing? For isn't it the artist's first duty to be transgressive and adventurous, to experiment wildly, and to chart new paths even if it is by attempting to mix what on the surface might appear unmixable? What must be objected to, in defining the African novel, is every attempt to reduce it to a sub-genre of anthropology, a pedagogical tool for teachers of African politics and history.

But, perhaps a better way of looking at the African novel is to retrace our steps and ask, what does the novel do, not just the African novel, but the novel in general, what is its *raison d'etre*? If, as has often been observed, the novel illustrates or examines the human condition, then it is logical to say that the African novel exists to illustrate the African human condition, and if that is so, the next question should be, what exactly is this African human condition? Is it different from the general human condition, something uniquely experienced by Africans due to certain historical and social factors? If the novel always looks at life as it unfolds – and this for me is the genius of the novel, it will always be a step, even two steps, ahead of the critics and the theorists; before the critics can formulate their critiques and highfalutin opinions, the novel has already moved on. If that is the case, then the African novel is that which illustrates the African human condition as it unfolds today. This is attested to in the way the African novel has evolved in the space of about fifty years since independence, it has moved from being the novel of anti-colonial sentiment, or what has been called the novel of culture clash, to embrace a multiplicity of themes. I must point out here that I am not undermining the importance of the historical element in the African novel, but even if the African novel goes back in time to tackle a historical subject, it must do so with a contemporary sensibility – the eye-end of its telescope must be firmly rooted in the concerns of the here and now.

The contemporary African novel must deal with contemporary African issues, it must unshackle itself from the excessive fascination with its colonial past that is beginning to assume an almost normative importance, as if the African novel cannot be relevant unless it continues to obsess about how or why Africans were colonised by Europe. What about travel, what about urbanisation, globalisation, what about the environment, what has the African novel got to say about them? To stay relevant, the African novel must set the agenda for its preoccupation, not continue to react to a petrified image of Africa created by Europe; a homogenous, monolithic, and static space suspended in time. The African writer must see himself as a free agent, free from the restrictions of tradition. He or she must share a table in that room imagined by EM Forster in *Aspects of the Novel*, sitting side by side with all the best writers in the canon: Henry James, Dickens, Achebe, Soyinka, Shakespeare, Thackeray, Tolstoy, Flaubert, Goethe – he must see himself as competing with them, for in this room there is no skin colour, no excuses about lack of opportunities for publishing, no excuse about anything, there is only the word processor and the imagination.

Below are some themes I like to think of as themes of the future – themes that might in a way even come to redefine the African novel. Some of the themes, interest ingly, have been touched upon by earlier African writers, even though they didn't treat them with the urgency and centrality they now deserve.

Novels of the City

Here are some facts to think about. Currently, Africa has the highest rate of urbanisation in the world. It has been estimated that by 2020, Africa will have more than eleven megacities – a megacity has a population of over five million people – and that by 2025 Africa will have seventy-three cities with a population of between one and five million people. It is logical then to assume that the city, as setting, as theme, even as aesthetic determiner – will continue to engage the African novel in the foreseeable future. How then, does the African writer approach it, illustrate it? To my mind few writers have captured the idea of the city, with its threats, its precarious modernity, as well as its possibilities, as Yvonne Vera does in the opening section of her novel *Stone Virgins*, describing the city of Bulawayo in pre-independence Zimbabwe:

> The city revolves in sharp edges; roads cut at right angles. At noon, shadows are sharp and elongated. Streets are wide. Widest at intersections. In this city, the edge of a building is a profile, a corner ... ekoneni. The word is pronounced with pursed lips and lyrical minds, with arms pulsing, with a memory begging for time. .. Ekoneni is a rendezvous, a place to meet. You cannot meet inside any of the buildings because this city is divided .... Here you linger, ambivalent, permanent as time. You are in transit. The corner is a camouflage, a place of instancy and style; a place of protest. Ekoneni is also a dangerous place, where knives emerge as suddenly as lightning.

This passage understands so well the idea of the city as conceived by the coloniser – an off-limits space, its square buildings on the European model, severe, and its open streets daunting to the outsider, designed not so much for comfort as to expose and deny the unwanted intruder a hiding space, banishing him to the corner, the shadow zone, the fringe. It is also a sight for protest, for creative dissidence and improvisation. And the question to ask will be: has all that changed with independence, or does the new African ruling class see itself as the rightful inheritor of the colonisers' space and therefore it has the right to banish its less privileged countrymen and women to the ghettos and townships? And if you think that is farfetched, just look at our cities today, Abuja, Lagos, Nairobi, Cape Town, how they are built without provision for the poor, forcing them to live in the shanty towns and ghettos on the city outskirts: close enough to be tapped for their labour, but far enough not to be seen.

Traditionally in African novels the city has been treated as a place of moral ambivalence, filled with temptations and spiritual perils. To me, and I am sure to most younger African writers, the city has been a place of great good. To become a writer I left my small Nigerian town and moved to Lagos where I found intellectual stimulation and encouragement from fellow travellers, people like myself, journalists, poets, writers. This is where the readers are, and the publishers, and the critics, and the bookstores. The city may have its many dangers, but it also has innumerable opportunities.

The Travel Novel

Currently I am working on a novel tentatively titled *Travellers*. It is about Africans living in the US. I read somewhere recently that among this year's most anticipated novels are novels by African writers, Chimamanda Adichie and a recent Caine prize winner, NoViolet Bulawayo, and they are both about Africans living in America. My good friend, the Zimbabwean writer Brian Chikwava, not too long ago, published a novel titled *Harare North*, about the experience of African immigrants in London. This, and future generations of African writers, will continue to write about travel the way the first generation of African writers wrote about colonialism and the clash of cultures; simply because there are more Africans currently travelling and living outside of Africa than ever before. And as they travel they create stories, some sad, some happy, but all serving to illustrate that ever-widening idea of the African human condition

One good example would be my friend, the writer, Chika Unigwe, who was born in Nigeria, now living in Belgium, married to a white Belgian, with Belgian children, writing sometimes in Flemish, and still calling herself an African writer. This is the new reality, the new African writer. Suddenly the earlier debates by African writers over what language an African writer should write in, or even who can be called an African writer, seem so irrelevant and dated, overtaken by the facts of modern living. Even though my friend Chika writes in Flemish for a largely Belgian audience, who is to say that she is not an African writer, that she doesn't examine the African human condition as it unfolds in Belgium?

Travel, in real life and as metaphor, is an expression of freedom, adventure, growth, curiosity, crossing of borders and breaking of boundaries. What colonialism did, with its delineation of arbitrary national boundaries, was to imprison the African in these imaginary borders, and the modern world, with its insistence on travel documentation and discriminatory travel policies, seeks to keep the African in Africa while others travel freely anywhere at any time. By asserting his right to travel, by asserting his right to live in other places other than Africa, the African is saying he also is part of this great world that God gave us.

That is why I like to refer to this new generation of African writers as the post-nationalist generation. They are a generation that questions the narrow idea of nationalism especially where it seeks to confine and limit both physical and mental movement.

The novel, *Open City*, by Teju Cole, published in 2011, has a main character, Julius, who is half-Nigerian half-Belgian, living in New York. And what is interesting about this book by this African writer is that it is a book about New York: a celebration of the complex history of that city, and the place of people like Julius in that space. Here is Julius at Ellis Island, contemplating the significance of this historic port of entry where refugees from Europe were once processed before being allowed into America to become citizens:

> From where I stood, the statue of Liberty was a fluorescent green fleck against the sky and beyond her sat Ellis Island, the focus of so many myths; but it had been built too late for those early Africans – who weren't immigrants in any case – and it had been closed too soon to mean anything to the later Africans like Kenneth, or the cabdriver, or me. Ellis Island was a symbol mostly for European refugees. Blacks, we blacks, had known rougher ports of entry ....

The Environmental Novel

Of all the emerging themes in African literature, the one that focuses on the environment is perhaps the least explored, and the one Africans seem least interested in, at least that is what I thought until I began my research for my last book, *Oil on Water*, dealing with the subject of oil pollution and violence in the Niger Delta. I discovered that the traditional African way has always been about conservation – there were always attempts, through ritual and religious observances, to maintain harmony between the human world and the animal and plant world. This is exemplified in the recognition that not only humans, but even animals have souls, and that plants can be homes to spirits and other unseen beings. And in most communities before a tree is cut down, certain rituals must first be carried out, this is the same with the killing of animals, which was always done for food, not for sport.

And now, when I read African novels like Ngugi wa Thiong'o's *Weep Not Child*, I realise that the anguish of the lead characters when their land is taken away from them by the British farmer, is not just anguish over the loss of their means of livelihood, it is anguish over being separated from the land, from that spiritual connection with their ancestors and all their dead who were buried in the land.

Since my book *Oil on Water* came out, I have become something of an environmental advocate, I go to give readings and people want to know about the activities of Shell and Texaco in the Niger Delta – as reluctant as I am to usurp the place of an environmental activist, I am also made aware that this is another aspect of the modern African experience that the writer simply can not afford to ignore. Every day oil is being discovered in yet another African country, every day another mine is started in Ghana or Congo or South Africa, which leads to another war, or another *coup d'état*. Our forests are fast disappearing, even as our mineral resources are being exploited daily by foreign corporations without regard to sustainability. Even though, unlike Achebe, I don't see myself as a teacher or prophet – my view of the writer is more as a student than a teacher, a student of life and nature and of himself – yet I believe it is important to speak out. And when I speak out I am not necessarily speaking out for my community or my country, I am speaking out for myself, for my conscience.

I will conclude, by urging the African novelist to always question tradition even as he or she remains rooted in culture. He must break away from tradition where necessary, for tradition is only there to guide us, it is a road sign, not a destination.

Lingua Franca

by Alain Mabanckou

Helon Habila, in his keynote, touched on the widely held notion that African novels should be written only in African languages. For him this was too extreme a position, but other delegates to the Conference mentioned having encountered analogous arguments elsewhere in the world. The Malay novelist **Chuah Guat Eng**, speaking in Kuala Lumpur, said that she had been reprimanded in Europe for writing in English rather than in Malay or in the Chinese of her forefathers. She said it seemed to make no difference to her critics that English was the language of her childhood home, or even that – her ethnicity notwithstanding – she speaks no Chinese. Writing in the local language – and a concommitant refusal to use the language of the coloniser – is seen to equate with cultural patriotism and a particular kind of national-historic authenticity.

But the fact is, language and nationality are not always contiguous. More often than not, language does not map onto nationality at all – neither in cartographic terms, nor in the psychological landscape of individual writers. One could, for example, make a persuasive argument that English literature is best defined as literature in English – but one would have to expect howls of protest from Anglophone writers who happen to be American, Scottish, Indian, Australian, Canadian ....

... or indeed African, since Africa, it goes without saying, encompasses many nationalities and languages, but some of its great fiction was produced in European languages. Any discussion of the parameters of the language of African literature is already a transnational, multilingual undertaking. And as it happens, **Alain Mabanckou**, in the keynote he delivered in Brazzaville, dwelt on this very question of language, literature and national (or supranational) allegiance – as if commenting on the passing remarks in Habila's speech. What follows is an abridged version of that address on the topic of African literature in French.

'The question of a national literature is very political,' said Mabanckou, 'especially when we are discussing writers from sub-Saharan Africa. The question implies that we disapprove of writers who prefer what became official languages, those of colonisation. We imply that Francophone Congolese literature cannot be called national literature, because it is expressed in a language incapable of understanding some of the 'codes' of specific local realities. There is in this a kind of nostalgia for times past, mingled with a gregarious africanism which denies writers the possibility of hearing the din of the world, the chaos of mutations born out of what the great Congolese writer Tchicaya Utam'si referred to as the 'bronze civilisation'. The notion of a national literature is used to confine spirits – to demagogical ends.

'This nationalistic and very afro-centred movement is now widespread among French black African elite writers. For them, a national literature represents the reconquering of an identity, a return to the source, a rejection of western domination. It is, in a word, a call for a real African conscience, since what makes up what we would call African literature – written by Africans for Africans – is the sum of the continent's national literatures. In order to achieve this reconquering, some writers challenge the use of the French language, and criticise those who defend the language of French writers, going so far as to call them hypocrites and corrupt because they 'write for white people'. The Cameroonian writer Patrice Nganang suggested a few years ago that the aim was 'to write without France'. And Patrice Nganang has asked: 'Shall we soon see the day when African writers truly stop being Francophone?' He is demanding that the writings of his continent be given a 'colour'. In other words, he is calling for the emergence or the recognition of so-called national literatures. And in Africa, these literatures can only exist if they stand clearly in opposition to western writing, which is seen as the grave of black conscience, as the place where African identity is erased.

'But in what way does writing in French prevent you from being an African writer, a Congolese, a Senegalese or a Cameroonian writer who speaks of the world? The main argument of those defending literatures written in local languages is that the French language is tainted with a crippling, insurmountable, and (should I say) inexcusable vice: it is the language of the coloniser. According to the proponents of this literature of authenticity, French carries the ciphers of enslavement, and turns of phrases that are inappropriate for African phrasing. Senegalese writer Boubacar Boris Diop declared he would henceforth be writing in Wolof, so as to be in tune with himself. He explained his decision as follows: 'French – and English – are ceremonial languages, and their codes, both grammatical and cultural, have something intimidating about them .... They make the African writer doubt the very meaning and purpose of his literary craft.' Boris Diop therefore published a novel in Wolof in 2003. It was called *Doomi Golo* (*The Monkey Children*). But two years later he published *L'impossible innocence* (*The Impossible Innocence*), a novel written in the most masterly French.

'The idea of a national literature implies a dangerous opposition between African writers 'from within' and African writers 'from without'. The African writer 'from without', who lives in Europe, is seen as someone who is disconnected from reality. The prejudice is that his vision of the world is skewed because he is uprooted. And a corrupt writer, caught in the quicksands of the Parisian editorial system, no longer speaks to his brothers and sisters, but to an audience of convenience which tells him what to write: 'books formatted for a western public' as Senegalese journalist Nabo Sene puts it. But then what is the literary nation of Salman Rushdie, of Vladimir Nabokov – or of David Diop, who was born in Bordeaux, but who is considered a powerful voice of the Negritude movement?

'Do we need a national literature, by which I mean a literature written in African languages? Of course we do, when these African languages are taught in order to enable the public to have access to another sort of literature. Yet most French-speaking writers of black Africa, though they speak their native language, are far from mastering it in writing. Many of those languages remain oral tongues. The policy-makers of those countries should first hold a debate around their languages. It is essential to work on building a grammar, or rethinking it if it already exists; reorganising it, setting up regional education authorities, drafting dictionaries, designing newspapers. In a word, people need to be prepared to go from an oral stage to a much more demanding written stage.

'And we must stop boasting about the role of elders in transmitting culture. Nothing keeps us from translating the French book of an African author into an African language! *The Guardians of the Temple*, by Cheikh

Hamidou Kane, was written in French and later translated into Wolof! The issue isn't just writing in an African language, but also preparing Africans to read that language the way the French, the Chinese or the Russians are prepared to read their respective languages.

'Simply branding a literature as national serves only to strengthen prejudices concerning the themes that African writers should address. The elements of that literature would be predictably inevitable: a certain vocabulary, a predictable colourfulness. Every cultural field would be affected by this. In film there would be a specific national, perhaps even African colour – and the same would go for paintings, sculptures and so on. The national writer would be the clerk of his nation, the guardian of the nation's desires and customs, and indirectly, his mission would be to tell of his space, and of that alone. And if he deviated from that mission, he would be called a black man in a white mask.

'We give back to the world what we have received from it. We are the product of our exchanges and of our movements. At a time when the artist is as mobile as the work he creates, it is not surprising that some of Cuba's soil should be mixed with that of South Africa or of some Amazonian land. Books take us to unknown territories. And art erases borders, allowing the thoughtful observer to add meaning to it, so that the language of thought becomes secondary. What matters is our ability to enter a universe, to make it ours, to read the creative trance of the writer, this universal creative trance, seeing beyond each sign, each colour. This peregrinatory age is set to redefine space, to open up minds. The world is at our door with its noises, its fury, its oceans, its thick forests, its species that we must tame. When we go to faraway lands, we initiate the process that will enable us to rebuild our humanity .... We need only to open our eyes and look to the horizon to see how varied the firmament is, especially that ever-changing rainbow. This is what art is. This is what artists offer us: a chance not only to brighten our future, but also to revisit our past.'

Categorisation is reductive

by Marlon James
Keynote, Trinidad, April 2013

A soon as I heard what was to be the topic of this discussion, I thought of two things immediately. Chimamanda Adichie's groundbreaking TED talk on the danger of the singular story and an incident I experienced recently where after being asked to interview the Jamaican poet Mutabaruka, I was, without my knowledge then demoted to asking prepared questions from the audience. All because a Jamaican organisation found me unsuitable, too volatile a voice to represent Jamaica in an international forum – which was sort of like me telling Bunny Wailer that you can't hang with Peter Tosh because you've been known to smoke weed.

But what both instances reminded me of was the immediate pitfall, the danger in the term 'national literature', the same danger in terms like 'black music' or 'women's fiction.' That this is a categorisation and any attempt at categorisation is reductive, like the library of congress reducing your novel to three words. Take away literature and substitute any other art and this is quickly apparent: a national music, a national painting, a national dance step, especially in this post-everything age where national boundaries are not only irrelevant but sometimes anti-art. Because at the core of categorisation is an attempt not only to make something smaller, but also easily definable. Great art resists paraphrase, but isn't 'national lit' an act of paraphrasing?

And we're already seeing this happening, a move certainly in my country Jamaica to decide what is acceptable and unacceptable national literature. At the core, this acceptance versus rejection is a moralising; sprung from both religiosity and jingoism, an attempt to enforce the singular story. Sometimes with the delusion of diversity. So sure, let's have a gay story as long as it fits an acceptable arc of sadness, but what if it involves actual gay sex and what if the two or more involved quite like it? Moralising disguised as nationalising rears it ugly head when we talk about violence. There's an acceptable limit, which can be crossed if there's an acceptable comeuppance. But what if you're Irish playwright Martin McDonagh and you're a master of violence, that your poetry is gore, guts and buckets of blood? And what if you're totally amoral about the whole thing? What if you're Jamaica's Jean Genet, or even closer: an actual Jamaican who navigates queer space to international acclaim yet all but unknown in her home country, Patricia Duncker? Is Thomas Glave national lit? Or what if you're none of these things, but someone who simply wants to write about the middle class? You end up in that situation where your national lit isn't national enough.

And what are teachers supposed to do with a national literature? Teach art or nationalism? I was part of a generation where this was first enforced, not just nationalism but regionalism, clearly with good intentions, after all if you spend your early years with Enid Blyton you're going to need all the cultural correctives you can get. But the result was not a national literature or the appreciation of it. It was a steady diet of simplistic poems, leaden dramas, and failed novels that caused, certainly in my generation, an unhealthy association of local literature with mediocrity, nostalgia and sentimentality. That these were works to consume because it was your national duty, not because they had any inherent value. And another thing happens, where in the midst of your own literature you disappear. Because there was no one in these books like you. You unfortunately came from neither bush nor ghetto so your voice is illegitimate. It certainly explains why in the discussion of Jamaican literature for example, John Hearne and Louis Simpson rarely appear. What if you just don't look like a national writer? I remember when I was a student I was told that nobody in Jamaica writes about the upper middle class but John Hearne and nobody reads him. And lord knows the man should not be lionised, but he should not be ignored either. How do I get to be national enough? Who gets to define it? And will they be inclusive or restrictive, because that makes all the difference.

A good parallel example for this is hip-hop. Between 1981 and 1991, rap music had its most creative years, certainly it most expansive, driven by this unbelievable sense of possibility. A form that came out of nothing could now encompass everything. But growth makes us nervous. By 1993, there was a growing mood that hip-hop was *too* expansive, *too* inclusive and out of that came a new idea: What is *not* hip-hop. The music started to define identity by drawing lines. You want to grow up? Sorry, not hip-hop. You're neither bitch nor ho? Not hip-hop. Can't keep it real and represent? Not hip-hop. Now an art-form had a gatekeeper, and not only that, it made gatekeeping the legitimate means for defining the culture. What's the price we pay for this, of music, of literature becoming so easily defined because it is being protected? It becomes easily produced. Easily parodied. So take one small rural village, two grannies, a church sister named Dorcas, two wayward children named Lerlene and one Mas Joe (because there must always be a Mas Joe), throw in some rivers, a mountain and a brush with obeah and – poof! – you have a Jamaican novel. No movement has ever survived categorisation, not 1970s-style feminism that couldn't figure out what to do with non-American women, or the Black Arts movement that couldn't figure out what to do with James Baldwin. A national literature, if this is the way it goes forward, as it sometimes threatens to be, won't get very far either.

This is a problem that will stunt art. Every few years for example we have a rash of 'Britain for the British' fever, which is just a cutely racist way of saying British lit does not look like British lit unless it's white. You get a case of too many paintings and not enough mirrors. Even rebellion gets couched in a nationally approved way — always moralistic, never complicated. Sexuality if it happens is off-stage. Poverty is always confused with simplicity and the past is always suffused with nostalgia. A national literature whose first duty is to promote tourism, not art.

Now, a national literature, if it's supposed to happen, has to be so broad that it risks vagueness. Like Japanese literature it has to be constantly wrestled with and debated even at the risk of extinguishing the very idea of it. Like Indian literature it has to both accept and throw away the concept of Indian-ness and whether that has any bearing on literature at all. It has to include the next *Beloved*, but also the next *Story of O*. Criticism of it has to evolve as well beyond the petty sensibilities of critics and beyond the argument of whether a book should or should not have been published or whether or not it hurts the Brand. Japanese literature had to evolve from a very simplistic and jingoist idea of nationalism to something that celebrates both Murakamis: the one who writes dreamlike fantasies and the one who writes sadomasochistic violence. Swedish literature is at once immediately recognisable and unclassifiable. It recognises how essential it is, the contrary voice, the ambivalent voice, the deeply critical. Everybody of course knows of *The Girl With the Dragon Tattoo* but some are unaware that its Swedish title is *Men Who Hate Women* and it's a scathing critique of Scandinavian society's almost institutionalised brutality against women. And yet the book is held up as something to celebrate in a way that a book called *Men Who Kill Battymen* would never be in Jamaica. At least not yet.

Maybe we need to rethink the term, and it's not just the literature that needs to evolve, but also the national. National literature should never be anything that follows the word 'should'. There is no such word as 'should' in art. It can be cultural despite having no flag-waving purpose. Where speaking truth to power is a greater service than describing beautiful beaches and wonderful people, it resists a literary blackface. National Literature is worth fighting for, but also worth fighting over. That it should never be confused with a national story; that's an advertising agency's job. A national literature wrestles with form but also leaves it alone. A national literature reckons with how people actually speak. It recognises the fluidity and musicality of form and extends it. For a national literature to exist it must always be uneasy with the term 'national literature', distrusting it every step of the way.

Or a national literature is none of the above, but rather a blank space and safe space, a sponsored space but also a free space where nothing is beyond imagining but anything can happen.

Above the barriers

The Irish writer **Arthur Riordan**, speaking in Brussels, quoted James Joyce's famous mission statement: 'To forge in the smithy of my soul the uncreated conscience of my race'. The two key nouns in that phrase – soul and race – encapsulate the insoluble contradiction at the heart of the national-literature formula. **Jonathan Shainin** summed it up while chairing the discussion in Jaipur: 'If the novel is a humanist and individualist project, then it is a contradiction to ask that novels bear the burden of representing the entire culture.' **Imraan Coovadia**, in Cape Town, was inclined to agree: 'None of us writers want to take on national duties. We are far too busy. I am not sure what we are doing, but we *are* busy – worrying. It seems like a chore to think at a national level.' For **Melvin Burgess**, speaking in Krasnoyarsk, the problem was not so much to do with the workman as with the tool. 'Novels don't really deal with political constructs such as the nation,' he said. 'The Modernist writers such as Joyce were trying to be transnational, to write beyond the national tradition, but there are writers who are much more embedded in their culture, which is different from being embedded in your nation. But actually Joyce was writing specifically about Dublin.'

But was he was though? Is that was he was hammering out on his innermost anvil – a souvenir of Grafton Street? Surely Joyce was trying to say something truthful about himself in such a way as to say something meaningful about everybody. That's the aim of most art of every kind. Literature strives to be personal and at the same time universal, almost never national. Several delegates sought spiritual ways to parse the notion of homeland, so as to raise it above the irksome reality of the nation-state and define it in abstract or metaphorical terms that a collocation of writers could feel comfortable with. **Jose Rodrigues Dos Santos** quoted the Portuguese poet Fernando Pessoa, who said: 'My country is my language.'

Marina Warner, in Trinidad cited Derek Walcott: 'I have no territory now but the imagination.'

Ben Okri, in Edinburgh, also turned to remarks made by an earlier generation of writers, and wove around them one of his spellbinding bijou orations. 'Around the time that the original Edinburgh Conference was taking place here in the 1960s,' he said, 'there was a great African conference taking place in Nigeria. And this very same question of national literature – African literature – perplexed us then (and it continues to rage wherever I go). In 1966 the Nigerian poet Christopher Okigbo made an astonishing remark. He said: "There is no such thing as African writing; there is only good writing or bad writing." At that same conference there was a lot of talk of "negritude," as a way of describing the African spirit. Wole Soyinka stood up and said: "A tiger does not speak about its tigritude – it pounces!" I think we need to bring that spirit back here to this Conference. We need to remember that writers *write* – as well as they can, as truthfully as they can, from the depths of their spirit, about what burns them, annoys them, amuses them, shocks them, disgusts them. I am perplexed by the notion of a national literature because a nation is constantly unfolding, and the artist is an important part of that process. If you say "Scottishness is this shape", then you limit the possibilities of Scottishness for all time. The writer is constantly widening the boundaries of who we think we are.'

In Edinburgh, at least, the Conference seemed to be moving towards a sort of concensus around the universal, whatever the local context of any particular book. It also seemed to be generally agreed that national literature could be taken to mean that readers – especially unformed young readers – were best served by books that portrayed their own lives, that were populated with characters not unlike their own selves. But there were two slightly dissenting voices. First, **China Miéville** sounded this dissonant note. 'I think there is a problem with the opposite of localism being universalism,' he said. 'What if the opposite of localism is complete estrangement? Why should we recognise ourselves in literature? Why is the aim to see our own lives reflected? Surely literature can also be fantastic by reflecting nothing that we've ever seen before, by completely shocking and astonishing us. In the immediate aftermath of the Zimbabwean revolution there was a huge drive for a local Zimbabwean literature – for entirely legitimate and understandable nation-building reasons. Dambudzo Marechera's response was to set out to write something that would traumatise everyone – because he lived in a traumatic world. I think that is more interesting than producing literature in which we recognise our local surroundings.'

Ewan Morrison immediately stormed into the breach that Miéville had opened up by suggesting that national or regional literature should perhaps be subject to an *appellation d'origine contrôlée* – a protected status like that enjoyed by Arbroath smokies and Welsh laverbread. 'We as writers with indigenous backgrounds have to fight the homogenising forces of global culture,' he said, 'and one of the ways that we do that is to put up walls. France and Germany are very effective in protecting their culture – including their cheese and their sausages. It is not enough to write from your own language and your own culture, you have got to attack the source of the homogenisation, which is global capitalism. This is a little plea on behalf of the cheeses and the sausages.'

Morrison was being playful for sure: it must be hard for him, as for anyone else, to see how a national or international authority could forbid a French writer to set a story in Glasgow, or license an Australian writer to tell a tale about Vietnam. Stories – until they are shared – are the property of the person who dreamed them up. And as **Reza Aslan** said in Jaipur: 'Stories are about people, not about events or ideas. The only thing that has the power to break through the walls that separate us – into different nationalities, peoples, cultures, religions – is story. And story can reach us in such an intimate visceral way that it doesn't matter what god we pray to, or what state we are a citizen of.'

Jonathan Bastable (ed.)

Citizens of the cosmopolis

by Kapka Kassabova
Keynote, Brussels, March 2013

Last year at the Olympic event Poetry Parnassus, I represented Bulgaria. I accepted the invitation because it was an honour, but felt like a fraud – our family emigrated from Bulgaria twenty years ago, and I write in English. In the past, because I was living and publishing in New Zealand, I attended festivals as a New Zealand writer – and again, I felt like a fraud. Today, I'm honoured to be here as a writer from Scotland, a country I love and feel at home in, and I'm still struggling with that fraudulent feeling.

In short, the idea of national literature gives me a headache. The headache escorts me to public events where you must appear not just with your name and your book, but with your nation too. You must be escorted, as if you can't be trusted on your own.

The headache comes from a clash between the private and the public. Between my instinct, shared by many writers, to unsubscribe from the collective, and the collective claim which is what all things 'national' do, they claim – national literature, national identity, national sport, national pride, national shame, national history .... The list is long and to me, as someone from the Balkans, depressing. The nineteenth century was in love with nationhood. And the twentieth demonstrated in detail just how nationality, like ethnicity and religion, is an accident – sometimes a lucky escape, sometimes fatal. An unnamed child during the 1990s wars in Yugoslavia, clearly a born poet, had the last word on this: 'I love my country, because it is small and I feel sorry for it.'

When we say 'national literature', we are uttering an anguished cry. The very construct is an expression of a nostalgic desire for a home that can be written in terms of nation. It's a desire for innocence. Nation as family, mother tongue as home. How lovely. And how dangerous.

We understand a place through the art that comes out of it. Books, pictures, music, this is what endures when other things go – political fashions, golden ages, nature itself. I live in the Highlands, an area of sublime natural beauty, and every day I see another forest come down, and a pylon replacing it. When the forests are gone, what is left are the stories of the forests. Sooner or later, a place becomes its literature. So the real question we're asking when we say 'national literature' is: Where is my home? What is this place? Who are my people?

We might say that in the global era, this is an irrelevant question, and I think it *is* privately irrelevant to most people. But it acquires momentum in public. I've seen it discussed in Bulgaria and Britain among others, each country like a family carrying its ancestral baggage and looking for somewhere to lay it down.

So here's a suggestion. What if, in this young century where we are simultaneously victims and beneficiaries of globalisation, there are *already* two meanings of the word nation: the traditional and the spiritual. We are familiar with the traditional nation-state. It has a capital and a periphery (the diaspora), it's attached to an approved language in which it writes its literature, and it's in love with its own myths and monuments. The Roma make other Europeans nervous because they are a nation without a state – you can't even tell them, in the international language of the thug – to 'go home'. They don't have one, except in music. From Rajasthan to Andalusia, via the Balkans and Eastern Europe, the Romany Gypsies are a nation of music. This is not to say their plight is romantic – being the underdog is not romantic. It is to say that Gypsy music distils all human exile. Not unlike jazz, the blues, and the tango, created in Argentina and Uruguay by immigrants and the dispossessed, and now consecrated by UNESCO as intangible human heritage.

Back at Poetry Parnassus, I discovered that the poet from Turkmenistan Ak Welsapar lives in Sweden, and Nikola Madzirov, the poet from Macedonia lives, in his own words, out of a suitcase. The poet from

Australia, John Kinsella, is so opposed to nationhood that he once asked for a Red Cross passport (he was denied it). When I asked Christodoulos Makris, the poet from Cyprus who lives in Ireland, how he felt about the Olympic thing, he said: Well, I could equally be representing Ireland, or Britain. Many poets of course lived in their original homelands and wrote in their first language. The point is, this Parnassian gathering was a mini-nation in itself: a nation of poetry. I was among my people – those for whom poetry is more important than other things. I felt at home, because home, as the poet Christian Morgenstern said, is where they understand you.

On the question of home, here is a haiku by the seventeenth-century poet Basho:

Even when I am in Kyoto
When I hear the call of the cuckoo
I miss Kyoto.

I've never been to Kyoto, but I miss Kyoto too, because this haiku is not a patriot's song, it's a spiritual incantation. A yearning for the union of the material – which is not enough – with the imagined. Kyoto chiming with the idea of Kyoto.

I spent my childhood in Bulgaria in the company of books and languages, as if they were passports that would lead me out into the world. Like many kids, I was homesick for the world. Home ceases to be home when the door is removed, and the Berlin Wall was the opposite of a door. Reading was my 'internal emigration', my cure for homesickness. Even though I was in Sofia, when I heard the tinkling of the trams, I missed Sofia. Which is why I wrote the memoir *Street Without a Name* twenty years later. When we leave our families or homelands to become more fully ourselves, they haunt us, doubly real with the call of the cuckoo.

Joyce Carol Oates says that for most writers, 'the art of writing is the use to which we put our homesickness'. It makes sense: exile is our essential condition. We are all exiled – from a landscape, from an original homeland, from our own unlived lives. In German, it's *Weltschmerz*. In Portuguese, *saudade*. In Spanish, *tanguidad,* a state of tango.

I am yet to hear a writer say they write to be included in a canon of national literature. How could you? People move countries. Countries move people. The literature of a nation is a mirage because the concept of nation is a mirage. Stories, however, remain.

The Scottish-born Robert Louis Stevenson, one of the world's most translated authors who died in Samoa and is buried there with his American wife, is to world readers simply a favourite writer. And so with favourite books: *Treasure Island, Peter Pan, Sherlock Holmes, Alice in Wonderland, The Little Prince*, these are books we grow up with, before we even learn the word nation. The novels of Ismail Kadare are read by people who know nothing about Albania. I first discovered Morocco – and Moroccan writers – through the fiction of Paul Bowles, an American-born writer. One of my favourite books about Argentina is written by the Polish-born Witold Gombrowicz who went on a 'casual' visit to Buenos Aires and ended up staying for twenty-four years. Kafka is almost his own noun, synonymous not with a country or a language, but with the twentieth century – that lover of ideas, that enemy of life.

These writers' worlds are cosmopolitan, yet pungently rooted in specific reality, with all the quirks of place and personality. Cosmopolitanism mustn't be confused with Coca-Cola. It doesn't have to breed cultural homogeneity. It is the freedom to come and go, or indeed stay, without the urge to wave a flag. We Europeans, especially, can't afford to snub that freedom – if we are to have a future.

We are surrounded by what Nabokov described with the Russian word *poshlost*, 'the falsely important, the falsely beautiful', a form of public kitsch. It's what advertising gurus and tribal rhetoricians specialise in. Tribal allegiances, like shopping, give us the illusion of a self, the sugar-pill of familiarity, but it's never enough if the spirit centre is missing. The real task in all our lives is to find a true spiritual home.

This is the point Diogenes was making when he walked around Athens with a lantern, looking 'for an honest man'. When asked where he was from, he said *kosmopolites* – a citizen of the universe. In defiance to the city-state which demanded citizenly obedience, his allegiance was to common humanity. He lived in an empty tin and he was a free man.

I'm not suggesting we all get ourselves an empty tin. I'm making a humanist call, in the spirit of the Scottish Enlightenment. Instead of going on a state-visit to the mausoleum of national literature, let's inhabit the living cosmopolis of books, art, and music. There are no borders and no one will ask the purpose of your visit, or tell you to 'go home'.

STYLE VERSUS CONTENT

Reading the reader

by Hannah McGill

For whom does a writer write – and what sense can we make of style?

'Kill your darlings,' creative writing students are traditionally advised. Excise, in other words, those parts of your manuscript that smack of self-conscious craft. Raymond Carver, doyen of minimalism, took from his university tutor John Gardner that he should use fifteen words instead of twenty-five; later, his editor Gordon Lish would be more stringent still, advocating five in place of that fifteen. Cut, edit, simplify; bad writing is over-writing; any colour as long as it's not purple – so still runs the bulk of the received wisdom, whether a writer studies formally or just gathers tips along the way. In a set of rules for fiction writing supplied by noted authors to *The Guardian* in 2010, the finger wagged again and again. And that construction in itself would be frowned upon by Esther Freud, whose counsel was 'Cut out the metaphors and similes'. Warned David Hare in the same piece: 'Style is the art of getting yourself out of the way, not putting yourself in it.' 'Cut ... only by having *no* inessential words can every essential word be made to count,' scolded a nearby Diana Athill. And – oh dear – 'Never use a verb other than "said" to carry dialogue,' bellowed Elmore Leonard.

And yet ... and yet. And yet poetry. And yet jokes. And yet rules being made to be broken. And yet James, Faulkner, Nabokov, Carter, and the fun Dave Eggers was having in *A Heartbreaking Work of Staggering Genius* compared with the much less fun he seems to be having now that his prose has grown all sort of clipped and sad. And yet the seductiveness of gilding and embellishment versus the spare sensible greyness of self-control. Purple can be a pretty colour, after all. To Alice Walker's character Shug Avery, who gives her most famous novel its title, it's evidence of the Almighty going out of his way to please us: 'I think it pisses God off if you walk by the color purple in a field somewhere and don't notice it.'

In a 1985 *New York Times* essay entitled 'In Defense of Purple Prose', Paul West has similar appreciation for purple in its literary application: it is, he argues, not excess, but 'a homage to nature and to what human ingenuity can do with nature's givens.' Plain writing, by contrast, is a field no-one's bothered to plant. To West, fashionable minimalism constitutes 'a refusal to look honestly at a complex universe … an excuse for dull and mindless writing, larded over with the democratic myth that says this is how most folks are.'

Raymond Carver, though never inclined to what one might call purplism, withdrew his work from Gordon Lish's heavy hand in the end, bemoaning the 'surgical amputation and transplant' he saw Lish deploying in order to fit the established idea of 'what a Carver short story ought to be'. That particular relationship remains a matter of myth and of controversy – a cautionary tale either of how a writer can reap the rewards for an unsung editor's instincts, or of how an insensitive editor can override a writer's wishes, depending on your perspective. But the discussions that took place at the Conference under the banner of 'Style Versus Content' made it powerfully apparent that the matter of forced or elaborate style, as set against the disputed holy grail of unmediated, furbelow-free directness, remains a significantly contentious one. To some, the question of 'how most folks are' so slightingly referenced by Paul West deserved to be lent more weight. Writers, when not communicating on the level of some mythic lowest common denominator of readers, sinned *politically* – by implicit elitism; by using language to exclude. Others were aghast at the notion that any writer might owe it to anyone to limit his or her colour palette in the name of acceptability, comprehensibility or convention.

The Scottish novelist **Ali Smith** has taught on one of those very creative writing courses at which one might imagine darlings to be habitually condemned to death (the famed East Anglia one birthed by Angus Wilson and Malcolm Bradbury). She herself, however, has never been shy of wordplay and flourishes – though these tend in her work to co-exist with a chummy, good-humoured directness that precludes pretension, making her an interesting hybrid of stylist and populist. An appropriate choice, then, to deliver the opening salvo in the Conference's engagement with style and content, Smith did so with an address to the Edinburgh audience that determinedly merged the two concerns. Its points were inseparable from its wordplay and its digressions; its intellectual force was one with its surface dazzle. 'Everything written has style,' she said. 'The list of ingredients on the side of a cornflakes box has style. And everything literary has literary style. And style is integral to a work. How something is told correlates with – more – makes what's being told. A story is its style. A style is its story, and stories – like onions, like the earth we live on, like style – are layered, stratified constructs. Style is never not content. This is because words themselves when put together produce style, never lack style of one sort or another.'

In the debate that followed Smith's Edinburgh speech, her fellow Scot **Alan Bissett** raised the notion of style as exclusive of 'the people who are not convinced by literature, who find it intimidating'. Style carried risks, he thought, because 'we can disappear into it. There is the risk of that: that style becomes fetishised, and it's *very stylish people talking to each other*. I worry about the people we're not talking to.'

Worrying about people on the basis that they might not understand one's fancy writerly ways … it's a problematic tack to take, and indeed it rendered Bissett's fellow delegate **China Miéville** – a writer rarely accused of plainspeaking – 'slightly nervous'. He cautioned against condescension, and argued that 'second-guessing readers is a fool's game. For everyone who's put off by a style that they find difficult, you can find some autodidact who is delighted by not understanding a book, and really struggling with it, and finding their way into a love of words.' Deploying a call-to-arms he's used in interviews, Miéville called for a recognition of the writer's job as 'not to give readers what they want, but to try and make readers want what we give'. Only risk-taking writing would take literature to new places; and that meant embracing the possibility of failure. 'I would rather read an honourable failure than a dishonourable success.'

Is a complex understanding of one's inner – or outer – reality, in any case, the preserve of an elite? Smith quoted a remark of Angela Carter's: 'I've got nothing against realism. But there is realism and realism. I mean, the questions I ask myself, I think they are very much to do with reality.' An audience member in Edinburgh quoted David Foster Wallace's version of that thought: 'I don't know about you, but for me, real life doesn't feel anything like a linear narrative.'

Certainly you don't have to occupy the same lofty intellectual plane as Carter and Wallace to notice that lived experience can lack satisfactory coherence and include improbable leaps of logic. After all, the protagonist of *Ulysses* was no professor, but an advertising agent of patchy education; his wife Molly Bloom communicates in a restless stream-of-consciousness not because Joyce is adopting a high elitist literary style, but because he's striving to bypass exactly that, and replicate the spontaneous, disorganised rush of her thoughts.

But where is the reader in all of this? Charmed by a replication of life's chaotic rhythms? Or restless for some conventional structure and clarifying punctuation to point a way through the muddle? Interestingly, two defences of 'readability' in Edinburgh came not from Bissett's perspective of political – implicitly class – inclusiveness, but from the perspective of the reader's age. Young Adult authors **Patrick Ness** and **Melvin Burgess**, whose work, being for a specific age demographic, must take reader response into account in a different manner than adult fiction, both argued for the importance of *communication* between reader and writer.

This was a theme to which Burgess would return later in the Conference, as he prepared to deliver his keynote speech in Krasnoyarsk, Russia. 'At the conference [in Edinburgh] quite a lot of people were saying 'I only write for myself'', he noted, 'but I feel quite strongly that when you're writing it is an act of communication. To make out that your readers are merely stray passengers is, to me, disingenuous. It's a sort of 'romantic artist' concept – that writing is merely an act of self-expression. It is to some degree; but really I feel that kind of statement is a cop-out, it drives me mad.' Style, then, has an element of responsibility to it, for Burgess at least: the responsibility to communicate to one's selected reader.

Who might be a very specific individual – or two. In Toronto, the Norwegian author **Jo Nesbø** explained his approach. 'I don't write my books for myself, but I write them for two friends of mine,' he said. 'They're the readers I had in mind when I started. I studied with them, we shared tastes in popular culture ... I guess I wanted to impress those two guys. They don't know who they are. Sometimes if they're in a good mood they'll say 'I read your last book, it wasn't too bad' ... and they'll make my day. That's my audience.'

Communication to a wider imagined audience mattered to

Canadian novelist **Marjorie Celona**, also speaking in Toronto, to whom self-conscious style could be a block to empathy. 'If I have to struggle to understand what you're trying to say because you're so busy showing off how beautifully you can write, I don't really want to read your writing,' she said. Celona's fellow panelist **Anakana Schofield,** from Ireland, pronounced herself 'horrified' by the suspicious attitude towards style – the aversion to experimentation. 'The word "story" bothers me a lot more!' she told the Toronto audience. 'It's a dead end, in some ways.'

Dispose of your darlings, then, or stick resolutely to a predefined idea of 'story': either way, it seems, something can end up dead. A subtler rule than 'kill your darlings' might be one of equal use to handy householders as to writers: beware of decoration unless you're really, really good at it. But in fiction writing, as in home improvements, identifying one's own skill level can be a challenge; and somehow it can be those with the least skill, taste and judgment who most enthusiastically undertake the hanging of new curtains. Ah, taste: there's another loaded word. Perhaps the handiest advice after all is that of Burgess and Nesbø, which might be persuaded to co-exist with the more uncompromising stance of Miéville. Know who your reader is. Mainstream reader; friend; bright teenager ill-served by existing literature; imagined external manifestation of yourself. Bring that person with you. But don't ask what he or she wants; make him or her want what you've got to give.

'Fight! Fight! Fight!'

by Ali Smith
Keynote, Edinburgh, August 2012

Point 1: 'What's it all about?' v 'What's it all – a bout?'

Fight! Fight! Fight! In the style corner, a battered old copy of *Ulysses*. In the content corner, the Brazilian writer Paulo Coelho. 'Writers go wrong when they focus on form, not content,' Coelho once told a São Paulo newspaper. He explained to the paper that his ability to make complicated things simple was what made him a great modern writer. 'One of the books that caused great harm was James Joyce's *Ulysses*,' he said. The problem with *Ulysses*? It's 'pure style. There is nothing there. Stripped down, Ulysses is a twit.'

Or did he mean 'Ulysses is a tweet'? That sounds more likely – and handy too, because it lets us add new technological reference to the same old age-old fight. The great rollicking world of invention, the book whose rewrite of tradition, whose fusion of ordinary, legendary, fictional and real made the everyday and the man in the street an epic, and vice versa – a tweet. I think Joyce would have made a really good tweeter, it being his habit to transform characters – whether fictional human beings or the letters that form words – into something unexpectedly expansive.

Nothing is harmful to literature except censorship, and that almost never stops literature going where it wants to go either, because literature has a way of surpassing everything that blocks it and growing stronger for the exercise. Personally, I don't care if everybody or nobody reads *Ulysses* or if nobody or everybody reads fifty shades of Coelho. There's room in the world for all of us. We are large. We contain multitudes. A good argument, like a good dialogue, is always a proof of life, but I'd much rather go and read a book. And I like a bit of style, myself, so it'll probably be *Ulysses*.

Maybe the Cyclops chapter, a fusion of pugilism with the parodies of written styles over the centuries, in which there's a description of a boxing match between Irish colonised and English coloniser; it's the chapter in which Bloom, talking in his own faltering way about the little things – violence, history, hatred, love, life – faces a bar-room of brawlers and a legendary one-eyed bigot.

Or maybe I'd read one of the most original writers at work in the novel in English right now, Nicola Barker. I'd open *Clear: a Transparent Novel*, a book published a hundred years after Joyce's Bloomsday. What's it about? Ostensibly reality, a real-life event: David Blaine the magician, and how he survived on nothing in a see-through box strung above the Thames for 44 days in 2003. But from page one of this novel, all transparencies and deceptions, is a dissection of the infatuations, the seductions, the things we ask of books and art and culture. Like *Ulysses*, it's also a discourse on heroism. Its speaker is one of Barker's appalling and glorious wide boys, and all he can talk about, as it opens, is prose – specifically the opening lines of another book, Jack Schaefer's *Shane*, a 'Classic Novel of the American West'.

I was thinking how incredibly *precise* those first lines were, and yet how crazily effortless they seemed; Schaefer's style (his – ahem – 'voice') so enviably understated, his artistic (if I may be so bold as to use this word, and so early in our acquaintance) 'vision' so totally (and I mean *totally*) unflinching. 'I have huge balls.' *That's* what the text's shouting. 'I have *huge* balls, d'ya hear me? I have *huge* fucking *balls*, and I *love* them, and I have *nothing else* to prove here.' ... When you've got balls that size, you automatically develop a strange kind of moral authority ... a special intellectual *certainty* which is very, very seductive ...'

Then he sums up the power the literary styles we love have over us:

> I am putty – literally *putty* – in Schaefer's hands ... To be manipulated, to be led, to be *played*, and so artfully. It's just ... I've just ... I'm very, very happy to be a part of that process.

Barker's writing is a 21st-century force of energy, playfulness, marginalia, bombast, emphatic tic and formal courage, and – as with all high literary processes – not every reader's happy to be a part of it, though lots are.

Would I call it balls, what Barker's got? No, though I'd stay with the procreational possibilities. I'd use something a lot more gender non-specific. Jouissance? No, still too gendered. Life force? it certainly roars with something like life.

Let's just call it style.

Point 2: Style as more than one thing at once

Barker's multivocality is a display of just one of the versatilities natural to literary style. Here it gives us both her character's cockiness and his vulnerability, his blindness at being ironised. Plus there's the chat-up line, the beguiling, the way we'll readily let something remake us. There are inferences of territory and pioneering, and even moral authority. At the same time she undermines it; style's authority dismantles authority, reveals it as a load of macho balls.

The late Gore Vidal said, characteristically: 'Style is knowing who you are, what you want to say, and not giving a damn.' So is there something that risks being damned, in style? Something about bravado, defiance, the defiance that rings of individuality?

Is there a sense, too, in which some writers use style as a marker of existence? A proof we're here? But good working style is powerful whether it's bullish or showy or quiet. Style's existence is a matter of verbal precision, nothing else.

And what exactly has happiness to do with the process?

Point 3: Style as content

It's the easiest argument in the world, and one of the most specious, style v content. The clichéd view of literary style, especially style which draws attention to itself as style, is that it's a surface thing, a thing of appearance, a skin-deep thing; a fraudulent thing, not the real thing, blocking us from what it's trying to say even as it says it.

But everything written has style. The list of ingredients on the side of a cornflakes box has style. And everything literary has literary style. And style is integral to a work. How something is told correlates with – more – makes what's being told. A story is its style. A style is its story, and stories – like onions, like the earth we live on, like style – are layered, stratified constructs. Style is never not content. This is because words themselves when put together produce style, never lack style of one sort or another. Otherwise we could junk, say, one of the most recent translators of *Madame Bovary*, Lydia Davis (who went back and looked at Flaubert's edits and took into account for her translation his removal, from draft to draft, of metaphoric or lyrical elements in the language of the novel), and just run *Madame Bovary* through Google Translate.

Style isn't the ghost in the machine, it's the life that disproves the machine. There's nothing ghostly about it. It's alive and human. More, style proves not just individual human existence, but communal existence.

It's an act at once individual and communal, to read a book, which is why the question of how much we're asked to engage is such a loaded and interesting one (do you read to escape? Or to think, learn, understand? Or to be entertained?). For a style may not be to your taste. It may not be your style. But that's an important issue, one that marks style's power. The last thing literary style is is a matter of indifference; that's why it's so powerful a stirrer of love and passion, anger and argument. That's why it can really trouble us. That's why a style you don't take to can feel so like a personal assault.

And style is so versatile that it can carry all the opositions simultaneously. I'm thinking of a novel like Uzodinma Iweala's *Beasts of No Nation*, or Helen Oyeyemi's *The Icarus Girl*, stories of bloody murderous fracture told via child-innocence, or novels like Vonnegut's *Slaughterhouse-Five* or Heller's *Catch-22*, which clarify historic foulness yet masquerade as, and are, comedic entertainments. Style can and will do many things at once, be ironic, ambiguous, challenging, questioning, quicksilver. It might not be easy on the eye. Not everything is. Not everything's simple.

Austen, for one, wanted her readers to be clever. What writer doesn't? 'I do not write for such dull elves / As have not a great deal of ingenuity themselves,' she wrote in a letter to her sister. We don't need to know she's playing on a reference to a couple of lines from Walter Scott's long romantic poem *Marmion* here. Not knowing doesn't stop what she wrote being witty. But it's interesting to know, since the original lines she's improvising on concern the power of the imagination. This rewriting and reforming, in miniature here, is what she does in a major way in her novels, playing on and finding a new style in reaction to the styles of Sterne and Fielding and Richardson and Defoe before her. It's what writers do. Books beget books, styles beget styles. Flaubert wrote *Madame Bovary* against what he saw as the foul falseness, the romantic excrescence of the contemporary French novel, which is why his book addresses so closely the effects of style and its responsibilities and moralities. Words and styles have import and impact beyond themselves. In Ben Marcus's *The Flame Alphabet*, parents begin to suffer terrible physical symptoms because they're being literally poisoned by the words used by their kids, a daughter talking 'like a tour guide to nothing'. Style is chemical and reactive, and – both daunting and exciting – it can go where it likes, do what it likes.

Point 7: Style as reality

Where style goes – what it does – is always telling. Naturally, some writers are more attentive to language and structure, and some want to draw more attention to these, than others.

But style is not language – it's bigger than language. Style is not voice. Style is not form. It's not stylistics or parataxis or rhythm or metaphor. Style is what happens when voice and form meet and fuse into something more than both.

With a writer like Muriel Spark or Angela Carter, consciousness of artifice allows for an admittance of artifice. This is simply true. Look, the work says. This is a novel/a story. (This isn't new – the novel's been doing this since Tristram Shandy. It's long been a facet of style.) The heroine of Spark's first novel, *The Comforters*, thinking she's living a real life in a real world, suddenly finds that, no, she's fictional and she's being dictated by a narrator in the form of a giant typewriter. So she argues with the narrator about metaphysics and free will; and it's a mark of Spark's lifelong style, this use of fiction to question truth. As Carter famously said, in defence of a fiction that went to new heights of literary stylistic extreme: 'I've got nothing against realism. But there is realism and realism. I mean, the questions that I ask myself, I think they are very much to do with reality.'

Carter thought Austen and Dickens were cartoonists, not novelists. It's why she could break the mould. One of the exciting things about the novel as a form is that it is traditionally revolutionary. In this debate fifty years ago, Mary McCarthy said about the nouveaux romanciers: 'I think the new novel is really simply a form of dressmaking. You know – Robbe-Grillet began it and he lowered the hemline, and everyone followed, somewhat hesitant .... The French novel seems to me experiments with the shears in cutting .... I don't think it has much to do with the novel as a serious thing.'

But it's about the seriousness of the novel and it reveals the novel as a serious thing, this taking to task of the shape it tends towards. It might not always work; it might look like or end up being just fashion (though style and fashion are not spuriously connected, since style is what makes fashion). But the structures of what we make are bound to parallel the structures of our cultures, how we're living, how we're thinking. And the ability to perceive and question and even alter the structures of things is related to and touches on issues of revelation, question and change in our art forms. You might be able to spray fashion on like a perfume. But style is integral. It's what things really smell like.

Point 153: Style as implement, adornment, toothbrush, protector, mother, art, love

The word style comes in its English form from the Latin *stilus*, primarily the word for a writing implement, possibly fused with Greek *stylos*, the word for a pillar, one that either architecturally supports or adorns a structure or place.

A stylite was an ascetic who lived, usually for religious reasons, perched day in, day out on top of a pillar. It's hard to get a whole novel balanced, in all its ranginess, with all its chairs and cups and toothbrushes, on a pillar (maybe, of all the novelists, only Woolf did it and kept one foot on the ground). But look, there's TS Eliot up there in his long black coat intoning *Four Quartets* for all our good. 'Humankind cannot bear very much reality.'

The word content means both that which is contained and a kind of happiness close to peace of mind. Are being held and happiness connected? Ask any baby. Style is also an aesthetic means of containing something for us and allowing us both distance from and proximity to it. It will hold us up against the darkest things, as well as up against the throwaway lightness of life.

Style will also discomfit us, since art's about both, being held and being flung open. There's a telling moment in Alison Bechdel's graphic novel, *Are You My Mother?*: the main character sends her mother a piece of memoir specifically about the evening when she was a small child and her mother decided to stop kissing her good night. The mother sends it back, five months later, annotated. Bechdel's meticulously drawn frame shows a page of black typescript held in two hands – and, scrawled all over its margins, comments in red pen. 'Pay more attention to verbs'. 'Good use of color: visual memory from child's p.o.v'. 'Am I being too critical? I am probably jealous because you are writing and I am not.' The mother steadfastly ignores what it says, by concentrating on how it says it. Style gives us that – what shall we call it? – grace, I suppose. But anyone reading it can see that a stylistic critique doesn't just protect, it also reveals, allowing the safe surfacing of all the unsayables, the primal responses.

Now I'm going to quote Alain Badiou, from *In Praise of Love*, because I think what he says here about love could also be a working definition of the powers and gifts of literary style.

> At the most minimal level, people in love put their trust in difference rather than being suspicious of it. Reactionaries are always suspicious of difference in the name of identity … if we, on the contrary, want to open ourselves up to difference and its implications, so the collective can become the whole world, then the defence of love becomes one point individuals have to practice. The identity cult of repetition must be challenged by love of what is different, is unique, is unrepeatable, unstable and foreign.

Point 7,000,000,000: How should the novelist approach the novel?
With ingenuity. With humility. With a hammer. With energy. With erudition. With naivety. Traditionally, anarchically, adventurously, brokenly, wholly, any adverb you want, but always only with an eye to what the story asks, because that's more than enough. The story will dictate its style. (And you won't need adverbs anyway. Lose them in the edit.)

I asked two writers younger than me, whose work is very different from each other's, how they thought we should approach the novel. Kamila Shamsie said: 'Boldly, and with a certain fear in the heart.' This reminded me of Charlie Chaplin in *The Circus*, locked by mistake in a cage with a sleeping lion. That's quite close to what it feels like, to write a novel. You're brave, or you'd better be, and you're an idiot. Tread carefully. I texted Helen Oyeyemi. How should the novelist approach the novel? She replied: 'With courage and vigour and flexibility, I think.' Then her text said: 'What do you think?' Yes, it's always a matter of dialogue.

And clearly a matter of courage. Oh! but it is only a novel, as Jane

Austen puts it in chapter five of *Northanger Abbey*, the most postmodern of her works, where she tells us with a flirtatious combination of real/feigned modesty and indifference what the novel can do. Best chosen language = greatest powers of the mind, most thorough knowledge, human nature, liveliness, wit, humour, world.

A world, in a novel, in a tweet, in a grain of sand. In that newsworthy fistfight, that lively discussion the delegates had here fifty years ago in the shadow of the H-bomb and still in those long shadows of the Second World War, Rebecca West talked at one point about Austen's style and the wildly opposing universes it unites: 'She said it like a lady, but the intention was strictly revolutionary.' The novel as a form, West said, would never die. She cited Salinger's characters, 'people who are dealing with eternal problems, ancient problems, and they simply cannot use a phrase that was made more than twenty-five years ago ... fighting, fighting, fighting into a means of self-expression.'

Fight, fight, fight. Language is never not up for it. It's a fight to the life. All we need to do, reader or writer, from first line to final page, is be as open as a book, and be alive to the life in language – on all its levels. Then style, as usual, will do what it does best. Then you, and I, and all of us (all seven billion of us here now in the world, not forgetting all the people in the future, and the past) with all our individualities, all our struggles, all our means of expression, will find ourselves, one way and another, when it comes to the novel, content.

Thought's clothing

Even before Ali Smith gave her speech, **Nathan Englander** (who chaired the session) proposed an intriguing mind experiment in which he tried to identify a piece of writing that was pure style, and another that was pure content. The piece he saw as pure content was 'the "begat" section of Genesis, which goes down through the generations from Noah to Abraham. It's basically a Biblical phonebook, but I remember it as this really moving thing. I looked at it in Hebrew and in English and to me it is marvellous and mellifluous and beautiful and true poetry. So here's a thing that's just content, but to me it's all style.' So already, even before Englander reaches the end of his thought, style and content are merging back into each other, inseparable (the loose, collusive nature of these two concepts was a feature of the 'Style versus Content' conversation as it moved around the world). But Englander was undeniably right to point out that the passage was intended merely to convey the genealogical information. The fact that it tolls like an ancient bell, the rich stateliness of the passage, these things are a happy accident arising from the repetition of one obsolete but redolently beautiful word. The cascading begats make a pattern that runs through the listed names like the stitching on a piece of embroidery; they assert themselves like a bloodline....

'And then I was trying to think of something that's all style,' continued Englander. 'And all I could come up with was Donald Barthelme's *Manual for Sons* which doesn't make any sense except in the way fiction makes sense, which is truer than truth.' He quoted these lines:

'If their dress is covered with sewn-on tin cans and their spittle is like string of red-boiled crayfish running head to tail down the front of their tin cans, serious impairment of the left brain is present. If, on the other hand, they are simply barking, no tin cans, spittle held securely in the pouch of the cheek, they have been driven to distraction by the intricacies of living with others.'

'It makes no sense except in the way it makes story sense,' said Englander. 'But honestly, this touches me so deeply. It moves me to tears. It is its own universe, everything is contained within, it has no content except its own style, which becomes the content.'

But is this passage really all style and no apparent content? If so, if it is all style, why does the text affect Englander so deeply? Wouldn't it be truer to say that the gaudy, wordy façade deliberately masks the truth of the words, the unacknowledged pain and emotional anguish behind the language? Isn't it the case that the firework phrases dazzle only because they burst against a background of nocturnal blackness? The fact is: there is a story unfolding in Barthelme's passage, and story *is* content – or so said many of the participants in the subsequent debate.

So what then is content? Is it the truth, or the arc of the story, or the anxiety to be expressed through the story? And what is style? Is it merely the suitcase in which the tale is carried to the left-luggage locker of the reader's imagination? Is the same thing as form, or is form – as **Kirsty Gunn** maintains later in this chapter – something else entirely (see p.310)? Is style the author's voice, or (as the fashion sense of the word suggests), no more than the changeable garb in which a story is clad – 'the clothing of thought' as **Hubert Haddad** said, quoting Seneca (see p.322).

The global conversation on this topic contained many brave attempts to pin down the twin terms. Some of these definitions took the form of complex and considered metaphors, others were ad hoc, spur of the moment, off the cuff; some delegates cited writers from the past (such as Smith's quotation of Gore Vidal) and then sought to enlarge upon them. One of the most striking style/content comparisons was this: 'I find it hard to think of these things without a concrete image,' said **Margo Lanagan** in Melbourne. 'And the one that comes to mind is when you are coming up to the birth of a baby, setting up a birthing plan. I think of the content as the baby itself – it represents the plot and the themes that the work of fiction is trying to carry. Form is like the bigger decision as to whether you are going to have a hospital or a home birth or whether you are just going to go out into the fields and sit under a bush. Style is partly a matter of choice, and partly a matter of the exigencies of the moment – whether you are up on your feet walking back and forth, or whether you are curled in a foetal ball and screaming for anaesthetic, whether you have scented candles in the room.'

It goes without saying that only a woman could have elaborated that simile. Male writers, one suspects, would be much more likely to see their work as a thing that they had made or invented, rather than something that they had grown or given birth to. But in fact it was another woman – **Sophie Cooke** speaking in Edinburgh – who eloquently expounded the obvious constructional metaphor. 'I think you can view style as separate from content, in the same way that in architecture form is separate from function,' she said. 'In a building, the form is not inevitable, and doesn't necessarily spring from the function. As writers we do make choices about style. If content is the story, and style is the way that we tell the story, then we know that we can tell that story in any number of different ways. To use the building analogy again, what we want to do is to build a beautiful edifice that still has plumbing and stairs and works properly. There is a danger of creating beautiful things that don't actually function.'

But function must have an effect on form: an aircraft hangar has to be broad and tall enough to contain an aircraft, or else it is an absurd failure as a hangar, a waste of effort. In St Malo, where the discussion was haunted from the start by Flaubert's famous wish to 'write a book about nothing', some delegates were insistent that a book had to say something – and something worth saying. **Pinar Selek**, whose writing had earned her a horrifying spell in a Turkish jail, spoke up for the primacy of content, when content is conveying an urgent truth. 'When you live through difficult times you need to express them,' she said. 'Writing can help you express the inexplicable. Literature can be about that as well as about Flaubert.' The French-Algerian writer **Azouz Begag** agreed. 'I have never wondered about style, thank God, because if I had I wouldn't have dared try to write,' he said. 'I grew up in a slum in Lyon. My parents didn't know how to read. But we, the children of poor and illiterate parents, find ways of drilling down through the layers of sediment in our heart to find the oil, the book inside, something that is beautiful, true and useful. There are some young people in this room who have come to learn what style is about so that they can start writing a book that has style. This is what I say to them: use a direct style.'

Sophie Cooke, like Begag, saw the search for content as descent into the self. In the Beijing address that follows, she expresses it in terms of diving down to a wreck (having borrowed the image from Adrienne Rich). And like the dignified Pinar Selek, she equated content with truth – with the added implication that it can be individual and internal as well as external and political. 'Content is our telling the truth; style is the way we make it fiction,' she said in the course of the discussion in Beijing. 'There is a balance, they are aspects. If you concentrate too hard on style and neglect the truth-telling content, then you are not doing your job as a writer.'

Jonathan Bastable (ed.)

The tao of writing

by Sophie Cooke
Keynote, Beijing, March 2013

Ali Smith, in her wonderful speech on this topic of style versus content, proposed that we shouldn't try to separate style from content. That the two are truly inseparable.

In my opinion – and of course everything I say here is simply my own opinion – style *does*, content *is*. Style without content is vacant doing, meaningless activity. Content without style is unexpressed. Style is *yang*, content *yin*. They are opposites. Yet in harmony they create each other, and in the end become each other. So I agree with Ali, that it is impossible to conceive of one without the other. But it is very possible – desirable – to conceive of them as separate aspects of a whole, of writing in the sense of *tao*.

Why is it desirable to see these aspects separately? What does it matter, really, in a world troubled by global warming, unnecessary wars, soaring inequality and unrestrained greed? Why are we here talking about style versus content in literature?

Let me quote from the great, late poet, Adrienne Rich.

I came to explore the wreck.
The words are purposes.
The words are maps.
I came to see the damage that was done
and the treasures that prevail.
I stroke the beam of my lamp
slowly along the flank
of something more permanent

than fish or weed
the thing I came for:
the wreck and not the story of the wreck
the thing itself and not the myth
the drowned face always staring
toward the sun
the evidence of damage
worn by salt and sway into this threadbare beauty
the ribs of the disaster
curving their assertion
among the tentative haunters.

I think we use stories to help us locate the shipwrecks. Knowing someone else has been here before us can make us braver, more able to shine a lamp into the proof of our own forgotten storms. Perhaps the reason why writing feels like discovery rather than creation, is because it is really an act of remembering what we know.

Language, style: these are how we communicate the content that we find, when we dive down to the wreck – the truth beneath the surface of things. It is pointless to go there without them. We need to be able to express what we have found. Retrieving that lost content is important because it is:

Amazing how the forgetting
enables deathly ruins to be reborn
the fortunate nourished by the decomposed

– in the words of the imprisoned poet Liu Xiaobo. Remembering the truth about oppression helps us avoid becoming part of new injustices. Something that is difficult to do, because most societies contain unjust structures of privilege which seem natural or normal to us – or perhaps simply inevitable.

Ali Smith also mentioned the courage a writer must have, to approach their work well. I agree. I would like to observe that to be stylish is not a courageous act. In fact, the more outrageous and apparently provocative your style, the more, as a writer or a fashion designer or a pop star, you will be celebrated. The courage is not for style. No. It is needed for the long, dark, lonely dive, down to the wreck. The content of the writing.

To go there completely is a frightening thing. To fully witness your personal losses, and your shame and your vulnerability; and the scale of humanity's tragedy. The space between the wrecks and the world in which you – or all of us – might not be drowned. Between the sunlit breathing surface and these depths where the truth lives; where things have happened.

But treasures, in that dark world, do prevail. We find the gifts of love and wisdom that sank inside the ships, under the weight of the storms. And we make our maps.

I would like to re-tell two stories from Greek mythology. Both are stories of seeing what should not be seen, of giving up one's innocence. First there is Pandora. The first woman, sent to man as a punishment for his arrogance, with a box which she is forbidden to open. Of course – she opens it. And all the evils in the world fly out – death, disease, greed, war, famine. It is the end of Eden. But at the very end of this dreadful emanation, one last thing flutters from the jar – for it is really a jar, and not a box. This thing is hope. Hope comes last.

To quote from Liu Xiaobo again:

> I am merely
> a discarded wooden plank
> powerless to resist the crushing of steel
> still, I want to save you no matter if you're
> dead or still barely breathing, breathing.

As writers, we can say: what your heart knows, is true. Here are other hearts that felt the same. You're not crazy, to have these hopes and dreams. Listen, and move.

The second story I wanted to re-tell is the story of Psyche and Eros.

Psyche's husband Eros forbids her from seeing his face. He comes to her by night: she does not even know who he is. Psyche, the mind, is ignorantly wedded to Eros, the heart, and she is happy. But then her jealous sisters begin to whisper. Perhaps we can compare them to the jealous sisters of the Weaver Girl in Chinese mythology, when she goes to visit the Cowherd. What Psyche's sisters tell her is this: that her husband is a ghastly monster, a semi-human beast – this is why he will not let her see him. They encourage her to wait til he is sleeping, after love-making, and then sneak up on him – with a lamp and a knife. A lamp to see, a knife to sever the awful head.

But what the mind sees is not a monster. Instead, she sees beauty. So beautiful, the heart, that the mind stands transfixed. A drop of oil falls from her lamp onto his skin, and wakes him. Furious at her disobedience, he leaves her. He will not return, because she looked at him.

For me, this is a truer story than Pandora's. What we see when we look inside ourselves is not only the pain of ugly feelings. It is also the pain of impossible hopes, uncynical love.

Why does Eros forbid Psyche to see him? Why does the heart flee when it is seen?

If writing has its yin and yang of content and style, of being and doing, the heart has a yin and yang also. The heart that *does* – the heart that wants, and loves, and desires – this heart is easy to see. It speaks to our minds all the time. It tells us what it wants, and asks us to get it. Go make safe the things that are dear to me! Get me things I can give to the ones I love. Avenge the wrongs done to my darlings. We know how to listen to this. We pursue our desires; we protect our homes and our children. We care for the people we love, and we seek to fulfil our ambitions. Perhaps we exact vengeance.

But the heart has another side we can not see. The heart that *is*. This heart does not come out: it is unexpressed, by itself. And this heart knows that it is crazy. Because it belongs in a world of peace and harmony, a world that's in such perfect balance, no action is needed. It simply wants to be love. The quiet heart can't be acknowledged by the mind, because it's at odds with the heart the mind already knows. It is its opposite, and that other heart could devour it in an instant. The mind expected to see ugliness, and instead saw gentleness and beauty.

Psyche is, literally, broken-hearted. She begs the gods for a chance to regain Eros. She is set three seemingly impossible tasks by Eros' mother, Aphrodite, which she completes. But there's a final hurdle. She must go down to hell, and return with a box of beauty cream – which she must, on no account, open. You can see where this is going.

Psyche enters the underworld. The mind travels down into the depths: sees the faces of the shipwrecked. Psyche sees the truth. She gets the cream and she carries it back. She brings this treasure up to the sunlight. She's out on the open fields. And she thinks – perhaps this cream will make me so beautiful, my lost heart will come back to me. So she lifts up the lid.

No demons fly out: no evils. Because she has already encountered them, underground. She has dealt with them. Instead, a gas that puts her to sleep. And this was always Aphrodite's plan, of revenge. She knew that Psyche would open up the box; just as it was always known that Pandora would pull the cork from the jar. But Eros has been watching Psyche. He knows what she has been through, knows she has gone to hell and back, gone through the greatest loneliness and suffering – maybe now she can grasp him. He returns to her, and wakes her – how else? – with a kiss. Mind and hiding heart are consciously united. The mind, because of what it has been through, can finally see the *yin* heart and understand it. The *yin* heart knows and trusts this. So it reveals itself. No need, any more, for the mind to sneak up on it with tricks and suspicions.

We go to see, as writers and as readers, what we are discouraged from seeing in our everyday lives. We go looking for the truth beneath the image.

In our everyday lives, we are surrounded by lies. Lies in our personal lives, or our workplaces. Lies in our cultures and societies, in our media and in our educational establishments. Lies about our national histories, the airbrushing of empires; lies about our economic systems: the unimproveable rule by global capitalism; lies about the reasons for our wars, in which inconvenient states must be our enemies. In their specifics, in different locations and on different scales, the lies vary. They can be so ingrained in the worlds in which we have grown up, our busy clamouring hearts don't notice the discrepancies. But our quiet hearts have always known, and *if we want to see them* they will send us out, until we have gone far enough from what we thought we knew, to see – the evidence of damage.

What we find is, partly, terrible. But it's as we suspected! The urges behind the crimes are in our own noisy hearts too: that's how we knew we'd find them. The surprise is that we can also find the quiet heart, in the process of acknowledging the truth. We find hope, and forgotten dreams. Dreams we had when we were innocent. The part of us that experienced loss is the part that had those dreams, before it gave them up.

Our minds – and our speaking hearts – tell us to accept a situation of managed violence, injustice, and inequality. We're only human, after all. What do we expect? To live in the world our hidden *yin* hearts dream of? Well – yes. A world without greed or violence. A place of balance.

This hope, which we find on the other side of truth, can revivify us even if our hearts are dead or barely breathing, breathing …. Because the hope is common to all of us, it can be passed between us – in love, in words, in books.

So we read the maps, the ones gifted to us by others. We write new ones. We do it differently, because our style is our manner of living, as unique as our personal histories. We make our own versions of the truth. The truth itself, though – that is our shared source of content. The wreck and not the story of the wreck.

The relativists were right that truth belongs to to no-one in particular. Two things they forgot: firstly, if you follow it from the obvious tentacle of your life, to its centre, and return – there is hope; and secondly, the undefinable place at its centre belongs to all of us. Just because we can't define something, doesn't mean it isn't there.

Voice, gait, watermark ...

In her keynote address in Beijing, **Sophie Cooke** quoted two vanished writers: the recently deceased poet Adrienne Rich; and the Chinese thinker, poet and Nobel laureate Liu Xiaobo, who disappeared from view in 2009 when he was sentenced to eleven years' imprisonment for 'inciting subversion of state power'. In some countries literature is inseparable from politics, much as in literature style is inseparable from content.

If, with that subtle reproach, Cooke risked offending her Chinese hosts (and in fact the authorities put a stop to the Beijing Conference when it seemed to them to have become too political and critical) then she also paid them a gracious compliment with the title of her address, and with her apt use of the concept of yin and yang to express the interdependence, and opposition, of style and content. Everywhere that the topic was discussed, delegates and members of the audience tussled with this duality and tried to pin it down. **Zhang Yueran**, in conversation with Sophie Cooke, said that 'style and content are two sides of a paradox: you have me, I have you. There is no division. I think that, in successful and comfortable writing, you should not sense any clash. You will be thinking: this particular content requires this particular style. It is a fixed relationship. Only in respect of the external factors would we consider the idea of a conflict between content and style. Some styles cannot be translated, for example, not all works can break through the wall of language. Sometimes only content makes it through. What's worse, most of the Chinese novels published overseas in the past few years are Chinese tragedies; they just need a sad story – and in this sense the content is all that matters. This is one of the external factors.'

She added that: 'I don't think styles are like seats on a bus: it's not like you can't have one because they are all taken. I think style is like this: I am talking now, and the way I describe what is going on is uniquely my own.'

Kirsty Gunn, delivering her keynote in Melbourne, touched on a similar way of thinking about style when she used the term 'idiolect'. Perhaps it is fruitful to think of style as nothing other than the writer's own voice (though **Ali Smith** was chary of the term – see p.291). It is the written equivalent of a person's accent, tone, timbre – plus all the verbal idiosyncracies of that individual: mannerisms and tics; plus habits of terseness or loquacity or allusiveness that are an expression of personality, and that make, say, a recording of a person's voice instantly recognisable as that person and no other. (**Hubert Haddad,** quoting Cocteau, was making exactly this point when he described style as a 'gait' rather than a 'dance' – see p.322).

You might ask: what is it that makes one person's account of an incident deadly dull, while another person can recount the same events and make them gripping or hilarious? It can only be the speaker's or writer's style. To quote the Northern Irish comedian Frank Carson, 'It's the way I tell 'em'. Style is the magic ingredient that turns a bald witness statement into tale worth telling or hearing, the style is what turns the bland facts into a worthwhile anecdote. So here again, style and content elide and emulsify and become parts of the same whole.

It follows that there can be no such thing as a piece of writing that has no perceptible style. As **Nick Laird** commented in Edinburgh: 'I want to talk about this idea that style is quantitive, that you can have a high style or more style. A plain style is also a style – think of Hemingway and his plain books. But Nabokov would have read a page of Hemingway's dialogue and thought it was a load of crap. To Nabokov, the world is numinous and extraordinary, and so the prose is ecstatic. A style is a way of insisting on something, it is like a watermark.' **Francesca Rendle-Short**, who chaired the meeting in Melbourne, quoted a recent broadcast interview with the Australian writer Kim Scott. 'Kim speaks of a disapproving review he received for his book *That Dead Man Dance*, where he is accused of having "more style than substance". Kim's response: "That's what fiction is, isn't it? It's all style. Fiction is style".'

Jonathan Bastable (ed.)

On form

by Kirsty Gunn
Keynote, Melbourne, August 2013

Generally, it seems to me, when people get together to talk about style and content in the novel they talk about just that: there's the way a story is written and there's what is written about. And the two, as any literature professor in charge of any introductory undergraduate course on the novel would say, are inextricably linked. But nobody talks much about form. Or if they do, they use it as another word for style.

And we need to talk about form. Form that's not just another word for style – but 'significant form', as Roger Fry and Virginia Woolf had it. Form that is the shape and idea and *raison d'être* of the novel. Form that sits behind the style and generates it, that informs the presentation of content and makes sense of it, giving context. If content is the 'what' of a novel – what it's made of – and style the 'in which way' – in which way you choose to write it – then form is the 'how'. How a story is made in the first place, the plan for its very being. And it is form, the mother of style and content, I may say – if I want to be rather classical and eighteenth-century about things! – that I want to concern myself with here.

As I say, form is something we don't hear much about, do we? Form is fancy. It's 'highbrow'. Form is the word used by Modernists and for Modernism, it's for academic papers and critical theory and discussions about aesthetics. Form, for all that it is talked about in general literary circles, in the papers and at writers' festivals such as this one, may as well be a dirty word.

Yet, I return through the mists of time to my undergraduate English programme, headed up, no doubt, by that same professor I talked about earlier, who tells us that 'style and content are inextricably linked', and the core course: Introduction to the Novel 101. And what I remember is this: that as we marched our way through the canon that year, and in those that followed, from *Pamela* and *Clarissa* through to *Robinson Crusoe* and *Tristram Shandy* and *Tom Jones* and all the rest, stopping resolutely as we did in those Oxbridge syllabus dominated days with DH Lawrence, it was form that gave instruction to the writer I wanted to be. I had no or little interest, not really, in what went on in those books. All the stuff that was happening, riveting and dramatic as it may have been. I wasn't turned on by the stories' historical contexts, either; I didn't care to keep track of the characters' individual actions and remember what happened to whom, and when. No, I was interested in how they were made, those books, for what purpose their authors deemed they were fitted. I was interested in the *modus operandi*, how those writers were going to make an imaginative idea as real to me and as necessary and vital as anything else that might be going on in my life. Once the form of the novel was in place, I could figure, all the rest would follow.

And follow it did. The exam questions kicked in and I knew exactly what to do: 'In what way does the world of *Middlemarch* reflect a changing England?' Forget it. 'At what point in the novel and why does Dorothea realise her sense of independence has been challenged?' Pass. 'Show passages of speech and description that reflect class predjudice.' Not now. But once I got to 'How has George Eliot gone about creating a social document within a novel?' I was off and running. And everything else? Well all that came into the picture, too, but it wasn't the beginning of my thinking. Not the way thinking about the 'how' of the writer's project was.

Form was my way in, then, to these often lengthy, densely written, character-rich narratives that have all of us flipping back pages in the midst of our reading to remind ourselves of whether such and such was the same one who had said something to so and so in the first section, or whether he was her uncle. There was so much content! And then the paragraphs, the circumlocutions of period speech, the details of descriptions that were needed in a world before photographs and films. There was so much style! Getting through the canon of English language literature in three years – it's a relentless business, all right! But what books! What mighty books! And each one utterly unlike the other. No two the same and every story with its own unique shape. Like exciting novels we read now that transport us, that take us fully into their reality and keep us there, that aren't just some copycat project based on research, or that follow a trend, or trick us with a fancy style or overwhelm us with plot. The books that have form have unity and wholeness. They answer fully and with integrity the question: how am I going to create a world for this story to live in? That's what form does. It brings content and style together in unity in a novel. Form gives authority. Without it, the style, original as it may be, is just echoing in an empty chamber. The content, box-new perhaps but without its own form, dull and secondhand and boring to read.

I have a million examples of writing of the other kind, that miss the point of form, and still the books are praised and bought and read. Seemingly, just because we're talking about novels, that great ragbag of a genre that can hold anything from chick-lit to *War and Peace*, we can throw form out the window. Because in the novel, anything goes. But should it be that way? That a writer putting together a novel about, say, insanity in rural Ireland in the 19th century, (and I'm making up the examples here, by the way, to be polite) a novel with an uneducated central protagonist who is keeping a diary from her cell, has not considered a form for that book that would make sense of that woman's status and condition? So, for example, she would not write at all – because she can't. She's not educated. She wouldn't be able to fill the pages of a journal in her cell. But still there would be some other way of the writer creating that character's thoughts and life on the page? Can't that writer think about that, instead of just relying on the substance of his content, to make the story real? James Kelman knows how to solve that kind of challenge. He knows about form. He has characters who don't read, who've gone blind, yet still move through the pages of their stories in a way that's rich in literary terms because of how he has invented his books, to have come up with a form where, as the great late Dr Gavin Wallace, former head of literature at Creative Scotland described it, 'the life being lived is contiguous with the writing that describes it.' Kelman's form is made up of his very characters, who talk to themselves continually, apprehending, sensing, understanding, not understanding. What we read on the pages of his books are the entire contents of their minds. It's a world away from the tried and tested journal style used by that other writer, and countless like him, who've all copied in turn from Defoe – because Kelman has form. He's not like anyone else. Form doesn't *want* to be.

Or, to take another example, that a book, say, written from a child's point of view might consider issues of vocabulary and sentient understanding in a young mind, that it might encapsulate a sensibility more fractured and acute than the sophisticated adult who's writing it? Yet how many writers – some of them very successful – really capture in their words what it is to be a child? Carson McCullers did, perfectly, in *The Member of the Wedding*. She knew about form. Frankie's world, in that book, is complete, but made up of parts of disparate seeing and understanding and she grows up in the story with different ways of being, and speaking. Everything about the construction of *The Member of the Wedding* is idiosyncratic and wild, mixed up as a dream. That's what a child's world is like. It's not a version of an adult novel cut down to size. It's not a controlled narrative, or masses of character and interiority. It's scattered and intense. Why don't so many authors who write from a child's perspective get it? That kids' worlds aren't like theirs? Why doesn't form seem to matter to them, that they should think that just by inventing a young voice they'll pull off the trick of making childhood seem like childhood?

As I say, I could go on and on here, with examples. Books written from the first person that have never considered what it is about a first person sensibility that might be exciting actually, that the reader might not feel she's been stuck in someone's solitary company for too long. Books written that seem to be about character, until, ten pages in, you realise they're only about stereotypes; or books set in ancient times with all the research in place, all those details about iron vessels and agriculture, only the teenagers who live in the freezing hovels sound like they come from LA. Or books that seem to be about fancy writing but the writing has no context because there's been no central aesthetic governing it, nothing to put it in. Or books that seem to be about plot but really it's the setting that the writer loves, that could have been the plot in itself, if only the author had thought about form. If only, if only, if only the writer had thought about form, so many of the novels might come together.

But then, form is a challenge. It's the hardest part. It's why most writers stick with the tried and tested, that good old workhorse, the realist novel. Broken and harnessed to plough the fields of nineteenth-century fiction, we know what to expect of it, what it's supposed to do. Indeed, how many other, very different kinds of books are always held up to it for comparison? If you listened to enough of the hugely successful realist novelists at work today talk about the novel, their novels, you'd be forgiven for thinking that the canon stopped its march right there, in the turned earth of the classical English novel, with its showing and telling and character development and narrative arc.

But the examples I've given describe two ways form may have stepped in and created something new and exciting from the materials in hand without having to revert to tried and trusted methods. And I gave two masters of form, two mighty artists, as examples of how one might find solutions to the basic challenge of writing fiction, that is, making the words on the page believable and real. These are writers whose every book shows them having thought through completely the requirements of what they need to do to tell their stories. They know that idiolect does not form make. Nor crazy-looking chapter headings or multiple fonts. Nor content designed to impress or overwhelm. They know that form is not just tackling certain challenges of plot or character in isolation – but is the very 'how' of their work, as I said at the beginning of this talk, its beginning and its end.

Virginia Woolf's novel *The Waves* tells the unbroken story of six friends from childhood into age. By creating a kind of banner of prose, without punctuation or break, that segues from the mind of one character to the next, she tells about the private and public circumstances of their lives. So that's the style, that's the content. But the 'how' is how she gets started. Two places divided by a corridor, is how she first thought of *To the Lighthouse*. For *The Waves*, it was music. Yes, the work unfolds, as it does to any writer as she or he is writing, but it took shape first as a concept, an idea that was abstracted from the imagination and the intellect and sometimes too from the psychological make-up and even the psyche of the author. I can imagine writing a novel that would be like a ship at night 'strung about with lights', Mansfield wrote as though in response to Woolf's own definition of the novel as a row of lamps. How far these ideas are removed from the rigid, rectilinear narratives, that flinty mass-produced form, that constitute so many novels today. How wild, by contrast, how trippy, how exciting and involving …. This other kind of novel that has as its beginning a complex, aesthetic idea to do with the story's origin and design, that is nothing to do with what is safe and familiar.

In a recent lecture to writing students, critic and author Gabriel Josipovici talked about the 'terror' of creation. He was addressing the modernist condition of making art in the void, described so beautifully in his polemic 'Whatever Happened to Modernism?' as the 'fading of the numinous', the relaxing of a religious medieval mind, content with its world order and heaven, into the troubled, questioning condition of humanism. There is time in which to create, Jospipovici said, and out of that time can come the excitement – of making something new – but alongside it is the terror, too, that the writing may not succeed. All we have to hold onto is the sense of the form of the project. He was reading from his latest novel, *Infinity: the Story of a Moment*, a singular, uninterrupted interview between an unknown narrator and the manservant of a famous avant-garde conductor 'To listen to the *how* of music' is something the conductor talks about in that book. Once we have the how we have everything.

So to finish: there's writing as representation, and there's writing as a living thing. There are novels that are about, and like, and for. And there are other novels that … simply are. To consider form, the shape, the concept of a work of fiction, is to go at reading from the most exciting perspective – one that gifts us with fresh sight, that makes reading not passive, part of our consumer consumption, an extension of the entertainment industry, but something active, engaging, affecting and real.

Let me conclude with a remark made by science-fiction writer China Miéville. The word he has for what I'm wanting to get at here, in this talk of mine about what novels are made of, is 'uncanny' – the notion of a thought, or a sentence that is homeless, somehow, in the text. He is referring to future-fiction and fantasy, and also the modernist idea of looking at something anew, so that the familiar seem strange – saying that both these concepts need to find a home in the story so the reader can make sense of them. But the idea works beautifully for us here, today, too. Because that's what form does.

So style and content, yes, and always. Wild and clever and interesting that they may be. But it's form that gives them a home. And that gives us a place, readers and writers alike, where we can sing and sing and sing.

You've either got, or you haven't got ...

Once in a while, during the global discussion of the style/content theme, someone suggested that the goal of written style was to be invisible, that if readers' attention snagged on some literary device or turn of phrase, then the something has gone wrong in the crafting of the work. In Toronto, **Marjorie Celona** mentioned a piece of advice that she had heard Michael Cunningham hand out to creative writing students: 'Grade all your sentences as As or Bs, then delete all your As ...'. In the same discussion **Susan Cole** noted how 'some people say that you shouldn't even sense the style, that if the style is apparent you have failed.' She quoted Elmore Leonard's dictum: if I sense I am writing then I delete it. 'But of course he does have a style,' Cole added dubiously. 'So who knows what he means.'

Who indeed, and – come to that – why the striving for total transparency? No-one, after all, would ever say that the style of a piece of music ought to be inaudible to the listener, that music-lovers should bypass the noise and just get the sense and the emotion behind it. And no-one thinks it amounts to a failure on the part of a composer or a songwriter if listeners' focus drifts for a moment from the general to the particular – if they rewind a beloved few bars of melody, or make mention of the great musicianship in a guitar solo, or linger on a favourite line or two in a lyric. The same applies to any art form – apart from literature. All paintings have a style of some sort: style is the unmissable clue that we are looking at a Poussin rather than a Picasso. How could we fail to notice those painters' style, and why would we want to? But as **Gaspard-Marie Janvier** said in St Malo, 'Literature is an abstract art form, and therefore different from sculpture and painting. In literature there are only words.' That is, typography apart, all books look identical: they all consist of the inevitable serried ranks of black, in which every last stem, bar and serif makes up the same small handful of endlessly recycled sound-symbols. It is surely the abstraction of print, the superficial and artificial repetitiveness of the shapes on the page, that allows some to think that style in writing can be hidden, sidestepped or pared away to nothing. It never can; it's always there. As Janvier said: 'Even the telephone directory has a style.'

But a piece of writing certainly can have too much style. Which is to say that the style can draw too much attention to itself, it can be ill-suited to the subject matter, or it can be uncomfortably self-conscious. There is the obvious analogy with fashion. While in music, an excess of style might equate to an egotistical singer who so overdoes the trills and arpeggios that the melody is obscured; or to orchestration so rich that it leaves no room for refreshing changes of mood. Seen this way, good style is almost indistinguishable from good taste. **Margo Lanagan** touched on this in Melbourne when she said: 'A lot of writers, particularly when we are in the early stages of our craft, think of style or voice as a matter of adding embellishments that are actually superfluous to the central business of delivering the content. Style can sometimes mean getting fancy, it's being writerly all over the content instead of just leaving it be to say its thing simply. And the result can be difficult to read.'

The Beninese writer **Florent Couau-Zotti**, speaking in Brazzaville, had a couple of personal examples of youthful stylistic solecism – drawn from the misapprehensions of his student days, and from a recent conversation with a young writer. 'There was a time when I worshipped at the altar of style.' he said. 'I had managed to convince myself that the way you say something is more important than what you have to say. This had even conditioned my literary reflexes, so much so that when browsing through books by unknown writers, I could only form an opinion by reading the first few pages to assess the style. Not only did I believe that style maketh the man, but to my way of thinking any literary work exists through the effect it produces and the joy the writing procures. To quote Tola Toukoui: "We are on a stage, we are on a podium, and in order to seduce the viewer, we have to be as creative as we are impertinent."

'A week ago,' continued Couau-Zotti, 'I was talking with a young writer from Benin who lamented, in talking about the work of a promising young poet, his nauseating style, bland verse and lack of daring that failed to rattle comfortable habits and usage. "Nothing that would give the reader goose bumps or induce a feeling of magic." He then stated emphatically that he could not conceive of a literary text that would not attempt to use syntax provocatively, or to display stylistic extravagance, or in some way flout tradition. I decided to take a look at that writer's own work. I was expecting to be immersed in a special universe, yet I experienced a familiar malaise. His work is dense, at times striking in its poetic bursts and rustlings but also hermetic and obsessive in its search for aesthetic effect. Of the content, little do I remember. Between genres, his writing makes liberal use of puns, invents new words that sound contrived, and strives too transparently for uniqueness. All of which makes the work rather inconsistent and in the end detracts from his overall purpose. This raises the question: of what use is style if it fails to lift the text it is meant to enhance? Is there not a risk that the content of a novel, a poem, or a short story will be simply stifled if the language meant to deliver it stops short of intent?

'If my instinctive beliefs as a student had not matured, if I had continued to be primarily concerned with questions of style, I would never have taken the slightest notice of works such as *The Little Prince* by Saint-Exupéry, *The Stranger* by Camus, *The Sacred Night* by Tahar Ben Jelloun, *Ambiguous Adventure* by Cheikh Hamidou Kane – or many other works written in a pared-down, almost classical style. I would have missed out on these novels – because I would not have ranked them as great works of literature.'

Jonathan Bastable (ed.)

The feeling of the world

by Hubert Haddad
Keynote, St Malo, May 2013

'Style is the feeling of the world.' – André Malraux

The representation of a country, a people, a continent, or the world on the move in the media rests – *a priori* – on nothing human: the factual description of any phenomenon tells you nothing intimate or key about it, apart from a tremendous amount of documentary evidence which is soon locked back up in the archives. Only literature gives reality its full dimension, at the same time allusive, lethal, unpredictable, marvellous, and wildly open to interpretation. Just as the description of a language does not tell us anything about the breadth of its uses through history, its mores or its mythical and legendary foundations, any purely formal rendition fails the basic test of transmission because of a tautological, incomplete or cryptic form of communication.

Literature, along with the rest of the arts, is just reality becoming aware of itself in its enigmatic, symbolic and secular activity. The origin of the world is to be found in the mind of a poet admiring Courbet's painting, or the depths of the Milky Way. There is no place of places other than speech in the process of designation. Ancient Greece is still alive in Homer. Without Shakespeare – who knew only his own tongue – so many languages would be deprived of a metaphorical break as a source of transversality and illumination. While science establishes itself in a necessary object-based face-to-face loaded with so many presuppositions, literature emerges in all haste and speaks of the vanity of power and of the sleepy utopia of the most biting freedoms.

Through questioning, dreamlike deconstruction, inexpiable passion, humour or challenges, literature teaches us that there never is any absolute power; that hierarchies are acts of violence; that the organs of intimidation that institutions of knowledge are should never be accepted without a quarrel; and that writers or artists at work know one single, obvious thing: the absolute closeness of humans with their fragility, their struggles, their lack of knowledge at the heart of their lives, given that we all share a condition marked by the scars of language. The most glaring differences are mere nuances, the exquisite rustling of nuances: provided they are both on the lookout in symbolic spaces, there is no more than an angel's breath between an illiterate child and a brilliant scholar in the minute, unidentifiable thing we call culture.

Novels explore the infinite field of Nuance, this human truth every one of us experiences directly and differently without realising how fragile and transient it is; as does poetry which reveals its surprising nature through language. Therefore, there can be no decent writer without style, whatever its breadth – as majestic as the nebulae or as tight as metaphorical constriction. In the best instances, clinical writing can avoid repetition through prosody and rhythm. Writers distort language and put it through the kaleidoscope, forever and unexpectedly changing combinations and associations, offering hope and structuring in spirit the unfathomable wanderings of phenomena.

Just as composition commands eurhythmic representation in Pierro della Francesca or Cézanne's works, novels-as-object include a living structure, a driving energy derived from writing itself. As Sartre said, writers are made not by what they choose to say but by how they choose to say it: 'Every sentence hold the entirety of language and refers back to the universe'. Therefore an acute strategy of style summons, for an instant or for centuries of delight, all knowledge acquired both out of a legitimate concern for their durability and thanks to the floating investigation into the unknown lands of sensitivity. Flaubert dreamed of writing a book about nothing, a book which 'would hold through the internal strength of style'. As he marvellously put it: 'in and of itself, style is an absolute way of seeing things'.

Nothing is more foreign to classical French, kept in courtiers' tight grips to support national conquests, than the fates of language. Style is not just the wordsmith's showcase or the rules of clear speech; it is a native and structuring impulse, the quiet interaction of feeling, intuition and concept, the switch from lexicon to the dizzying heights of syntax, a unique way of moving within a language for an unprecedented interception and capture of meaning. Content is therefore nothing but what the particular intensity of language's impulses and trajectories in a given body, mind and memory yearns for at a given moment, in a given life context, and aiming for something that is immediately part of writing, of its haste or hesitations, of its destructive tetany or the lightning bolts of multi-faceted speech, leaping from height to height as Empedocles' speech.

For Proust style is an issue of vision not technique, it is 'the revelation of the qualitative difference in the way the world reveals itself to us'. As we can imagine, the distant prospect of the finished work pervades the worrisome act of writing in the present, it is a creative dialectics, a *Weltanschauung*, a constant to-ing and fro-ing between form and content, between appearance and substance or rather between obverse and reverse. Indeed, the writer presents the readers with a strange mirror wherein, compared to the slow pace and backtrackings of the workshop, everything occurs wholly and hurriedly, the inevitability of events being triggered by the spinning or fanning of pages until the synaptic lights go out. The writing that is more or less irresistible – as a painting or an architecture of words, as an abstract construct of concepts or as a succession of platitudes – is acknowledged as *style* as soon as a qualitative and emotional change occurs in the readers' flow of consciousness: something new seeps into the reading, repetition gives way to rhythm, focused images blaze onto the white screen of the page, and language shines through poetics in action.

You could almost say style is the other, the reconstruction by the reader of the necessarily intertwined values of expressions and beliefs at play in the text, given that, whatever the language, very few tales, short stories or novels are not surreptitiously poetic.

Granted, literature does not cover the entire scope of the written word. We could easily come to believe it is but an exception in the ideological and functional space of discourse. Yet when it appears, unexpectedly or after a lengthy maturation, amid the din of misunderstandings, general distraction or the silence of censorship, you can be sure style is at play; a project carried by a wild desire for fulfillment towards some known, or unknown, but always dangerous prospect. Indeed style is the sign of a sovereign march across the minefields of our representations and the unstable realm of the unconscious, the netherworld of the psyche against whose backdrop an inventive reality emerges, gesticulates or disappears according to a thousand fictions.

But what more is style but the resistance of language to the emphatic attraction of words and grammar? We must first challenge the ineptitudes and approximations found in quotations compendia.

Style is an instrument, not an end in itself. (Norman Mailer)

Only a literary orderly could say that. If style is an instrument then Proust and Rimbaud are operating theatres. No, style is no more an instrument than art, in and of itself, would be 'an instrument of propaganda and education'. On the contrary, it distorts all instrumentations and is life itself, replicated *ad infinitum* in the mysteries of a language.

Cocteau pleasantly said: 'Style is not a dance, it is a gait', probably referring to the catwalk or the rolling shoulders of the angel Heurtebise. Yet the author of *La difficulté d'être* knows that style is the constant tension of the mind, the dance of a million Theseuses before the labyrinth of work. He will readily admit to it in *Le Grand Écart*: 'It can happen that a road offers so many different views on the way out and the way back that hikers on the way back will feel lost'. That is how the written road feels to lost readers.

In a letter to Lucilius, Seneca claims 'Style is the clothing of thought'. Thought dressed up is no more than rhetoric. Style is movement, gesture, thought itself!

Stendhal, that least somatic of writers, stated *ad absurdum* that 'The best style is that which goes unnoticed'. And the ludicrous idea of covering the Civil code with a coat of 'transparent varnish'. Would anyone claim that the best music or the best poetry is the one that goes unnoticed? Without style, without a specificity assumed to its rightful climax, without the constraint of being awake which underpins the moment on the obsequious angels' wings, there would only be Father Delille on the one hand and the town clock on the other. *Going unnoticed* is the epitome of Stendhalian style, its inimitable dramatic strategy.

In a vaguely Beylian way, Jean-Paul Sartre wrote in his *Situations* that 'Obviously, style determines the value of prose. But it mustn't get noticed'. He adds along the same lines: 'As words are transparent, and sight goes through them, it would be preposterous to slip frosted glass in amongst them'. More DIY. He writes that 'With prose, aesthetic pleasure can only be unadulterated if it comes on top.' *On top*? It sounds like a little extra thrown into the bargain at the cattle market!

'Therefore, language is beneath literature. Style is almost beyond it: images, delivery and lexicon are born from the writer's body and past, and become progressively the reflexes of his art'. We recognise Roland Barthes' handsome rhythm but cannot follow him. Is the exclusive call to becoming other, expressed by Rimbaud, Marina Tsvetaeva or Antonin Artaud, therefore merely abandonment to some intimate formalism prior to the deliberate consummation of the mind?

The author of *Writing Degree Zero* echoes the thought: 'under the name of style a self-sufficient language emerges that delves only into the private and secret mythology of the author, into the hypophysics of speech where the first association of words and things form, where the major verbal themes of a lifetime are established once and for all.'

With Barthes and a host of arbiters of letters, the appearance of archaeo-semiotic thought on the battlegrounds of arts meant, strangely, that as the symbolic dimension was rightly being freed from reproductive fatality, innatism and outdated essentialist ideas, the University was managing to put literature, the object of its studies, under close supervision through the use of determinist shortcuts, almost derived from the slumber of sociobiology. For instance: 'style is always somewhat crude: it is shape without meaning, the product of an urge not of intent .... It refers to biology or to the past not to History ... it is not the product of choice or reflection about Literature. It is the decorative voice of an unknown and secret flesh .... Style is truly of a germinal nature, it is the transmutation of a Mood.'

So, at degree zero, you have a light-hearted reconciliation with a kind of literary physiologism which Paul Valéry practised, following in Taine and Balzac's footsteps. He was happy to see 'the dealings and productions of the so-called 'mind' as the dealings and productions of an organic system'. But can we ever understand what freedom the void produces in the harmonic cracks of language? We suspected writing contained 'the being and the appearances of power', in doctrinal spaces, as a privilege, as a function of time, reign, social status, barbaric elitism or deep sleep. Yet style is elsewhere. All remains to be invented in reality! A child brighter than lightning warned us a long time ago: 'The language will be a soul for the soul ... thought holding on to thought, and pulling.'

Not much further, Léon Paul Fargue, the master of delectable internal claudication, says: 'a perfect sentence sits atop the greatest vital experience'. For Victor Hugo, our perpetual contemporary, 'truly great writers are those whose thought occupies every recess of their style'. Let us close with the evanescent Emily Dickinson, the magic scribbler, for she alone, beyond language and beyond all authoritative pronouncements, uttered the only truth. What, really, is style?

A something in a summer's day,
As slow her flambeaux burn away.

AFTERWORD

The new publishing

by Hannah McGill

The book in its traditional form is the end result of two separate industrial processes: the creative one that turns a raw concept into a finished and edited manuscript, and the physical one that makes that manuscript into multiple printed objects ready for distribution and sale. In discussions of the coming fortunes of the book as we know it, at stake is not only its imperilled future on paper, but also its survival as the end product of a publishing process that has entailed more than the writer simply hitting 'Upload Now'. As demand for physical books declines, and dissemination of a work of literature becomes a mere matter of an internet connection, why does a writer need to offer up his or her baby to a publishing house at all? Time was when distribution was a significant power: without a publisher, your book stood no chance of being seen in big heaps in big bookshops. Now, it's big bookshops themselves that are rarely glimpsed, with just Waterstones clinging on to multiple prominent high-street sites, and the online retail behemoth Amazon dominating the book market.

Traditional publishers still have other means of positioning a title in the public consciousness, should they choose to 'push' it. They can assist in getting a book reviewed in mainstream publications; they can make entries to major prizes and arrange book tours and appearances at book festivals; they have marketing budgets for advertising and other promotion. But that push, or the lack thereof, is key – and is not offered to every title in a publisher's catalogue. With marketing budgets ever more drastically squeezed, promotional activity is limited for most titles, and only certain books command major publicity campaigns, commonly those blockbuster titles that have a guaranteed waiting market. As many delegates of the EWWC were heard to grumble, less well-known authors are increasingly called upon to generate their own publicity via punishing personal appearance schedules, diligently maintained websites and a steady drip of social media witticisms.

At the closed session on marketing instigated by Denise Mina at the Edinburgh Conference, the analogy was raised of musicians increasingly being expected to generate their income via live appearances rather than through music sales. Were writers being pushed in the same direction? Delegates observed that musicians are primarily performers, whereas writers are not; a number of the writers also noted the thanklessness of book tours, as well as querying the competence of publishers' publicity departments in mobilising audiences to attend readings. The expectation is that a writer will work tirelessly – and without additional recompense – to promote his or her own brand; broad-based contractual agreements regarding the scale of promotional activity required can render this hard for writers to query. Not only are writers thus corralled into being their own press and publicity departments, but their online lives are redirected through professional channels. The common Twitter disclaimer 'All views expressed here are my own' becomes complicated when a personal Twitter account is being used for promotion. 'All views are my own within the boundaries of the online persona agreed between me and my publishers in promotion of my next book' might be more accurate in some cases.

And whether their enthusiasm for the form is self-generated or at the behest of their publishers, some writers have damaged themselves with over-zealous Twitter presences. Writing in *The Guardian* in 2013, Nesrine Malik noted that 'most of us expect writers, especially novelists of a certain stature, to be ascetic, lofty creatures, occupied with the intricacies of the human condition – which explains our surprise when they turn out to be hard-nosed publicists seeking to maximise book sales by promoting their product as aggressively as one would push a new shampoo.' She cited the immodest Twitter activity of – among others – Salman Rushdie and Mohsin Hamid, both dedicated retweeters of praise and good reviews. Striking a balance between necessary self-promotion and unappealing self-aggrandisement is yet another daunting demand of the digital age. Yet more insidious and potentially damaging is the practice of actually writing positive reviews of one's own work pseudonymously, and posting them online via fictional 'sockpuppet' identities. In a letter to *The Daily Telegraph* in 2012, a group of indignant authors including Joanne Harris, Susan Hill, Charlie Higson and EWWC delegate Ian Rankin decried the practice as 'fraudulent and damaging to publishing'. But it's an area with a few of its own shades of grey. Writers enlisting friends or publishers calling on their other writers for sympathetic cover blurbs and reviews isn't even an open secret; it's accepted common practice. And when scabrously negative online reviews can be so easily and thoughtlessly generated, perhaps we can find a scrap of sympathy for writers who have succumbed to the temptation of skewing the balance their own way.

Although digital booksales continue to expand as the physical book declines – with the Publishers' Association rating 2012 as a record year for a UK industry it called 'very strongly competitive', few delegates of the World Writers' Conference seemed inclined to argue that it was boom time for their sector. The dominance of bestsellers bulk-bought by supermarket chains, the decline of the independent book shop, the massive pressure to hit big with a successful first novel rather than build a voice over time, the competition from other, less demanding media, and the low prices expected for e-books all contribute to a climate in which one of the Conference's most pertinent questions was 'How do we earn a living?' And if even those established and well-respected authors are haunted by that question, whither the aspiring author? Such hopefuls have always been counselled to expect multiple rejections. In this day and age, they might be forgiven for wondering whether to shell out the price of postage.

There is, if course, another option: self-publishing, that old refuge of the unorthodox, the highly specialised and the multiply rejected. Self-publishing once meant writers covering their own costs to be put into print by a small press. Today's authors can keep it even simpler, avoiding a bill for paper or printing by simply uploading to the internet, for download or printing on demand. Though self-publishing has long carried the taint of desperation (thanks in part to confusion with vanity publishing, the shady subset that involves a writer actually paying to be published), it's not hard to see its advantages in a choked and under-resourced market. Professional marketing and bookshop table-top displays might be factored out for the self-published author, but so too are overheads, and corporate decisions that exclude, disempower or misrepresent the author. Moreover, if self-publishing was once regarded as the compromise choice of the needy amateur – 'an outlet for scribes demanding that their hard work be read … a something versus nothing sort of situation', as Canadian author **Liam Card** put it at the Toronto Conference – it now slots more comfortably into a culture unembarrassed by unmediated online self-revelation. Just as online dating bears little stigma for a generation that has grown up conducting the bulk of its personal business on screens, so self-publishing is less of a poor relation in an age when it is utterly commonplace to promote creative or business pursuits as well as personal thoughts and ideas via websites, blogs and social media. The influence of critics and other facets of mass media has, we continually hear, dwindled to near-naught.

The blockbuster authors of our time are as likely to find their own audiences online as to be discovered through conventional publishing channels. And even those who do make the big time via the traditional route frequently amass countless rejections along the way from publishers who didn't spot their potential. JK Rowling famously faced down a dozen rejections before the Harry Potter series became the phenomenon of its age; more recently Paul Harding won a Pulitzer Prize for fiction not long after seeing his novel *Tinkers* turned down time and again. Who needs the approval of gatekeepers, if the gatekeepers keep getting it wrong – and if the realm to which they keep the gate is looking increasingly parched and depopulated anyway? It may be that literary fiction can no longer offer a living wage to more than a select few. It may be that it never really did – if stories have always have been needed and sought, they've rarely been big business, and the stereotype of the penniless writer scratching away in a garret is as old as that of the painter offering a landscape in exchange for lunch. Still, few would deny that the expansion of entertainment culture reduced the commercial demand for novels, or that the internet's vast glut of free and illicitly-traded diversions has further shrunk the market.

So is any stigma carried by self-publishing simply an outdated prejudice, a hangover from the old-media days when panels of men in suits stood between artists and consumers designating levels of quality? The Conference panels around the world revealed variable thinking on the subject (although it should of course be borne in mind that book festivals themselves and conference gatherings of this ilk might be considered part of the old, closed-off system, being to no small extent gatekeepers themselves, and favouring as they do writers who have risen via conventional means and are represented by agents and publishing houses). **Konstantin Milchin**, speaking in Krasnoyarsk, presented the internet as 'a friend to the novel', and he for one liked the view without gatekeepers. 'This new era is all about removing the mediators between writers and readers. We are moving towards a world without literary agents, publishers, printers, and booksellers.' But for **AL Kennedy**, speaking in Toronto, the sense of the second-rate still clings to self-publishing: 'I have to think that all of the self-publishers are really just looking for a respected publishing house to come along and snatch them up'. To her fellow panellist Liam Card, what he calls 'a heaping tablespoon of romance' is lost in the process. 'For me, there is an inescapable beauty in an unbiased, third-party group of individuals gathering around a table and selecting your book against hundreds of other choices because they have reached a consensus regarding the quality of the craft and the quality of the storytelling.'

Mainstream publishing – romantic? When did that happen? It's interesting how conceptions of beauty and romance can alter as technologies mature and industries shift. Once, the instantaneousness of email seemed miraculous compared to stuffy, slow 'snail mail'; now a letter that has been handwritten and physically transmitted seems the far more splendid thing to receive. Similarly, video technology, once a wondrously freeing advance for filmmakers, earns the scorn of 35mm snobs, and clunky C90 cassettes are cult objects to the generation that grew up on compact discs. That the once-formidable publishing industry should be defended on the grounds of its approval offering a writer romance might itself be read as evidence of a drastic depletion of its standing. Implicit in Card's take is the notion that by going through traditional channels a writer links him- or herself to the glorious literary past, when the knowledgeable sat in judgment of artistic quality and published on that basis, rather than accepting a frightening future (or, arguably, present) in which market trumps merit and the making of art should be considered a hobby. Is publishing 'romantic' the way that printing one's album on vinyl, or writing one's screenplay on a typewriter, is romantic – in that it clings to the old ways and denies the flashy temptations of progress? Or is it, as is also implicit, romantic because it more neatly fits the writer's preconceived fantasy of how it would be to be published – an acceptance letter, an advance, a stroked ego, approval from on high. Why is there more 'beauty' in the process Card describes than in thousands of unbiased readers discovering and embracing a book online?

The difference, in a manner of speaking, is the table around which Card's imagined readers gather. The table is in an office; the office is owned or rented by a publishing firm; the readers had to submit CVs and undergo interviews in order to work there. They have authority; they have discretion; they are trained. Those thousands of online readers, by contrast, could be anyone. And can they be trusted? To many writers and scholars, the runaway success of *Fifty Shades of Grey* indicates not. Of course, books without literary credibility succeeded long before the internet existed, and continue to flourish via traditional publishing – ask Jacqueline Susann and Barbara Cartland, Jeffrey Archer and Dan Brown. But the phenomenon of *Fifty Shades*, extreme as it is in terms of both the success and the perceived badness of the book, seems to have triggered a new level of fear amidst the respectable literati regarding the coming stampede of barbarians and the dearth of gatekeepers to hold them at bay. EL James and her book stalked the Edinburgh World Writers' Conference like the Ghost of Christmas Yet to Come, rattling its (whips and) chains and stirring envy, resentment and fear of imminent obsolescence amid the attending writers. At the Edinburgh Conference, **Nick Laird** pronounced *Fifty Shades of Grey* 'fucking dangerous' for its naked commercialism, while **Alan Bissett** took issue with its sexual politics. In Lisbon, **João Tordo** noted that book shops 'flooded' with such cynically-conceived bestsellers as James's had no space to display books like his own prominently enough for them to sell; everywhere, audiences seemed compelled to reference *Fifty Shades* as damning evidence of the decline and fall of literature. At the Toronto Conference, it fell to **China Miéville** to observe that the endemic 'kicking' of that particular book was becoming 'a little bit neurotically over-determined', and to suggest that writers 'let it go a bit.' Responding to an audience member who suggested that readers of *Fifty Shades* would not 'know what to do with' a piece of fiction from the pen of a George Pérec or a William Burroughs, he questioned why there should not be some degree of crossover between readers of EL James and readers of George Pérec.

The existence or otherwise of objective standards of 'good' and 'bad' writing, and whether the publishing industry could be trusted to protect the former, was a further preoccupation of the Conference sessions. In their discussion in Cape Town, **Anjali Joseph** and **Imraan Coovadia** circled ideas of 'real' novels versus 'junk' novels, with Coovadia arguing that the latter offer 'indirect rather than direct wish-fulfilment', and that 'there are certain slightly suspicious desires perpetuated by this kind of novel'. For Joseph, genre novels – thrillers, romances – could be categorised as offering a specific narrative arc that she termed 'masturbatory ... in that it's always going to reach a certain end'. But how do we sort the real from the junk – or are such distinctions inevitably subjective? **Teju Cole,** speaking in Melbourne, said he was not interested in the kind of book 'whose main purpose is to help the reader pass some hours on a plane.' His listeners and readers would doubtless have their own ideas as to what books those might be, and there might well be crossover – but not complete crossover.

Such decisive designations of quality or worthiness must surely be regarded as unstable, not only because they are subjective, but because they can alter over time. There may not be a great deal of debate regarding the quality of Dan Brown's or EL James's prose, but one need only look as far along the bestseller shelves as Stephen King to find a massively prolific and popular genre writer whose stock has shifted in recent years. Once regarded as a guilty pleasure, King has become fashionable as a 'real' writer, as evidenced by his receipt in 2003 of the Medal for Distinguished Contribution to American Letters from the National Book Foundation, and his 2006 inclusion in the Paris Review's series of author interviews. In the course of that encounter King discussed popularity versus credibility. 'The keepers of the idea of serious literature have a shortlist of authors who are going to be allowed inside, and too often that list is drawn from people who know people, who go to certain schools, who come up through certain channels of literature,' he said. 'And that's a very bad idea – it's constraining for the growth of literature .... The real breaking point comes when you ask whether a book engages you on an emotional level. And once those levers start to get pushed, many of the serious critics start to shake their heads and say no.' One person's emotional engagement, clearly, is another's 'masturbatory' pandering to easy expectations. But a postmodern age in which guilty pleasures – disposable pop music, comfort food, trash television – are embraced by the chattering classes would seem to have enabled a certain rehabilitation of King. As a 2013 *Guardian* interview noted, 'kids who read and loved him in the 1970s now run publishing houses and newspapers; he is revered, these days, as a grand old man of American letters.'

But writers of less contested status than King also serve to complicate our thinking on 'good = difficult / bad = easily pleasurable' – which seemed to be the closest that Conference delegates came to a consensus on determining a measure for literary value. Raymond Chandler and Philip K. Dick failed in their attempts to become known for their 'literary' fiction, but are now seriously celebrated for what they thought of as their hack work – mysteries in Chandler's case, science fiction in Dick's. Teju Cole's Melbourne keynote deployed Randall Jarrell's pleasing definition of a novel as 'a prose narrative of some length that has something wrong with it', setting this awkward product in opposition to what he called 'the neat and untroubled novel that has nothing wrong with it'. But where does that leave the pleasure-giving novel that also has an outsider quality to it, an edge of the strange? Chandler and Dick both appealed to mainstream audiences with work that was off-centre; disturbed; peculiar. And then where do we place comic novels, which are expressly designed to give pleasure and appeal to mass audiences, but do so with sophistication and intelligence? Whither, say, Anita Loos's *Gentlemen Prefer Blondes*, the American bestseller of 1925 that was sneered at by critics, counted James Joyce and Edith Wharton among its fans, and retains its sparkle to this day?

Certainly the 'genrefication of everything', as **Corey Redekop** called it in Toronto, is apparent to anyone visiting a book shop, whether online or in the flesh. From Painful Lives to Paranormal Romance, books seem ever more segregated into sectors; and e-books have encouraged the trend, with readers favouring genre books for their e-readers, and publishers increasingly responding with specialised ebook imprints. Random House has gone all out, introducing a science fiction/fantasy label called Hydra; a mystery label, Alibi; Flirt, for young adult readers; and Loveswept, for romance. HarperCollins, meanwhile, has introduced a digital mystery imprint named Witness. Digital suits genre because readers will sneak onto their e-readers those directly wish-fulfilling works that they might be embarrassed to buy for the bookshelf (famously a boon for *Fifty Shades of Grey*); because cheap production favours quick, insubstantial reads, in that readers will risk a few pounds or dollars where they might not part with twenty; and a rapid route to market allows publishers to respond to fast-flowering and short-lived trends. The low costs associated with digital-only publishing also permit publishers to take a chance on authors whose commercial prospects might not merit a full print commitment; and to embrace forms they wouldn't touch on paper, such as the short story and the novella.

There is of course nothing to say that a new *Gentlemen Prefer Blondes* shouldn't be lurking somewhere on the Loveswept catalogue, or a latterday Chandler penning pulp for Witness. But even where the work is bad, a further significant point should be considered with regard to *Fifty Shades of Grey* and its ilk – one raised during the Conference by **Denise Mina** (who is herself marketed as a genre novelist, albeit of a high-end stripe). We need 'shit books' that sell in millions, she reminded the Conference: whether on paper or in pixel form, the revenue that they bring in permits publishers to buy the good but less commercial stuff.

Another argument arising at the Conference had it that the declining influence of literary gatekeepers and the openness of the internet could harbour interesting creative possibilities. To **Teju Cole**, this experimental phenomenon is already happening – we just know it by another name. 'Isn't Twitter the most vivid illustration since Ulysses of what full inclusion might mean?' he asked. 'There are 200 million people on Twitter. They are all writing, and all are writing under a formal constraint.' Certainly individual Twitter projects – such as the account @Horse_Ebooks, which tweeted snippets of random text, falsely purported to be unauthored, and upon being unmasked was called 'the most successful piece of cyber-fiction ever' by *The Atlantic* – have been celebrated as avant-garde art; but Cole's intriguing notion is that the entirety of Twitter is collective authorship in full, ungoverned flow.

A world in which fiction-writing separates itself entirely from the concerns of the publishing industry – and not only from genre distinctions but feasibly from definitions of what constitutes 'fiction' at all – is of course slenderly attractive to many writers, however future-focused they may be in theory. The idea of copyright-free, collaborative, rewritable or communally forged literature might be fascinating, but in practice a writer's text reproduced the way he or she wrote it is both the fruit of his or her graft, and the sum of his or her creative and commercial identity. Is a collective approach to writing a necessary and potentially positive adaptation to the future of literature? Or is the struggle to retain one's creative control the latest challenge to the serious and committed author – whether self-published or traditionally launched – in the face of a digital revolution that may threaten the very concept of authorship?

BIOGRAPHIES
OF KEYNOTE SPEAKERS

Tamim Al-Barghouti is known for the capacity of his poetry to draw the attention of thousands from various age groups. The reception of his poetry among such a diverse audience is a testimony to the vitality of the centuries-old tradition of classical Arabic poetry.

Al-Barghouti was born in 1977 to Palestinian poet Mourid Al-Barghouti and Egyptian novelist Radwa Ashour. That year, the Egyptian government had embarked on a peace process with Israel and expelled most Palestinians of prominence, including Al-Barghouti's father. Since childhood, Al-Barghouti has been immersed in the political realities of the Arab world, the way they affect the most personal aspects of an individual's life, as well as in the literary means to express them. He published his first poem at 18. In 1999, at age 22, he was able to return to Palestine for the first time. There, he wrote his first poetry collection, "Mijana," in the Palestinian spoken dialect of Arabic and published it in Ramallah. His second collection, "Al-Manzar," followed shortly thereafter, written in Cairo using the Egyptian spoken dialect. In 2003, on the eve of the American invasion of Iraq, Al-Barghouti left Egypt in opposition to the war and the Egyptian government's position. The experience resulted in two works that gained Al-Barghouti a degree of fame in Egypt and the Arab world; the first was "Aluli-Bethebbe-Masr" (They Ask: Do You Love Egypt), written in the Egyptian spoken dialect, and "Maqam Iraq," in Standard Classical Arabic. Both works were well received. "Maqam Iraq" in particular was described by one critic as "something of a classical Arabic masterpiece … a lengthy epic-like diwan on Iraq comprising a variety of stylistic forms: song, narrative, and prose … that established Al-Barghouti as a master of Arabic language and history."

In 2007, Al-Barghouti's work "In Jerusalem" became something of a street poem. Palestinian newspapers dubbed Al-Barghouti "The Poet of Jerusalem". His posters hang on the streets of Jerusalem and other Palestinian cities, where keychains are sold with his picture on them. Sections of the poem have even become ring-tones blaring out from mobile phones across the Arab world, and children compete in memorizing and reciting it. The poem, which describes an aborted journey to the city, became the basis for a number of performances in Nablus, Ramallah, Hebron, Bethlehem, Jericho, Amman, Beirut, Muscat, Berlin, The Hague, and Vienna, among others.

Al-Barghouti studied politics at Cairo University, The American University in Cairo, and Boston University, where he received his Ph.D. in Political Science. He has written two volumes of history and political thought, Benign Nationalism: State Building Under Occupation (The Egyptian National Library, Cairo, 2007) and The Umma and the Dawla: the Nation State and the Arab Middle East (London, Pluto Press, 2008). Al-Barghouti was an assistant professor of Politics at the American University in Cairo, the Free University of Berlin, and Georgetown University in Washington DC. He was a fellow at the Berlin Institute for Advanced Studies, and is Currently a Consultant at the United Nation's Economic and Social Commission for West Asia.

Prof. **Larissa Behrendt** is the Professor of Law and Director of Research at the Jumbunna Indigenous House of Learning at the University of Technology, Sydney. She has published numerous textbooks on Indigenous legal issues. She is a member of the Academy of Arts and Sciences and a founding member of the Australian Academy of Law. Her most recent book is *Indigenous Australia for Dummies*. Larissa wrote and directed the feature film, Innocence Betrayed. Larissa won the 2002 David Uniapon Award and a 2005 Commonwealth Writer's Prize for her novel *Home*. Her second novel, *Legacy*, was released in October 2009. Larissa is Chair of the Bangarra Dance Theatre and a board member of NSW Museums and Galleries. She is the Ambassador of the Guwara Aboriginal Campus at St. Andrew's Cathedral School in Sydney and a board member of the Sydney Story Factory, a literacy program in Redfern. She was awarded the 2009 NAIDOC Person of the Year award and 2011 NSW Australian of the Year.

Melvin Burgess, writer of acclaimed and often controversial children's fiction, was born on 25 April 1954 in Twickenham, Middlesex. He grew up in Ilfield, near Crawley in Sussex, and moved to Reading, Berkshire at the age of twelve. After leaving school with two A-Levels in Biology and English, he enrolled on a six-month journalism course. He moved to Bristol at the age of 21, and began writing, between periods of work and unemployment. He continued writing after he moved to London in 1983, experimenting with short stories, radio plays and children's fiction. His first published book, *The Cry of the Wolf* (1990), was shortlisted for the Carnegie Medal. It was for his controversial teenage novel, *Junk* (1996) that he gained wider recognition. Winner of the Carnegie Medal an the *Guardian* Children's Fiction Prize, it is an honest and disturbing account of teenage homelessness and heroin addiction on the streets of Bristol, and has been adapted for television. In 2007, it was shortlisted for the Carnegie of Carnegies. *Bloodtide* (1999) was joint winner of the Lancashire County Library Children's Book of the Year Award. His comedy*Lady: My Life as a Bitch* (2001), also received a great deal of publicity for its frank exploration of the sexual behaviour of a teenage girl. Also in 2001, his novelisation of the film *Billy Elliot* was published, based on Lee Hall's screenplay. His controversial teenage novel, *Doing It*, was published in 2003 and won the LA Times Book Prize for Young Adult Literature in 2004, and *Sara's Face* in 2006. His latest books are *Kill All Enemies* (2011), *The Hit* (2013), e-book *Krispy Whispers* (2013) and *Hunger* (2014). Melvin Burgess lives in Yorkshire.

Teju Cole is a writer, art historian, and photographer. He was born in the US in 1975 to Nigerian parents, raised in Nigeria, and currently lives in Brooklyn. He is the author of two books, a novella, Every Day is for the Thief, and a novel, Open City, which was awarded the Internationaler Literaturpreis 2013, 2012 PEN/Hemingway Award, the Rosenthal Family Foundation Prize of the American Academy of Arts and Letters, the New York City Book Award for Fiction, and the Internationaler Literaturpreis; nominated for the National Book Critics Award, the New York Public Library's Young Lions Award, and a prize from the Royal Society of Literature; and named one of the best books of 2011 by Time Magazine, the New

Yorker, Newsweek, the Guardian, the Atlantic, the New York Times, and many others.

Sophie Cooke is a Scottish novelist, short story writer, poet, and travel writer. She was born in London in 1976. Her novels The Glass House, shortlisted for the Saltire First Book Of The Year Award, and Under The Mountain are both set in the Scottish Highlands. Cooke's short stories have been published in anthologies and literary magazines in the UK and Continental Europe, and have been broadcast on BBC Radio. She won the Genomics Forum Poetry Prize and has been long-listed for the Montreal International Poetry Prize, the largest poetry prize in the world. Her travel writing appears in The Guardian newspaper. Cooke lives in Edinburgh.

Emmanuel Dongala (b. 1941), the exiled Congolese chemist, novelist and playwright, is regarded as one of the most important figures in African literature. Although he has lived and worked for much of his career in the USA and France, since the 1970s Dongala has also chronicled the revolutionary changes that have occurred in Africa. Following on from his novel *Johnny Mad Dog* (2002), a gripping portrait of the extraordinary violence of the Congolese civil war, Dongala's work has assumed a more feminine perspective with his most recent novel, Photo de groupe au bord du fleuve [Photo of a group on the banks of the river]. A powerful humanist novel that is both vivid and full of humour, it won the Ahmadou Kourouma Prize in 2011.

Sahar el Mougy is an Egyptian novelist and short story writer. A lecturer of American and British poetry (Cairo University), a presenter of a weekly radio show concerned with the art of writing (Radio Cairo) and a columnist in the Egyptian daily Almasry Alyoum. She is also a gender and creative writing trainer and translator. Elmougy has published two collections of short stories and two prize-winning novels.

Li Er, novelist and short story writer, was born 1966 in Henan Province. He is the author of five story collections, two novels and approximately 50 novellas and short stories. His work appears regularly in Zuojia, Shouhuo, Renmin Wenxue and a variety of other mainland literary journals. German Chancellor Angela Merkel famously gave the German translation of his novel Cherry on a Pomegranate Tree as a gift to Premier Wen Jiabao. His novels The Magician of 1919 and Truth and Variations, about the mired physical and psychological circumstances confronting revolutionary poet Ge Ren in the 1930s and 1940s are now available in English.

As a teenager, **Keith Gray** went from reluctant reader to passionate reader – then straight on to being a dedicated writer. He published *Creepers*, which was shortlisted for the Guardian Children's Fiction Prize, when he was only 24. Since then he's written a number of critically-acclaimed novels which have won, or been shortlisted for, several major awards including the Carnegie Medal, the Costa Children's Book Award, the Scottish Children's Book Awards and the Smarties Book Prize. Never an author to shy away from difficult subject matter Keith's novels are often deemed 'controversial' and he recently edited two ground-breaking, if provocative, anthologies for teenagers – *Losing It* which tackles first sexual experience, and *Next* which explores ideas about the afterlife. His novel *Ostrich Boys* has been adapted for the stage and will embark on a UK tour in 2013. Keith lives in Edinburgh with his partner, their daughter and a parrot called Bellamy.

Kirsty Gunn is the author of six works of fiction, including short stories and a collection of fragments and essays. Translated in over twelve territories and widely anthologised. Her books have been broadcast, turned into film, dance and theatre, and are the recipient of various prizes and awards including Scottish Book of the Year. She is also Professor of Writing Practice and Study at the University of Dundee where she established and directs the writing programme. She lives in London and Scotland with her husband and two daughters.

Helon Habila is an Associate Professor of Creative Writing at George Mason University. He worked in Lagos as a journalist before moving to England in 2002 for a writing fellowship at the University of East Anglia. His novels include, *Waiting for an Angel* (2002), *Measuring Time* (2007), and *Oil on Water (2010)*. In 2006 he co-edited the British Council's anthology, *New Writing 14*. He also edited of *The Granta Book of African Short Story* (2011).

Habila's novels, poems and short stories have won many honours and awards. In 2003 he was awarded the Commonwealth Prize for Best First Novel (Africa Section), in 2005-2006 Habila was the first Chinua Achebe Fellow at Bard College, New York. His second novel won the Virginia Library Foundation's fiction award in 2008. In the same year Habila's short story, 'The Hotel Malogo' won the Emily Balch Prize. 'The Hotel Malogo' was also selected by the Best American Non-Required Anthology, edited by Dave Eggers. *Oil on Water*, which deals with environmental pollution in the oil rich Niger Delta, was shortlisted for the Commonwealth Writers Prize (2011) and the Orion Book Award (2012). It was also a runner up for the PEN/Open Book Award (2012).

Habila has been a contributing editor for the Virginia Quarterly Review since 2004, and he is a regular reviewer for the Guardian, UK. From July 2013 to June 2014 Habila was a DAAD fellow in Berlin. Helon Habila lives in Virginia with his wife and three children.

Born in Tunis in 1947, **Hubert Abraham Haddad** went to France with his parents several years later, first to Belleville, Ménilmontant, and then to the housing projects. He lived the difficult life of the immigrant growing up, with a shop-keeper father and a mother of Algerian origin. He evoked this childhood in his story *Le Camp du bandit Mauresque (The Camp of the Moorish Bandit)* (Fayard, 2005). His first collection of poems, *Le Charnier déductif* (*Deductive Mass Grave*), appeared in 1967. His first story, written at the same time and entitled *Armelle ou l'éternel Retour (Armelle or the Eternal Return)*, was not published until 1989. Starting with *Un rêve de glace (A Dream of Ice)* (Albin Michel, 1974; Zulma, 2005), he has continuously produced novels and collections of stories, alternating with essays on art or literature, plays, and collections of poems. Haddad's use of different genres and subjects combined with his extensive experience with writing workshops led him to write Le Nouveau Magasin d'écriture (The New Writing Store), a sort of encyclopedia of literature and the art of writing. This volume was followed in 2007 by the Nouveau Nouveau Magasin d'écriture (The New New Writing Store). Haddad has received literary prizes for a number of his works, including the 1983 Georges Bernanos Prize for Les Effrois (The Terrors); the 1991 Maupassant Prize for Le Secret de l'immortalité (The Secret of Immortality); the 1998

SGDL (Société des gens de lettres/ Literary Society) Grand Prix for the Novel for La Condition magique (The Magical Condition); the 2008 Five Francophonie Continents Prize and the 2009 Prix Renaudot Poche for Palestine.

Marlon James is a Jamaican writer, currently a professor of literature and creative writing at Macalester College in Minnesota. He is the author of *The Book of Night Women* and *John Crow's Devil*.

Anjali Joseph was born in Bombay and grew up in England. She has lived and worked in London, Paris and Bombay. Her first novel, *Saraswati Park,* won the Desmond Elliott and Betty Trask Prizes and the Vodafone Crossword Book Award for fiction. Her second novel, *Another Country,* has just been published. Reading, writing, and living in India and England has left her sceptical of the idea of simple, linear literary traditions that remain politely within national boundaries. The real lines of affinity between readers and writers, and writers and other writers, are elective, and sometimes unexpected.

Kapka Kassabova grew up in Sofia and after the fall of the Berlin Wall, her family emigrated to New Zealand where she studied French literature and published her first poetry and fiction in English. After moving to Britain in 2004, she wrote the childhood memoir *Street Without a Name,* short-listed for the Prix du livre européen. Her novel *Villa Pacifica* is set in South America, and her travel memoir, *Twelve Minutes of Love* (short-listed for the 2012 Scottish Book Awards) is a story of Argentine tango and the search for home. Kapka's latest poetry collection is *Geography for the Lost.* After years in Edinburgh, she now lives in the Scottish Highlands.

Georg Klein was born in Augsburg in 1953. He studied Literature, History and Sociology in Berlin. His big literary breakthrough came in 1998 with the publication of his debut novel, "Libidissi", followed by "Barbar Rossa" and "Sünde Güte Blitz" as well as the publication of his short stories "Anrufung des blinden Fisches" and "Von den Deutschen". He was awarded the Brüder-Grimm Prize and the Bachmann Prize. For his novel "Roman unserer Kindheit", published in 2010, he won the Prize of the Leipzig Book Fair. Klein lives with the writer Kathrin de Vries in Berlin and East Frisia.

Rachida Lamrabet is a Belgian author and lawyer descended from a Moroccan family. She works for the Centre for Equality of Opportunity and Opposition to Racism in Brussels. In her work with the Centre, Lamrabet regularly encounters discrimination due to race and ethnicity. These experiences largely influence her writing which focuses heavily on minorities' struggles with identity and migration. In addition, she speaks out against perceived xenophobia in Belgian politics and has been especially critical of the right wing *Vlaams Belang* party. She made her literary debut in 2006 with her story 'Mercedes 207' for which she won the 'Colour the Arts!' award. The book describes the experiences of a Moroccan man who regularly travels between Morocco and Antwerp. In 2007, she wrote *Woman Country* which tells of a woman's struggle between her adopted Western identity and her Moroccan roots. Her 2008 book *A Child of God* was very well received, winning the BNG Literature Award.

Michel Le Bris was born in Britain in 1944. As the director of the *Cause of the People*, he was sentenced to 8 months of prison before Jean-Paul Sartre took over the role. He was a co-founder of the daily newspaper *Libération*, and, together with Jean-Paul Sartre, he created and directed the Wild France collection published by Éditions Gallimard. In 1990, he founded the festival Étonnants Voyageurs (Astonishing Travelers) to promote the idea of "world literature", and he is also at the origin of the movement known as the "travel writers". Together with Jean Rouaud, he wrote the "manifesto for a world literature in French", which was signed by 44 writers including JMG Le Clézio and Édouard Glissant, and was published in Le Monde on March 15, 2007.

Amanda Lohrey's first novel was *The Morality of Gentlemen*, published in 1984. It was followed by *The Reading Group* and then *Camille's Bread*, winner of the Australian Literature Society's Gold Medal and a Victorian Premier's Literary Award in 1996. Her most recent novel is *The Philosopher's Doll* (2004) which was longlisted for the Miles Franklin Award and the International IMPAC Dublin Literary Award. She is the author of the novella *Vertigo* (2008) and of the short story collection *Reading Madame Bovary* (2010) which won the Fiction Prize and the Steele Rudd Short Story Award in the 2011 Queensland Literary Awards.

China Miéville's first novel was *King Rat* (1998), a dark fantasy relocating the Pied Piper to contemporary London. His second, *Perdido Street Station* (2000), is the first set in the city of New Crobuzon, and won the 2001 Arthur C. Clarke Award for Best Science Fiction and a 2001 British Fantasy Award. Two further books in this series are the British Fantasy award-winning *The Scar* (2002) and *Iron Council*, winner of a further Arthur C. Clarke Award. His other books include the young adult novel, *Un Lun Dun* (2007), and a collection of short stories, *Looking for Jake* (2005). *The City & The City* (2009) is an existential thriller, winner of a further Arthur C. Clarke Award, Hugo Prize and World Fantasy Award for Best Novel. His non-fiction includes a study of international law. China Miéville is Associate Professor of Creative Writing at Warwick University and an Honorary Research Fellow at Birkbeck College School of Law.

Njabulo S Ndebele wrote *'Fools' and Other Stories* (1983) which won the Noma award as the best book published in Africa in 1983; *Rediscovery of the Ordinary: Essays on South African Literature and Culture* (1991, 2006) a seminal collection of essays; the novel *The Cry of Winnie Mandela*, (2004) which received the Noma Award Honorable mention for 2005; and *Fine Lines from the Box: Further Thoughts About our Country* (2007) which received the K. Sello Duiker Memorial Award. He is a commentator on a range of public issues in South Africa. He has received honorary doctorates from universities in the UK, USA, The Netherlands, and Japan for achievements in literature, creative writing and higher education leadership.

Patrick Ness was born in the US and moved to England in 1999. He's the author of the *Chaos Walking* trilogy (*The Knife of Never Letting Go* which won the Guardian Children's Fiction Prize, *The Ask and the Answer* which won the Costa Children's Book Award, and *Monsters of Men* which won the Carnegie Medal). In 2012, he won his second Carnegie Medal for *A Monster Calls*, based on the final idea of Carnegie Medal winner Siobhan Dowd, whose premature death from cancer prevented her from writing it herself. His latest book for young adults is *More than This* (2013). He's also written two novels (*The Crash of Hennington* (2003) and *The Crane Wife* (2013)) and a short story collection (*Topics About Which I Know Nothing* (2004)) for adults. He's also a journalist and screenwriter, with his script of *A Monster Calls* going into production in late 2014.

Atiq Rahimi was born in 1962 in Kabul the capital of Afghanistan where he studied at the Franco- Afghan college Estiqlal. In 1984, he went from Afghanistan to Pakistan because of the war, and then he asked for and obtained political asylum in France, where he studied cinema at La Sorbonne. He now lives in Paris. From 1992 to 1995, he produced adverts and several documentaries for French television. As a writer he was first noticed in 2000 on the occasion of the publication of his first novel *Terres et cendres* at POL editions which has been translated in more than twenty-one countries. In 2002, Atiq Rahimi published *Les Mille Maisons du rêve et de la terreur*. In 2003 in Afghanistan, he shot *Terre et cendres*, a film that was selected in 2004 at the Cannes Festival where he obtained the Prix du regard vers l'avenir. This cinematic adaptation had a tremendous impact on Atiq Rahimi's career in fiction. In 2008, he became known as a major writer when he obtained the Prix Goncourt for his novel Syngué Sabour-Pierre de patience.

Boualem Sansal was born in 1949. He trained as an engineer and has a PhD in Economics. He occupied different jobs as teacher, consultant, and head of a company. He became a high-ranking civil servant in 1995 in the Department of Industry but he was dismissed in 2003 because of his criticisms of the system. He was encouraged by his friend Rachid Mimouni, the writer, to write and publish his first novel, *Le serment des barbares* when he was fifty years old. The novel was acclaimed by both the critics and the readers as soon as it was released in 1999. His other works include *L'enfant fou de l'arbre creux* and *Dis moi le paradis*. His book, *Poste Restante*, published in Algiers in 2006, is a short scathing open letter from Sansal to his compatriots. It was immediately censored by the Algerian government and so it never reached those it was meant for. He is a merciless witness of Algerian society today of which he paints a vivid picture in his very personal condensed and boisterous style. Boualem Sansal still lives near Algiers. Sansal has won the Grand Prix de la Francophonie, Prix de la Paix des Libraires Allemands, Grand Prix RTL-Lire, and Prix Edouard Glissant.

Olive Senior was born in Jamaica, has been based in Toronto, Canada, since 1993. She has published several prize-winning books, including the Commonwealth Writers' Prize-winning collection of stories, *Summer Lightning* (1986), three other books of fiction, and the poetry books *Talking of Trees* (1985), *Gardening in the Tropics* (1994, winner of the F.J. Bressani Literary Prize), *Over the Roofs of the World* (2005, shortlisted for Canada's Governor-General's Literary Award and Cuba's Casa de las Américas Prize), and *Shell* (shortlisted for the Pat Lowther Award).

Ali Smith was born in Inverness in 1962 and lives in Cambridge. Her books have won and been shortlisted for many awards. Her latest books are There But For The (2011), winner of the Hawthornden Prize, Artful (2012), winner of the Foyles / Bristol Festival of Ideas Best Book 2013, and, forthcoming, the novel How To Be Both (2014).

Ahdaf Soueif is a novelist and political commentator. She is the author of the essay collection *Mezzaterra*; two collections of short stories: *Aisha* and *Sandpiper*; and two novels: *In the Eye of the Sun* and *The Map of Love*, which was short-listed for the Man Booker Prize. Her latest work is *Cairo: My City, Our Revolution*, on the Egyptian uprising. Her articles on culture and politics appear in a wide array of Arabic and European papers including *The Guardian*, *Granta*, *al-Hayat*, *Le Monde*, *The Nation*, *El Pais*, and others.

Miriam Toews (pronounced tâves) was born in 1964 in the small Mennonite town of Steinbach, Manitoba. She has published four novels and a memoir of her father, and is the recipient of numerous literary awards including the Governor General's Award, the McNally Robinson Book of the Year Award (twice), and the Rogers Writers' Trust Fiction Prize. In 2007 she made her screen debut in the film Luz silenciosa. She was nominated for Best Actress at Mexico's Ariel Awards for her performance.

Irvine Welsh comes from Edinburgh, Scotland, and lives in Chicago, USA. He is the author of several novels, short story collections, stage plays and screenplays. He has lived in Scotland, England, Ireland, Holland and the United States, as well as travelling widely, and is interested in the issue of writing from a local culture within a globalized, consumerist era. As a journalist with the Telegraph, he was the first western correspondent in Darfur after the humanitarian crisis erupted in that region of Sudan. He also travelled to Afghanistan after the fall of the Taliban, to take part in a unique writing project on behalf of UNICEF. His current novel is the number one UK bestseller, Skagboys, and the film of his nineties number one bestseller, Filth, staring James McAvoy, was released in 2013. His interest in the issues and contexts of a national literature was fueled through being one of the Edinburgh-based group of Rebel Inc writers, who found national and international recognition in the 90's, in spite of, or perhaps assisted by, governmental and media antipathy.

INDEX

ACKNOWLEDGEMENTS

We are grateful to all of the writers who participated in the Edinburgh World Writers' Conference 2012–2013 for their permission to include quotations from their written and verbal contributions.

Copyright for specific keynote speeches is as follows:

Tamim Al-Barghouti, Poetry and Politics (*The state fell, the poem ruled*). Copyright © 2012, Tamim Al-Barghouti. All rights reserved.
Inci Aral, The Future of the Novel. Copyright © 2013, Inci Aral. All rights reserved.
Larissa Behrendt, Censorship Today, Censorship Tomorrow (*The whale on the rock*). Copyright © 2013, Larissa Behrendt. All rights reserved.
Tony Birch, A Post-National Literature? Copyright © 2013, Tony Birch. All rights reserved.
Theresa Breslin, A National Literature. Copyright © 2012, Theresa Breslin. All rights reserved.
Melvin Burgess, Politics and the Novel (*The power and the story*). Copyright © 2012, Melvin Burgess. All rights reserved.
Teju Cole, The Novel After the Novelist (*After the novelist*). Copyright © 2013, Teju Cole. All rights reserved.
Velibor Čolić, The Warriors' Cry – Nationalist Literature. Copyright © 2013, Velibor Čolić. All rights reserved.
Sophie Cooke, Style versus Content, or: The Tao of Writing (*The tao of writing*). Copyright © 2013, Sophie Cooke. All rights reserved.
Florent Couau-Zotti, Style above all. Copyright © 2013, Florent Couau-Zotti. All rights reserved.
Emmanuel Dongala, Writers Against Censorship (*A death penalty for thought*). Copyright © 2013, Emmanuel Dongala. All rights reserved.
Sahar el Mougy, The Egyptian novel: questions and challenges (*Egypt rising*). Copyright © 2012, Sahar el Mougy. All rights reserved.
Li Er, Talking About the Future of the Novel in China (*A shred of objectivity*). Copyright © 2013, Li Er. All rights reserved.
Keith Gray, Censorship Today (*The gatekeepers*). Copyright © 2012, Keith Gray. All rights reserved.
Kirsty Gunn, Style vs Content (*On form*). Copyright © 2013, Kirsty Gunn. All rights reserved.
Helon Habila, Reflections on the African Novel (*On the African novel*). Copyright © 2013, Helon Habila. All rights reserved.
Hubert Haddad, The Feeling of the World (*The feeling of the world*). Copyright © 2013, Hubert Haddad. All rights reserved.
Marlon James, A National Literature (*Categorisation is reductive*). Copyright © 2013, Marlon James. All rights reserved.
Anjali Joseph, A national literature: reading and writing across boundaries (*Writing across boundaries*). Copyright © 2012, Anjali Joseph. All rights reserved.
Kapka Kassabova, A National Literature? (*Citizens of the cosmopolis*). Copyright © 2013, Kapka Kassabova. All rights reserved.
Sema Kaygusuz, A National Literature. Copyright © 2013, Sema Kaygusuz. All rights reserved.
Georg Klein, ESCAPE TO BIG TIME: On the Novel and the Future (*Escape to the big time*). Copyright © 2012, Georg Klein. All rights reserved.
Antjie Krog, Should Literature Be Political? Copyright © 2012, Antjie Krog. All rights reserved.
Rachida Lamrabet, A National Literature (*Allochthoon, autochtoon*). Copyright © 2013, Rachida Lamrabet. All rights reserved.
Michel Le Bris, The Future of the Novel (*A new age of fiction*). Copyright © 2013, Michel Le Bris. All rights reserved.
Amanda Lohrey, Can Literature Affect Political